2

Defining Boundaries and Letting Go

In *Chapter 1, Architecting for Innovation*, we learned that the role of architecture is to enable change so that autonomous teams can confidently and continuously deliver business value. The key concept here is autonomy, but we need more than just autonomous teams. We need an architecture that promotes autonomy. We ultimately accomplish this by creating autonomous services with fortified boundaries. But first, we need to define the architectural boundaries of the subsystems within our system. Then we need to do the hardest thing of all, let go and trust the autonomous teams to deliver within their boundaries.

In this chapter, we're going to cover the following main topics:

- Building on SOLID principles
- Thinking about events first
- Dividing a system into autonomous subsystems
- Decomposing a subsystem into autonomous services
- Dissecting an autonomous service
- Governing without impeding

Building on SOLID principles

I had a run-in with architecture fairly early in my career that left an indelible impression on me. It was the 90s and n-tiered architecture was all the rage. I was the architect of a system with a middle tier that we wrote in C++ and ran on Tuxedo. This was well before **Continuous Integration (CI)** had emerged and we lived by our nightly builds. One morning I arrived at work and found that the nightly build was still executing. It was a large system with many subsystems, multiple services, and a significant quantity of code, but a nightly build that took all night was clearly an indication that something was wrong. The system was still growing, so things would only get worse if we did not identify and remediate the root cause.

It didn't take long to find the root cause, but the solution, although simple, would be tedious to roll out. In C++, we define classes in header files and include these files where we use the classes. However, there is no restriction on how many classes you can define in a header file. Our domain entities encapsulated our private persistence classes, but all these private classes were leaking, because we defined them in the same header files. We were building this private code over and over again, everywhere that we used the domain entities. As the system grew, the cost of this mistake became more and more expensive.

The SOLID principles did not exist at that time, but in essence, the system was in violation of the **Interface Segregation Principle**. The header files contained more interfaces than necessary. The simple solution was to move these internal classes into private header files. We immediately began to implement all new features this way and a few strategic updates brought the builds back under control. But the project was behind schedule, so the rest of the changes would have to wait. I took it upon myself to make those changes as time permitted. It took six months to retrofit the remainder of the system. This experience taught me the hard way about the importance of clean architectural boundaries.

Since that time, SOLID has emerged as a set of guiding design principles for implementing clean, flexible, and maintainable software. *Robert Martin* first promoted these principles for improving object-oriented designs. Since then, these principles have proven equally valuable at the architectural level. Although the implementation of the principles varies at different levels, it is convenient to apply a consistent mental framework throughout. Let's see how we will use these principles to guide the creation of evolutionary architectures that enable change.

Single Responsibility Principle

The **Single Responsibility Principle** (**SRP**) states that *a module should be responsible to one, and only one, actor.*

The SRP is simultaneously the most referenced and arguably the most misunderstood of all the SOLID principles. At face value, the name of this principle suggests *a module should do one thing and one thing only.* This misunderstanding leads to the creation of fleets of microservices that are very small and very interdependent and coupled. Ultimately, this results in the creation of the microliths and microservice death stars that I mention in the first chapter. The author of this principle, *Robert (Uncle Bob) Martin*, has made an effort to correct this misunderstanding in his book *Clean Architecture.*

The original and common definition of this principle states *a module should have one, and only one reason, to change.* The operative word here is **change**. This is crucial in the context of architecture because the purpose of architecture is to enable change. However, when we apply this principle incorrectly, it tends to have the opposite effect, because highly interconnected modules impede change. The coupling increases the need for inter-team communication and coordination and thus slows down innovation.

In his latest definition of the SRP, Uncle Bob is focusing on the source of change. **Actors** (that is, people), drive changing requirements. These are the people that use the software, the stakeholders, and the owners of external systems that interact with the system, even the governing bodies that impose regulations. After all, people are the reason that software systems exist in the first place.

The goal of this principle is to avoid creating a situation where we have *competing demands* on a software module that will eventually tie it in knots and ultimately impede change. We achieve this goal by defining architectural boundaries for the different actors. This helps ensure that the individual modules can change independently with the whims of their actors. Uncle Bob also refers to this as the **Axis of Change**, where the modules on either side of the boundary change at different rates.

Later in this chapter, we will use the SRP to divide our software system into autonomous subsystems and to decompose subsystems into autonomous services. The architectural boundaries will also extend vertically across the tiers, so that the presentation, business logic, and data tiers can all change together.

Open-Closed Principle

The **Open-Closed Principle (OCP)** states *a module should be open for extension but closed for modification. Bertrand Meyer* is the original author of this principle.

This principle highlights how human nature impacts a team's pace of innovation. We naturally slow down when we modify an existing piece of software, because we have to account for all the impacts of that change. If we are worried about unintended side effects, then we may even resist change altogether. Conversely, adding new capabilities to a system is far less daunting. We are naturally more confident and willing to move forward when we know that the existing usage scenarios have been completely untouched.

An architecture that enables change is open to adding and experimenting with new features while leaving existing functionality completely intact to serve the current user base. With the SRP, we define the architectural boundaries along the axis of change to limit the scope of a given change to a single service. We must also close off other services to any inadvertent side effects by fortifying the boundaries with bulkheads on both sides.

Events will be our main mechanism for achieving this freedom. We can extend existing services to produce new event types without side effects. We can add new services that produce existing event types without impact existing consumers. And we can add new consumers without changes to existing producers. At the presentation tier, micro frontends will be our primary mechanism for extension, which we will cover in *Chapter 3, Taming the Presentation Tier.*

Sooner or later, modification and refactoring of existing code is inevitable. When this is necessary, we will employ the **Robustness** principle to mitigate the risks up and down the dependency chains. We will cover common scenarios for extending and modifying systems with zero downtime in *Chapter 9, Choreographing Deployment and Delivery.*

Liskov Substitution Principle

The **Liskov Substitution Principle (LSP)** states *objects in a program should be replaceable with instances of their subtypes without altering the correctness of that program. Barbara Liskov* is the original author of this principle, hence the *L* in *SOLID.*

The substitution principle is essential to creating evolutionary architecture. Most innovations will consist of incremental changes. Yet, some will require significant changes and necessitate running multiple versions of a capability simultaneously. Following the LSP, we can substitute in new versions, so long as they fulfill the contracts with upstream and downstream dependencies.

We will use events to define the contracts for inter-service communication. This **design by contract** approach enables the substitution that powers the **branch by abstraction** approach. We can substitute event producers and swap event consumers. We will leverage the LSP to strangle legacy applications as we modernize our systems and continue this evolutionary process indefinitely to support continuous innovation with zero downtime. But zero downtime requires an understanding of all the interdependencies, and this leads us to the Interface Segregation Principle.

Interface Segregation Principle

The **Interface Segregation Principle (ISP)** states *no client should be forced to depend on interfaces they do not use.*

I provided an anecdote at the beginning of this chapter that highlights build time issues that can arise when we violate the ISP. These build time issues can have a big impact on a monolith. However, they are of less concern for our autonomous services because they are independently deployable units with their own CI/CD pipelines. We are still concerned about including unnecessary libraries because they can have an impact on cold start times and increase the risk of security vulnerabilities. But our real concern is on the deployment and runtime implications of violating the ISP and how it impacts downtime.

Our goal is to create an architecture that enables change so that we can reduce our lead times, deploy more often, and tighten the feedback loop. This requires confidence that our deployments will not break the system. Our confidence comes from an understanding of the scope and impact of any given change and our certainty that we have accounted for all the side effects and minimized the potential for unintended consequences. We facilitate this by creating clean and lean interfaces that we segregate from other interfaces to avoid polluting them with unnecessary concerns. This minimizes coupling and limits scope so that we can easily identify the impacts of a change and coordinate a set of zero-downtime deployments.

A common mistake that violates the ISP is the creation of general-purpose interfaces. The misperception is that reusing a single interface will accelerate development time. This may be true in the short term, but not in the long term. The increased coupling ultimately impedes innovation because of competing demands and the risk of unintended consequences. This is a main driver behind creating client-specific interfaces using the *Backend for Frontend* pattern. We will cover this pattern in detail in *Chapter 6, A Best Friend for the Frontend*.

For all our inter-service communication, our individual domain events are already nicely segregated, because we can change each of them independently. We do have to account for the fact that many downstream services will depend on these events. We will manage this by dividing the system into subsystems of related services and using *internal domain events* for intra-subsystem communication and *external domain events* for inter-subsystem communication. From here, we will leverage the **Robustness** principle to incrementally evolve our domain events. We will see this in play in *Chapter 9, Choreographing Deployment and Delivery*.

Even with well-segregated interfaces, we still need to avoid leaky abstractions. This occurs when details of specific upstream services are visible in the event payload and we inadvertently use those details in services downstream. This leads us to the Dependency Inversion Principle.

Dependency Inversion Principle

The **Dependency Inversion Principle (DIP)** states *a module should depend on abstractions, not concretions.*

At the code level, we also refer to the DIP as programming to an interface, not to an implementation. This manifests itself in the concept of dependency injection, which became an absolute necessity in monolithic systems. It eliminates cyclic dependencies, enables testing with mocks, and permits code to change and evolve by substituting implementations while holding interfaces closed to modification.

At the architecture level, I think we can best understand the value of the DIP by using the scientific method as an analogy. Holding variables constant is a crucial component of the scientific method. When we perform a scientific experiment, we cannot derive anything from the results if nothing was held constant because it is impossible to determine cause and effect. In other words, some level of stability is a prerequisite for the advancement of knowledge. Stability in the face of change is the whole motivation behind autonomous services. We need the ability to continuously change and evolve a running system while maintaining stability.

The DIP is a fundamental principle for creating architecture that provides for flexibility and evolution while maintaining stability. For any given change to a service, we have to hold something constant to maintain the stability of the system. That constant in an event-first system is the **domain events**. When we modify any service, all others will rely on the stability of the event types they all share. This will control the scope and impact of the change so that teams have the confidence to move forward.

Translating the DIP to the architectural level, we get the following:

- Domain events are the abstractions and autonomous services are the concretions.

- Upstream services should not depend on downstream services and vice versa. Both should depend on domain events.

- Domain events should not depend on services. Services should only depend on domain events.

In fact, many upstream services won't know or care that a downstream service exists at all. Downstream services will depend on the presence of an upstream service because something has to produce a needed event, but they should not know or care which specific upstream service produced an event.

This ultimately means that upstream services are responsible for the flow of control and downstream services are responsible for the flow of dependencies. In other words, upstream services control when an event is produced and downstream services control who consumes those events. Hence, the name of the principle still applies at the architectural level. We are inverting the flow of dependency (that is, consumption) from the flow of control (that is, production).

This event-based collaboration will be most evident when we cover the *Control Service Pattern* in *Chapter 8, Reacting to Events with More Events*. These high-level services embody control flow policies and other services simply react to the events they produce.

Taking this to the next level is the notion that downstream services react to domain events, and upstream services do not invoke downstream services. This is an *inversion of responsibility* that leads to evolutionary systems. It allows us to build systems in virtually any order and gives us the ability to create end-to-end test suites that don't require the entire system to be running or even completely implemented. This stems from the power of Event-First Thinking, which we will cover next.

Thinking about events first

In the first chapter, we covered a brief history of software integration styles and the forces that impact lead times. We designed autonomous services to enable teams to maximize their pace of innovation because they give teams the confidence they need to minimize lead time and batch size. However, to deliver on this promise, we need to change the way we act, which means we need a different way of thinking.

We need to do the following:

- Stop focusing on nouns.

- Treat events as first-class citizens.

- Turn our APIs inside-out.
- Shift the responsibility of control flow.

In other words, we need to think event-first. We can start to change our perspective by using a technique called event storming.

Event storming

Event storming is a workshop-oriented technique that helps teams discover the behavior of their business domain. It begins with brainstorming. The team starts by coalescing an initial set of domain events on a board using orange sticky notes. Next, we sequence the cards to depict the flow of events.

The following is a simplified example of the flow of events for a typical food delivery service. I will use and elaborate on this example throughout the book:

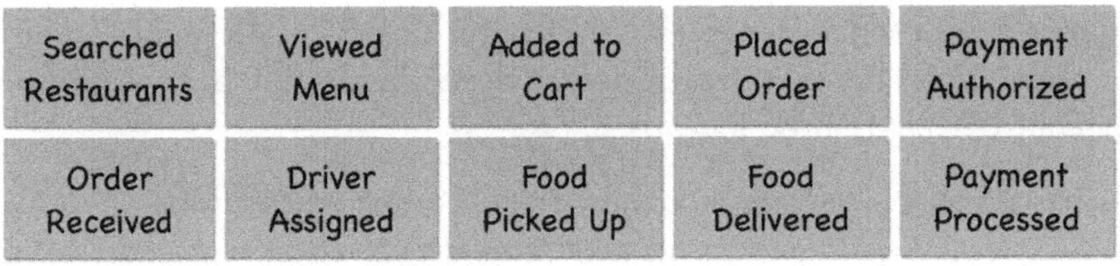

Searched Restaurants	Viewed Menu	Added to Cart	Placed Order	Payment Authorized
Order Received	Driver Assigned	Food Picked Up	Food Delivered	Payment Processed

Figure 2.1 – Event storming—flow of events

From here, teams can iteratively add more details with sticky notes, such as the following:

- The command (blue) that requested the action
- The users (yellow) and external systems (pink) involved in the activity
- The aggregate business domain (tan) whose state changed
- The read-only data (green) that we need to support decision-making
- Any policies (grey) that control behavior
- The overall business process (purple) that is in play

Note that event storming is not a substitute for user stories and story mapping. User stories and story mapping are project management techniques for dividing work into manageable units and creating roadmaps. Event storming ultimately facilitates the discovery of user stories and the boundaries within our software architecture.

Verbs versus nouns

The flow of events discovered in the event storming exercise clearly captures the behavior of the system. This event-first way of thinking is different because it zeros in on the *verbs* instead of the *nouns* of the business domain. Conversely, more traditional approaches, such as object-oriented design, tend to focus on the nouns. However, *when we focus on the nouns, we tend to create services that are resistant to change* because they violate the SRP and ISP principles.

As an example, it is not uncommon to find a service whose *single responsibility* is everything to do with a single domain aggregate. These services will end up containing all the commands that operate on the data of the domain. However, as we discussed in the *Building on SOLID principles* section, the SRP is intended to focus on the actors of the system. Different actors initiate different commands, which means that these noun-focused services ultimately serve many masters with competing demands. This will impede our ability to change these services when necessary.

Instead, we need to *segregate the various commands across the different actors*. By focusing on the verbs of the domain model, we are naturally attracted towards creating services for the different actors that perform the actions. This eliminates the competing demands that add unnecessary complexity to the code and avoids coupling an actor to unneeded commands.

Of course, now that the actors are the focal point of our services, we will need a way to share the nouns (that is, domain aggregates) between services without increasing coupling. We need a record of truth. To address this, we first need to start thinking of events as facts, instead of just ephemeral messages.

Facts versus ephemeral messages

Let's recognize that when we think about events, we are focused on the outputs of the system instead of the inputs. We are thinking in the past tense and thus we are focused on the *facts* the system will produce over time. This is powerful in multiple ways.

It turns out we are implicitly building business analytics and observability characteristics into the system. For example, we can count the `ViewedMenu` events to track the popularity of the different restaurants and we can monitor the rate of `PlacedOrder` events to verify the health of the system. We can also use this information to validate the hypothesis of each lean experiment we perform to help ensure we are building the right system and delivering on our business goals and objectives. In other words, event-first thinking facilitates observability mechanisms that help build team confidence and thus momentum.

However, to turn events into facts, we must treat them as *first-class* citizens instead of ephemeral messages. This is different from traditional messaging-based architectures, where we throw away the messages once we have processed them. We don't want to treat events as ephemeral messages because we lose valuable information that we cannot easily recreate, if at all.

We will instead treat events as *immutable* facts and store them in an *event lake* in perpetuity. The event lake will act as the record of truth for the facts of the system. However, to make the record of truth complete we must think of events as contracts instead of mere notifications.

Contracts versus notifications

Many event-driven systems use events for notifications only. These *anemic events* only contain the identifier of the business domain entity that produced the event. Downstream services must retrieve the full data when they need it. This introduces coupling because it requires a synchronous call between the services. It may also create unwanted race conditions since the data can change before we retrieve it.

The usefulness of notification events as the record of truth is very limited because we will often refer to these facts far off in the future, well after the domain data has changed. To fully capture the facts, we need events to represent a snapshot in time of the state of the domain when the event occurred. This allows us to treat the facts as an audit log that is analogous to the transaction log of a database. This is a very powerful concept because a database uses the transaction log as the record of truth to manage the state and integrity of the database.

We are essentially turning the database inside out and creating a systemwide record of truth that we can leverage to manage the state and integrity of the entire system. For example, we can leverage the facts to transfer (that is, replicate or rebuild) the state of domain aggregates (that is, nouns) between services. This eliminates the need for aligning services around domain aggregates and results in an immensely scalable and resilient system.

This means that we are turning our APIs inside out by using events as the contracts between services. This also implies a guarantee of backwards compatibility and we will therefore create strong contracts between services within a subsystem and even stronger contracts between subsystems. At first glance, it may appear that this way of thinking will make the system more rigid. In reality, we are making the system more flexible and evolutionary by inverting responsibility to downstream services so they can react to the events as they see fit.

React and evolve

The DIP, as we covered earlier in the chapter, was a major advancement in software design, because it decoupled high-level policy decisions from low-level dependency decisions. This gave teams the flexibility to substitute different implementations of the low-level components without breaking the logic in the high-level components. In other words, DIP facilitated the use of the **LSP** and the **OCP** to make systems much more stable and flexible.

We elevated the DIP to the architectural level by using events as the abstraction (that is, contract) between autonomous services. This promotes the stability of the system when we modify a service because we are holding the contracts constant to control the scope and impact of any given deployment. But we gain more than just stability, we also gain *flexibility*. The use of events for inter-service communication gives rise to an **inversion of responsibility** that makes systems reactive. The best way to understand this improvement is to compare the old *imperative* approach to the new *reactive* approach.

The traditional, imperative approach of implementing systems is *command* focused. One component determines when to invoke another. For example, in our food delivery system, we would traditionally have the checkout functionality make a synchronous call to an order management service to invoke a command that submits the customer's order. This means that we are coupling the checkout component to the presence of an order management service because it is responsible for the decision to invoke the command. This may not seem like a problem until we apply the same approach to retrieving driver status. We will need to invoke a service to retrieve driver status over and over again by any number of components and it will likely become a bottleneck.

Alternatively, we end up with a much more resilient and flexible system when we employ the reactive approach. The checkout component simply produces an `OrderPlaced` event. The order management service is now responsible for the decision to consume this event and react as it sees fit. The driver service simply produces `DriverStatusChanged` events when there is something useful to report. Any other service can take responsibility for reacting to driver events without impacting the driver service.

This inversion of responsibility is a key characteristic of autonomous services. It greatly reduces the complexity of the individual services because it reduces their responsibilities. A service is already aware of its own state and it can simply produce events to reflect the changes without taking responsibility for how other services will react. A service only takes responsibility for how it reacts to other events. This completely decouples services from one another. They are all autonomous. This simplicity makes it much easier for teams to gauge the correctness and impacts of any given change. Teams can be confident that the system will remain stable, provided that they uphold the contracts.

The reactive nature of event-first thinking is a paradigm shift, but the benefits are well worth the effort. A system becomes free to evolve in unforeseen ways by simply adding consumers. We can implement services in virtually any order because we can simulate upstream events and there is no coupling to downstream consumers. We gain the ability to create end-to-end test suites that don't require other services to be running at the same time. The bottom line is that the reactive nature of autonomous services enables autonomous teams to react much more quickly to feedback as they learn from their experiments.

Powered by an event hub

At the heart of our event-first architecture is the **event hub**. It brings everything together and pumps events through the system. There is a myth that event-driven systems are much more complex, but this couldn't be further from the truth. Event-first thinking enables the creation of arbitrarily complex systems with the simple fractal topology depicted in *Figure 2.2*:

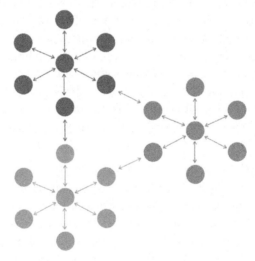

Figure 2.2 – Event-first topology

From a single service to many services in a subsystem and from a single subsystem to many subsystems in a system, the pattern of an autonomous service producing and consuming events repeats ad infinitum. We will dig into the details of the event hub in *Chapter 4, Trusting Facts and Eventual Consistency*, and we will see how to connect subsystems in *Chapter 7, Bridging Intersystem Gaps*.

Event-first is a very powerful approach, but adopting this way of thinking can be a journey. Let's continue the journey by learning how to divide a system into autonomous subsystems, then we will move on to the autonomous service patterns within each subsystem, and finally, we will dig into the anatomy of these services. Then we will be ready to bring all the details together throughout the remaining chapters.

Dividing a system into autonomous subsystems

The goal of software architecture is to define boundaries that enable the components of the system to change independently. We could dive straight down into defining the individual services of the system, but as the number of services grows the system will become unwieldy. Doing so contributes to the creation of microliths and microservice death stars. As architects, our job is to facilitate change, which includes architecting a system that is manageable.

We need to step back and look at the bigger picture. We must break a complex problem down into ever-smaller problems that we can solve individually and then combine into the ultimate solution. We need to divide the system into a manageable set of high-level *subsystems* that each has a single reason to change. These subsystems will constitute the major *bounded contexts* of the system. We will apply the **SRP** along different dimensions to help us arrive at boundaries that enable change. This will facilitate organizational scale with separate groups managing the individual subsystems.

We also need our subsystems to be autonomous, in much the same way that we create autonomous services. This will give autonomous organizations the confidence to continuously innovate within their subsystems. We will accomplish this by creating bulkheads between the subsystems. A system resembling the event-first topology depicted in *Figure 2.2* will begin to emerge. The purpose of each subsystem will be clear, and the subsystem architecture will allow the system to evolve in a dynamic business environment. Let's look at some ways we can divide up a system.

By actor

A logical place to start carving up a system into subsystems is along the external boundaries with the external actors. These are the users and the external systems that directly interact with the system. Following the SRP, each subsystem might be responsible to one and only one actor.

In our event storming example earlier, we identified a set of domain events for a food delivery system. During the event storming workshop, we would also identify the users and external systems that produce or consume those events, such as in *Figure 2.3*. In this example, we might have a separate subsystem for each category of the user: Customer, Driver, and Restaurant. We may also want a subsystem for each category of the external system, such as relaying orders to the restaurant's ordering systems, processing payments, and pushing notifications to customers:

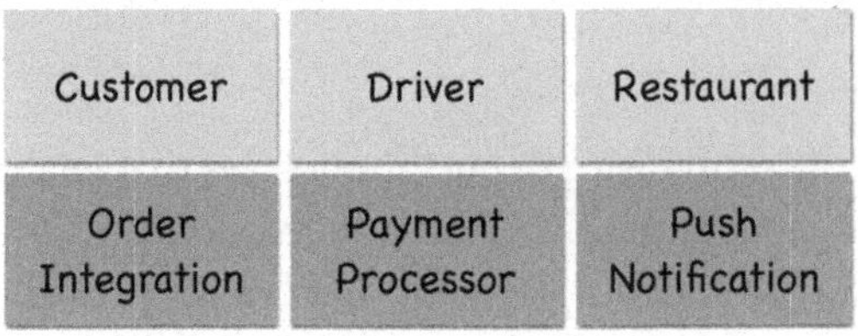

Customer	Driver	Restaurant
Order Integration	Payment Processor	Push Notification

Figure 2.3 – System context diagram

Of course, this is a simple example. Enterprise systems may have many kinds of users and lots of external systems, including legacy and third-party systems. In this case, we will need to look for good ways to organize the actors into cohesive groups and these groups may align with the business units.

By business unit

Another good place to look for architectural boundaries is between business units. A typical organization chart can provide useful insights. Each unit will ultimately be the business owner of the subsystems and thus they will have a significant impact on when and how the system changes.

Keep in mind that we are interested in the organization of the company, not the IT department. Conway's Law states *organizations are constrained to produce designs which are copies of their communication structure*. We have seen that the communication structure leads to dependencies, which increases lead time and reduces the pace of innovation. So, we want to align each autonomous subsystem with a single business unit.

However, the organizational structure of a company can be unstable. A company may reorganize its business units for a variety of reasons. So, we should look deeper into the work the business units actually perform.

By business capability

Ultimately, we want to draw our architectural boundaries around the actual business capabilities that the company provides. Each autonomous subsystem should encapsulate a single business capability or at most a set of highly cohesive capabilities.

Going back to our event storming approach and our event-first thinking, we are looking for logical groupings of related events (that is, verbs). There will be high temporal cohesion within this set of domain events. They will be initiated by a group of related actors that are working together to complete an activity. For example, in our food delivery example, a Driver may interact with a Dispatch Coordinator to ensure that a delivery is successful.

The key here is that the temporal cohesion of the activities within a capability helps to ensure that the subsystem as a whole will change together. This cohesion allows us to scale the SRP to the subsystem level when there are many different actors. The individual services within a subsystem will be responsible to the individual actors, whereas a subsystem is responsible to a single set of actors that work together to deliver a business capability:

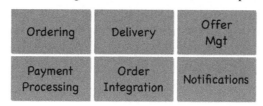

Figure 2.4 – Capabilities subsystems

Figure 2.4 depicts our food delivery system from the capabilities perspective. It is similar to the system context diagram in *Figure 2.3*, but the functionality is starting to take shape. But we may find more subsystems when we look at the system from a data life cycle perspective.

By data life cycle

Another place to look for architectural boundaries is along the data life cycle. Over the course of the life of a piece of data, the actors that use and interact with the data will change and so will their requirements. Bringing the data life cycle into the equation will help uncover some overlooked subsystems. We will usually find these subsystems near the beginning and the end of the data life cycle. In essence, we are applying the SRP down to the database level. We want to discover all the actors that interact with the data so that we can find all the actors and isolate these sources of change into their own bounded context (that is, an autonomous subsystem).

Going back to event-first thinking, we are stepping back and taking a moment to focus on the nouns (that is, domain aggregates) so that we can discover more verbs (that is, domain events) and the actors that produce those events. This will help find what I refer to as **slow data**. We typically zero in on the **fast data**. This is the transactional data in the system that actors are continuously creating. However, the transactional data often relies on reference data and government regulation may impose records management requirements on how long we must retain the transactional data. We want to decouple these sources of change so that they do not impact the flexibility and performance of the transactional and analytics data. We will cover this topic in detail in *Chapter 5*, *Turning the Cloud into the Database*:

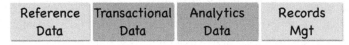

Figure 2.5 – Data life cycle subsystems

Figure 2.5 depicts subsystems from the data life cycle perspective. We will likely need a subsystem upstream the owns the master data model that all downstream subsystems use as reference data. And all the way downstream we will usually have an analytics subsystem and a records management subsystem. In the middle lies the transactional subsystems that provide the capabilities of the system, like we saw in *Figure 2.4*. We will also want to carve out subsystems for any legacy systems.

By legacy system

Our legacy systems are a special case. In *Chapter 7*, *Bridging Intersystem Gaps*, we will cover an event-first migration pattern for integrating legacy systems. We are creating an anti-corruption layer around the legacy systems that enable them to interact with the new system by producing and consuming domain events. This creates an evolutionary migration path that minimizes risk by keeping the legacy systems active and synchronized until we are ready to decommission them. This extends the substitution principle to the subsystem level because we can simply remove the subsystem once the migration is complete.

We are essentially treating the legacy systems as an autonomous subsystem with bulkheads that we design to eliminate coupling between the old and the new and to protect the legacy infrastructure by controlling the attack surface and providing backpressure. We will use the same bulkhead techniques we are using for all subsystems: separate cloud accounts and external domain events. Let's look at subsystem bulkheads next.

Creating subsystem bulkheads

What is the most critical subsystem in your system? This is an interesting question. Certainly they are all important, but some are more important. For many businesses, the customer-facing portion of the system is the most important. After all, we must be able to engage with the customers to provide a service for them. For example, in an e-commerce system, the customer must be able to access the catalog and place orders, whereas the authoring of new offers is less crucial. So, we want to protect the critical subsystems from the rest of the system.

Our aim is to fortify all the architectural boundaries in a system so that autonomous teams can forge ahead with experiments, confident in the knowledge that they are containing the blast radius when teams make mistakes. At the subsystem level, we are essentially enabling autonomous organizations to manage their autonomous subsystems independently. Let's look at how we can fortify our autonomous subsystems with bulkheads.

Separate cloud accounts

Cloud accounts form natural bulkheads that we should leverage as much as possible to help protect us from ourselves. Far too often we overload our cloud accounts with too many unrelated workloads, which puts all the workloads at risk. At a bare minimum, development and production environments must be in separate accounts. But we can do better by having separate accounts, per subsystem, per environment. This will help control the blast radius when there is a failure in one account. Here are some of the natural benefits of using multiple accounts:

- We control the technical debt that naturally accumulates as the number of resources within an account grows. It becomes difficult, if not impossible, to see the forest for all the trees, so to speak, when we put too many workloads in one account. The learning curve increases because the account is not clean. Tagging resources helps, but they are prone to omission. Engineers eventually resist making any changes because the risk of making a mistake is too high. The likelihood of a catastrophic system failure also increases.

- We improve our security posture by limiting the attack surface of each account. Restricting access is as simple as assigning team members to the right role in the right account. If a breach does occur, then access is limited to the resources in the one account. In the case of legacy systems, we can minimize the number of accounts that have access to the corporate network, preferably to just one per environment.

- We have less competition for limited resources. Many cloud resources have soft limits at the account level that throttle access when transaction volumes exceed a threshold. The likelihood of hitting these limits increases as the number of workloads increases. A denial-of-service attack or a runaway mistake on one workload could starve all other workloads. We can request increases to these limits, but this takes time. Instead, the default limits may provide plenty of headroom once we allocate subsystems to their own accounts.

- Cost allocation is simple and error resistant because we allocate everything in an account to a single cost bucket without the need for tagging. This means that no unallocated costs occur when tagging is incomplete. We also minimize the hidden costs of orphaned resources because they are easier to identify.

- Observability and governance are more accurate and informative because monitoring tools tag all metrics by account. This allows filtering and alerting per subsystem. When failures do occur, the limited blast radius also facilitates root cause analysis and a shorter mean time to recovery.

Having multiple accounts means that there are cross-cutting capabilities that we must duplicate across accounts, but we will address this shortly when we discuss continuous auditing and the automation of account creation in the *Governing without impeding* section.

External domain events

We have already discussed the benefits of using events as contracts, the importance of backward compatibility, and how asynchronous communication via events creates a bulkhead along our architectural boundaries. Now we need to look at the distinction between internal and external domain events.

Within a subsystem, its services will communicate via **internal domain events**. The definitions of these events are relatively easy to change because the autonomous teams that own the services work together in the same autonomous organization. The event definitions will start out messy and they will quickly evolve and stabilize as the subsystem matures. We will leverage the Robustness principle to facilitate this change. The events will also contain raw information that we want to retain for auditing purposes but is of no importance outside of the subsystem. All of this is OK because it is *all in the family*, so to speak.

Conversely, across subsystem boundaries, we need more regulated team communication and coordination to facilitate changes to these contracts. As we have seen, this communication increases lead time, which is the opposite of what we want. We want to limit the impact that this has on internal lead time, so we are free to innovate within our autonomous subsystems. We essentially want to hide internal information and not *air our dirty laundry in public*.

Instead, we will perform all inter-subsystem communication via **external domain events**. These external events will have much stronger contracts with stronger backward compatibility requirements. We will intend for these contracts to change slowly to help create a bulkhead between subsystems. Domain-Driven Design refers to this technique as **context mapping**, such as when we use domain aggregates with the same terms in multiple bounded contexts, but with different meanings.

In *Chapter 7, Bridging Intersystem Gaps*, we will cover the **External Service Gateway** (**ESG**) pattern. Each subsystem will treat related subsystems as external systems. We will bridge the internal event hubs of related subsystems to create the event-first topology depicted in *Figure 2.2*. Each subsystem will define an *egress* gateway that defines what events it is willing to share and hides everything else. Subsystems will define *ingress* gateways that act as an anti-corruption layer to consume upstream external domain events and transform them into its internal formats.

Now that we have an all-important subsystem architecture with proper bulkheads, let's look at the architecture within a subsystem. Let's see how we can decompose an autonomous subsystem into autonomous services.

Decomposing a subsystem into autonomous services

At this point, we have divided our system into autonomous subsystems. Each subsystem is responsible to a single dominant actor who drives change. Each subsystem is autonomous because they communicate via external domain events and they are each housed in a separate cloud account that forms a natural bulkhead. This autonomy allows us to change the subsystems independently.

Now we are ready to start decomposing our subsystems into autonomous services. Again, the SRP plays a major role in defining the boundaries within a subsystem. First, we need to place a subsystem in context, then we will set up common components, and finally, we apply the major autonomous service patterns.

Context diagram

We will apply a set of autonomous service patterns to decompose a subsystem into services. These patterns cater to the needs of different categories of actors. So, we need to understand the context of an autonomous subsystem before we can decompose it into autonomous services. In other words, we need to know all the external actors that the subsystem will interact with. During event storming, we identified the behavior of the system and the users and external systems that are involved. Then we divided the system into autonomous subsystems so that each has a *single axis of change*.

A simple context diagram can go a long way to putting everyone on the same page regarding the scope of a subsystem. The **context diagram** enumerates all the subsystem's external actors using *yellow* cards for *users* and *pink* cards for *external systems*. The diagram will contain a subset of the actors identified during event storming. We have encapsulated many of the original actors within other subsystems, so we will treat those subsystems as external systems. *Figure 2.6* depicts the context of the Customer subsystem:

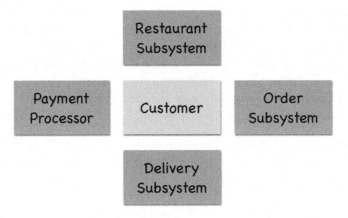

Figure 2.6 – Subsystem context diagram

The Customer subsystem of our example Food Delivery System might have the following actors:

- The Customer will be the user of this subsystem and the dominant actor.
- The Restaurant Subsystem will publish external domain events regarding the restaurants and their menus.
- A Payment Processor must authorize the customer's payment method.
- The subsystem will exchange OrderPlaced and OrderReceived external domain events with the Order Subsystem.
- The Delivery Subsystem will publish external domain events regarding the status of the order.

Now that the context is clear, we can start decomposing the system into its frontend, services, and common components.

Micro frontend

Each autonomous subsystem is responsible to a single primary user or a single cohesive group of users. These users will need a main entry point to access the functionality of the subsystem. Each subsystem will provide its own independent entry point so that it is not subject to the changing requirements of another subsystem.

The user interface will not be monolithic. We will implement the frontend using autonomous micro-apps that are independently deployed. The main entry point will act as a metadata-driven assembly and menu system. This will allow each micro-app to have a different reason to change and help ensure that the frontend is not responsible for increasing lead times and impeding innovation.

We will cover the frontend architecture in detail in *Chapter 3, Taming the Presentation Tier*.

Event hub

Each autonomous subsystem will contain its own independent event hub to support asynchronous inter-service communication between the autonomous services of the subsystem. Services will publish domain events to the event hub as their state changes. The event hub will receive incoming events on a bus. It will route all events to the event lake for storage in perpetuity, and it will route events to one or more streams for consumption by downstream services:

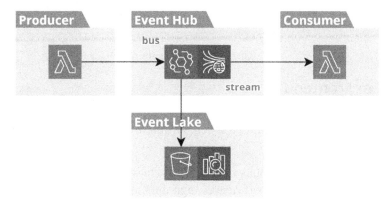

Figure 2.7 – Event hub

We will cover the event hub in detail in *Chapter 4, Trusting Facts and Eventual Consistency*. In *Chapter 7, Bridging Intersystem Gaps*, we will cover how to bridge the event hubs of different subsystems together to create the event-first topology depicted in *Figure 2.2*.

Autonomous service patterns

There are three high-level autonomous service patterns that all our services will fall under. At the boundaries of our autonomous subsystems are the **Backend For Frontend** (**BFF**) and **External Service Gateway** (**ESG**) patterns. Between the boundary patterns lies the **Control** service pattern. Each of these patterns is responsible to a different kind of actor, and hence support different types of changes:

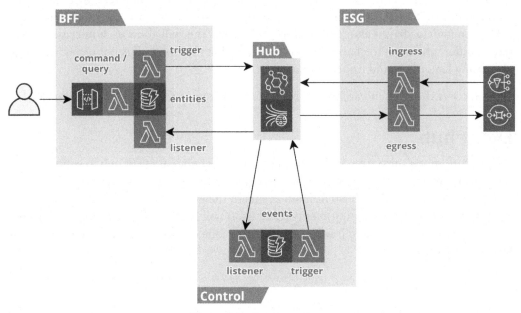

Figure 2.8 – Service patterns

Backend For Frontend

The **Backend For Frontend** (**BFF**) pattern works at the boundary of the system to support end users. Each BFF service supports a specific frontend micro-app, which supports a specific actor.

In the Customer subsystem of our example Food Delivery System, we might have BFFs to browse restaurants and view their menus, sign up and maintain account preferences, place orders, view delivery status, and view order history. These BFFs typically account for about 40% of the services in a subsystem.

A listener function consumes domain events from the event hub and caches entities in materialized views that support queries. The synchronous API provides command and query operations that support the specific user interface. A trigger function reacts to the mutations caused by commands and produces domain events to the event hub.

We will cover this pattern in detail in *Chapter 6, A Best Friend for the Frontend*.

External Service Gateways

The **External Service Gateway (ESG)** pattern works at the boundary of the system to provide an anti-corruption layer that encapsulates the details of interacting with other systems, such as third-party, legacy, and sister subsystems. They act as a bridge to exchange events between the systems.

In the `Customer` subsystem of our example Food Delivery System, we might have ESGs to receive menus from the `Restaurant` subsystem, forward orders to the `Order` subsystem, and receive the delivery status from the `Delivery` subsystem. The `Order` subsystem would have ESGs that integrate with the various order systems used by restaurants. The `Delivery` subsystem would have an ESG to integrate with a push notifications provider. These ESGs typically account for upwards of 50% or more of the services in a subsystem.

An `egress` function consumes internal events from the event hub and then transforms and forwards the events out to the other system. An `ingress` function reacts to external events in another system and then transforms and forwards those events to the event hub.

We will cover this pattern in detail in *Chapter 7, Bridging Intersystem Gaps.*

Control services

Control services help minimize coupling between services by mediating the collaboration between boundary services. These services are completely asynchronous. They consume events, perform logic, and produce new events to record the results and trigger downstream processing.

We use these services to perform complex event processing and implement business processes. They leverage the systemwide event sourcing pattern and rely on ACID 2.0 properties. In the `Delivery` subsystem of our example Food Delivery System, we might have a control service that implements a state machine to orchestrate the delivery process under many different circumstances. Control services typically account for about 10% of the services in a subsystem.

A `listener` function consumes lower-order events from the event hub and correlates and collates them in a micro `events` store. A `trigger` function applies rules to the correlated events and publishes higher-order events back to the event hub.

We will cover this pattern in detail in *Chapter 8, Reacting to Events with More Events.*

Dissecting an autonomous service

Up to this point, we have discussed using the SRP as a guide for defining architectural boundaries that help ensure the system has the flexibility to change with the needs of the different actors. We have covered dividing a system into autonomous subsystems and decomposing an autonomous subsystem into autonomous services. Now we move on to the anatomy of an individual autonomous service.

Each autonomous team has the ultimate responsibility for making the decisions that are best for the services they own. Embracing a polyglot-everything mindset and empowering the teams to make these decisions gives them the freedom they need to maximize innovation. Still, every service needs a starting point to jump-start the process of discovery and continuous improvement. The following sections cover all the common elements we need to implement the autonomous service patterns discussed in the previous sections.

One of the most interesting things to note is that there is much more to a service than just its runtime code.

Repository

Each service has its own source code repository. This is due, in part, because modern distributed source control tools, such as Git, make it is very easy to create and distribute new repositories. In addition, hosted offerings drive this point home by making the repository the focal point of their user experience. Furthermore, modern CI/CD pipelines tools assume that the repository is the unit of deployment. All these factors steer us towards this best practice.

Yet, the most important reason that each service has its own repository is autonomy. We want to drive down our lead times and sharing a repository with other teams will certainly cause friction and slow teams down. Separate repositories also act as bulkheads and shield teams from mistakes made by other teams.

They also protect us from ourselves in that we cannot accidentally create a dependency on the source code owned by another team, just because it is in the same repository. Instead, we have to explicitly create shared libraries that will have their own repositories and release cycles.

CI/CD pipeline and GitOps

Each service has its own CI/CD pipeline, as defined by a configuration file in the root of its repository. Modern CI/CD pipelines enhance the concept of GitOps, which is the practice of using Git pull requests to orchestrate the deployment of infrastructure.

The pipeline hooks into the state changes of the repository and pull requests to trigger and coordinate CI/CD activities. Each push to a repository triggers CI tests to ensure that the code is behaving as expected. The creation of a pull request triggers deployment to the staging environment and signals that the code is ready for review. Approval of a pull request triggers a production deployment.

This is a very powerful approach that becomes even stronger when combined with the concepts and practices of decoupling deployment from release, multiple levels of planning, task branch flow, and regional canary deployments. We will cover this in detail in *Chapter 9, Choreographing Deployment and Delivery*.

Tests

Automated testing plays a vital role in giving teams the confidence to continuously deploy. To this end, test cases make up the majority of the code base for a feature and unit tests make up the majority of the test cases. We execute unit tests, integration tests, contract tests, and transitive end-to-end tests in the CI/CD pipeline in isolation from all external resources. We continuously execute synthetic transactions for key usage scenarios in production with alerts set up for **key performance indicators** (**KPIs**). We will cover testing in *Chapter 9, Choreographing Deployment and Delivery*.

Stack

We deploy each service as a set of cloud resources that we will refer to as a stack. We declaratively define the resources of a stack in a `serverless.yml` configuration file in the root of the repository. We use the Serverless Framework to initiate deployments and execute the cloud provider's deployment management service, such as AWS CloudFormation. The deployment management service manages the life cycle of the resources as a group. It compares the current state of the stack to the latest declarations and applies any changes. It adds new resources, updates existing resources, and deletes removed resources. And it deletes all resources when we delete the stack to ensure there are no orphaned resources. We also define the least privileged permissions for these resources within the stack:

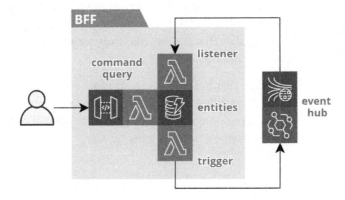

Figure 2.9 – A typical service stack

We use diagrams such as *Figure 2.9* to depict a service. The gray box logically equates to the service and physically equates to both the repository and the stack. The icons represent the cloud resources within the stack. We place icons next to each other to indicate communication. This results in tighter diagrams. The nearest arrow implies the flow of communication. A legend for all the icons is available in the preface.

We will cover the details of creating a stack in *Chapter 6, A Best Friend for the Frontend*, and *Chapter 9, Choreographing Deployment and Delivery*.

Persistence

Each service will own and manage its own data. Following polyglot persistence practices, each service will use the type of database that best supports its needs. These serverless resources are managed as part of the stack.

Services will consume domain events from upstream services and cache the necessary data as lean materialized views. The high availability of these serverless data stores creates an inbound bulkhead that ensures necessary data is available even when upstream services are not. This also greatly improves data access latency.

We will leverage the **Change Data Capture** (**CDC**) mechanism of a data store to trigger the publishing of domain events when the state of a service changes. We can also use CDC to control the flow of data within a service.

We will cover the details of the persistence layer in *Chapter 5, Turning the Cloud into the Database*.

Trilateral API

Each service will have up to three APIs: one for the events it consumes, another for the events it produces, and one for its synchronous interface. Not all of these interfaces are required. Most services will consume events, but not all will publish events. For example, a BFF service that provides a read-only view of data would only consume events, cache the data, and provide a synchronous API to access the data. Control services and most ESGs do not have a synchronous interface.

Events

Following our event-first approach, the APIs for events are the most important, because they dictate how a service will interact with other services. A service should document the events it consumes and those that it produces. This could be as simple as a listing in the README file at the root of the repository or an explicit enumeration in the metadata of the service code. We can document the JSON structure of the events using TypeScript notation. The cloud infrastructure may provide a registry for the schemas of all the event types in the subsystem. We will cover events in detail in *Chapter 4, Trusting Facts and Eventual Consistency*.

API Gateway

Services operating at the boundaries of the system, such as BFFs, will have a synchronous interface. We will implement these using an API Gateway.

We design the API of a BFF specifically for a single frontend. One team owns the frontend and the BFF, so official documentation of the API may not be necessary. However, we often use a self-documenting API, such as **GraphQL**. We will cover BFFs in detail in *Chapter 6, A Best Friend for the Frontend*.

Some ESG services will also require an API Gateway, such as implementing a webhook to receive events from a third-party system or providing an external API for your own SaaS system. We will cover various ESG patterns in detail in *Chapter 7, Bridging Intersystem Gaps*.

Functions

We will implement the business logic of a service as functions using the cloud provider's **Function as a Service (FaaS)** offering. Each function is independent, but it is important to point out that we manage functions as a group within the stack that controls all the resources used to implement the service. A service will usually have three to five functions. These functions work together to provide the capabilities of the service. The typical functions in our service patterns include a `listener` function that consumes domain events, a `trigger` function that produces domain events, and `command` and `query` functions or a `graphql` function that implement the synchronous API.

The code within a function will follow typical clean and hexagonal architecture practices, which structure the code so that internal dependencies are acyclic and external dependencies are decoupled. Domain entities and business logic will sit in the middle and ports and adapters (that is, connectors) will sit on the perimeter. This will give us our biggest benefit in the context of testing.

Micro-app

Each BFF service will work with a corresponding micro-app presentation tier that supports an explicit set of capabilities for a specific actor. These micro-apps combine to provide the suite of features offered by the subsystem. Each micro-app will live in its own repository and have its own CI/CD pipeline.

We will be covering this topic in detail in *Chapter 3, Taming the Presentation Tier*, and *Chapter 6, A Best Friend for the Frontend*.

Shared libraries

We will tend to shy away from using shared libraries for business logic to help avoid the false reuse that creates coupling and complexity. We will use open source libraries for crosscutting concerns. When a BFF service uses GraphQL, we will package the schema in a shared library for use between the BFF and the micro-app. Over time, duplicated logic can be refactored into libraries when it proves to not be false reuse. Each library will live in its own repository and its own CI/CD pipeline will publish it to a registry, such as **npm**.

Governing without impeding

As architects, once we have defined the architectural boundaries of the system, we need to let go and get out of the way, unless we want to become the impediment to innovation. But letting go is difficult. It goes against our nature; we like to be hands-on. And it flies in the face of traditional governance techniques. But we must let go for the sake of the business, whether it realizes this or not.

Governance has an understandable reputation for getting in the way of progress and innovation. Although it has good intentions, the traditional gated approach to governance actually increases risk, instead of reducing it, because it increases lead time, which diminishes a company's ability to react to challenges in a modern dynamic environment. But it doesn't have to be this way.

We have already taken major strides to mitigate the risks of continuous innovation. We define architectural boundaries that limit the scope of any given change and we fortify these boundaries to control the blast radius when honest human errors happen. We do this because we know to err is human. We know that mistakes are inevitable, no matter how rigorous a process we follow.

Instead of impeding innovations, we must empower teams with a culture and a platform that embrace continuous governance. This is a safety net that gives teams and management confidence to move forward, knowing that we can catch mistakes, and make corrections, in real time. Automation and observability are the key elements of continuous governance. Let's see how we can put this safety net in place and foster a culture of robustness.

Leveraging observability

I remember when a product owner asked me, many years ago, why her product had periodic performance issues. I didn't have a good answer because in those days it was typical to only monitor the infrastructure, with details limited to the likes of CPU and memory utilization and overall transaction volumes and latency. I could confirm that there was a periodic issue, but there was very little contextual information available in the production system to clearly identify the root cause.

Today, the opposite is true. We have significant observability of the inner workings of our systems. We are leveraging fully managed, serverless, cloud resources that emit many useful metrics out of the box. We receive these metrics in fine-grained details, so we can see exactly how individual transactions are performing.

Managing this information and leveraging it for continuous governance is a difficult challenge in and of itself. Attempting to provide this capability in-house will ultimately fall short in capabilities and have a higher total cost of ownership. More importantly, under-delivering on observability will impede innovation. Following our serverless-first mantra, it is best to leverage a SaaS monitoring service to provide teams with a one-stop, turnkey solution. These tools consume all the observability metrics from our cloud resources and provide a single-pane-of-glass view across all our services, cloud accounts, and cloud providers.

The ultimate goal is to turn all this valuable observability data into actionable information. Autonomous teams will only accelerate their pace of innovation if they are confident that they can control the impact of any potential mistakes. Bulkheads are one part of the equation because they help control the blast radius. Observability is the other part because it gives teams the information, they need to take the necessary action to fail forward and minimize the time to recovery.

We will dive into the relevant details of observability in the context of the various chapters. Here, we will cover a categorization of metrics, such as work metrics and resource metrics, that helps turn this data into information.

Work metrics

Work metrics represent the user-visible output of the system. They tell us what the system is doing from the external perspective. For example, are the users experiencing errors or increased latency. These are the **KPIs** we will use to determine if the system is healthy. We may also use them to gauge the success of our experiments.

Our BFF and ESG services are candidates for key work metrics because they operate at the boundary of the system. Our **domain events** are the facts that record the work that the system has performed. The **RED** method recommends monitoring *rate*, *error*, and *duration* work metrics. We will collect these metrics for the *API gateway* resources of our boundary services. We will track the rate that we publish *domain events* to the event hub, with special handling for *fault events*. We will perform *anomaly detection* on these metrics to identify and alert on variations over time.

It is important to avoid *alert fatigue*. If we over-alert, then the metrics become noise and we miss valuable, actionable information. This in turn leads to longer response times, then longer lead times, and ultimately less innovation. One of the objectives of *TestOps*, which we will discuss shortly, is to identify which metrics provide the most value.

Netflix provides the classic example. They have identified one work metric as the most important indicator of a significant problem with the system. This one metric is the rate at which users press the *Play* button. They will page people in the middle of the night when they detect an anomaly in this metric. Other metrics may be important, but not worth waking people up for.

The general guideline is to alert liberally, but page judiciously on symptoms rather than causes. All teams need to discover their most important work metrics so that they can page the teams about things that matter. For example, in our Food Delivery system, the rate of the `PlacedOrder` domain event is likely to be important. We will record all other alerts as **System Events** for root cause analysis, as we will discuss shortly.

Resource metrics

Resource metrics describe the internal workings of the system. They tell us at a lower level what the system is doing to produce the user-visible output. In other words, work metrics represent the symptoms, while resource metrics indicate the cause. When we see a degradation of work metrics, our resource metrics help us determine the *root cause* of the user-visible symptoms.

These resources are the serverless cloud services we are leveraging, such as databases, streams, queues, functions, API gateways, and so on. Although they are fully managed, we still need to monitor and tune them to optimize the system. The **USE** method recommends monitoring the *utilization*, *saturation*, and *errors* of our resources. When we provision these resources, we allocate capacity, either explicitly or implicitly. We need to monitor the percentage of *capacity* that is utilized so that we know when we are running out of headroom. *Throttling* and *iterator age* metrics indicate when we have exceeded (that is, saturated) our allocated capacity. Other errors are usually an indication of bugs in our code.

A spike in a resource metric may be temporary, auto-scaling may kick in and/or the resource may recover on its own. If this spike does not impact a work metric, then we will not page the team in the middle of the night. However, these spikes may be an early indication of a future problem. Therefore, we will record these alerts as `System Events`, so that we can use them in future root cause analysis and performance tuning. We may email the team so that they can take proactive action in the morning.

System events

System events are distinct from metrics. We collect metrics continuously, whereas system events occur at discrete points in time. The monitor system will record a system event when a work metric or resource metrics exceeds a threshold; our CI/CD pipelines will generate a system event when we perform a deployment; our intrusion detection monitoring will create a system event when it detects a breach; and our continuous auditing will raise a system event when a rule is violated.

Collecting all this information into a unified monitoring tool gives us comprehensive observability of the system. Overlaying these system events with the work and resource metrics provides context and a single pane of glass for performing root cause analysis. This will reduce response times, which gives teams the confidence to reduce lead times and ultimately increase the pace of innovation.

From a governance perspective, we are interested in the metrics of the system events themselves. These are higher-order metrics that provide observability into the inner workings of the teams. An excessive rate of system events may indicate that a team needs help. The underlining work and resource metrics help identify where they need additional mentoring. So, let's look into some important team metrics.

Team metrics

Autonomous teams are responsible for leveraging the work and resource metrics of their services as a tool for self-governance and self-improvement. In my experience, teams truly value these insights and thrive on continuous feedback. From an oversight perspective, we should focus on teams that are struggling. The following team metrics help identify which teams may need more assistance and mentoring:

- **Lead time**: How long does it take a team to complete a task and push the change to production?

- **Deployment rate**: How many times a day is a team deploying changes to production?

- **Failure rate**: How often does a deployment result in a failure that impacts a generally available feature?

- **Mean Time to Recovery (MTTR)**: When a failure does occur, how long does it take the team to fail forward with a fix?

The answers to these questions clearly, identify the maturity of a specific team. We certainly prefer lead time, failure rate, and MTTR to be low and deployment rate to be high. Teams that are having trouble with these metrics are usually going through their own digital transformation and are eager to receive coaching. We should track these metrics alongside all the others in our observability tool.

Cost metrics

An interesting benefit of our serverless-first approach is that cloud cost itself becomes a much more useful metric. The cloud provider calculates cost per transaction, and for some resources based on the time it takes to complete a transaction. Therefore, if we reduce the number of transactions, such as with low-cost edge caching, and/or if we reduce the transaction time, such as by optimizing an algorithm, then we can improve performance and user satisfaction, while also reducing cost.

This new reality is a bit mind-bending because we traditionally need to spend more money to improve performance. Even when we optimize an algorithm under the traditional approach, this usually just means that we get more headroom within the capacity we have already purchased. This totally changes the incentive equation. I might even say that performance tuning starts to become addictive.

Concerns over performance and scalability traditionally slow teams down and increase lead times. Instead, the implicit scalability and observability of serverless resources gives teams the confidence to move forward, with the knowledge that they can tune the system as they go. Then, each month, when the cloud invoice arrives, the cost metrics are a powerful motivator for self-governance and continuous improvement.

This is where **worth-based development** comes into play. Let's say that a specific transaction within an autonomous subsystem accounted for 60% of the monthly cloud cost. If the team identified that they could improve the performance of that transaction by 50%, then that would account for a 30% reduction in monthly cost. At this point, it becomes a simple matter of deciding whether or not the estimated cost of making the improvement is worth the expected reduction in monthly runtime cost.

Even if the cost is equal in the short term, it is still an improvement in customer satisfaction and goodwill. The power of fine-grained cost metrics, implicit scalability, and worth-based development is mind-boggling at first and liberating thereafter.

The bottom line is that observability, along with bulkheads, gives autonomous teams the confidence to exercise the power and freedom of self-governance. It also gives architects the insights needed to govern without a heavy hand and to help out where teams clearly need it.

The next part of the governance equation is facilitating a culture of robustness and providing the tools that make it practical.

Facilitating a culture of robustness

Our goal of increasing the pace of innovation has led us to smaller batch sizes and shorter lead times. We are deploying code much more frequently and these deployments must result in *zero downtime*. To eliminate downtime, we must uphold the contracts we have defined within the system. These include the contracts between a service and its database, between a service and its frontend, between services and between subsystems. Yet, to support innovation, these contracts must be flexible, they must support continuous change. Traditional *versioning* techniques fall apart in a dynamic environment with a high rate of change. Instead, we will apply the **Robustness principle**.

The Robustness principle states *be conservative in what you send, be liberal in what you receive*. This principle is well suited for continuous deployment, where we can perform a successive set of deployments to make a conforming change on one side of a contract, followed by an upgrade on the other side and then another on the first side to remove the old code. The trick is to develop a culture of robustness where this dance is committed to team muscle memory and becomes second nature.

In *Chapter 9, Choreographing Deployment and Delivery*, we will cover a lightweight continuous delivery process that is geared for robustness. It includes three levels of planning, GitOps, CI/CD pipelines, and more. It forms a simple automated bureaucracy that governs each regional canary deployment but leaves the order of deployments completely flexible.

To facilitate this process, each team needs an integrated suite of tools including issue management, source control, and CI/CD pipelines. These tools also need to integrate with the monitoring tool, as we discussed earlier, to provide observability of team metrics. Again, following our serverless-first mantra, it is best to use a SaaS provider that offers these capabilities as a one-stop, turnkey solution. High availability is another key characteristic of these hosted solutions. Using a hosted solution creates a natural bulkhead between our tools and our services to help ensure the tools are available when we need to deploy a fix to a failing service.

In my experience, autonomous teams are eager to adopt a culture of robustness, especially once they get a feel for how much more productive and effective, they become. But this is a paradigm shift, and it is unfamiliar from a traditional governance perspective. The transparency and observability provided go a long way towards bridging that gap. As architects, we need to facilitate cultural change.

The next part of the governance equation is performing continuous auditing to help fill the gaps that we once filled with time-consuming manual audit hurdles.

Audit continuously

A major objective of governance is to ensure that a system is compliant with regulations and best practices. These include the typical *-ilities*, such as scalability and reliability, and of course security, along with regulations, such as NIST, PCI, GDPR, and HIPAA. The traditional approach includes manual audits of the architecture. These gates are the reason governance has a reputation for impeding progress. They are labor intensive and worse yet, they are error prone.

Fortunately, we now have a better option. Our deployments are fully automated by our CI/CD pipelines. This is already a significant improvement in quality because **infrastructure-as-code** reduces human error and enables us to quickly fail forward. We have also added observability, which provides timely, actionable information so that we know when to jump into action. We can take this further by hardening our build processes and adding continuous auditing in our cloud accounts.

Modern build pipelines have become very robust, thanks to strong open source community support. Dependency management tools have built-in security auditing to identify third-party dependencies with known vulnerabilities. Open source static code analysis rules do a great job of enforcing well-established design patterns. And we have shifted all the traditional testing, including unit, integration, contract, and end-to-end testing, into the build pipelines with significant levels of code coverage.

We still have some manual gates for each deployment. The first gate is code review and approval of a pull request. We perform these gates quickly because each task branch has a small batch size. The second gate is certification of a regional canary deployment. We deploy to one region for continuous smoke testing, before we deploy to other regions. We will cover CI/CD pipelines in detail in *Chapter 9, Choreographing Deployment and Delivery*.

After deployment, we continuously audit our cloud resources, with tools such as AWS Config, to ensure that we have configured them properly and they remain so. These audit rules hook into cloud administration events, such as AWS CloudWatch events. The rules evaluate whenever resources change. When a rule fails, it generates a system event in the monitoring system to alert the team and provide observability.

Of course, we must pair auditing with mentoring. The teams need to understand the rules and best practices before they can comply with them. A great place to start is with project templates for each of the major service patterns so that teams can seed new projects that are compliant from the start. For example, the first pull requests for a new repository should seed a complete and compliant CI/CD pipeline that deploys a default service stack all the way to production to verify that all the governance plumbing is in place. From here, we can leverage the observability provided by system events, team metrics, and cost metrics to help identify teams with additional mentoring needs.

The reality is that continuous auditing provides better risk mitigation than the traditional gated approach because we find and fix mistakes faster in real time. It allows teams to focus on their functionality and gives them the confidence to move forward with their experiments so that they can mitigate the risk of building the wrong solutions.

The next part of the governance equation is securing the perimeter of the system along the entire software development life cycle and pushing the perimeter to the edge of the cloud, far away from our private resources.

Securing the perimeter

First and foremost, companies have to value security and invest in it accordingly. Security is everyone's responsibility, the teams', the team members', the architects', and the business', everyone's. Fortunately, the serverless-first approach draws the line of the cloud security shared responsibility model significantly high in the technology stack. This means the providers of fully managed, serverless cloud services are responsible for securing a significant portion of the stack. This frees teams to focus on securing their business domain, such as identifying what data we must protect and redact. Continuous auditing rules help to ensure that we follow security best practices.

This still leaves the all-important task of securing the perimeter of the system. This includes locking down access to our cloud accounts and monitoring the entire system for attacks and breaches. Thankfully, these are crosscutting concerns that we can manage centrally and provide to the teams for self-service.

Before anything else, we have to lock down access to our cloud accounts. Otherwise, anything else we do is irrelevant. This includes requiring **multi-factor authentication (MFA)**, following the principle of least privilege and practicing good access key hygiene. Furthermore, this all must extend to the third-party tools that have access to the cloud accounts, including the monitoring system and CI/CD pipelines. In larger organizations, this usually includes setting up **Single Sign-On (SSO)** for the cloud accounts and tools to the corporate directory system. When regulations are in play, this includes ensuring separation of duties. And more so than ever, VPN access with IP address whitelisting is necessary to support remote workers.

Next, we need to leverage the fully managed cloud services that are available to create a secure runtime perimeter at the edge of the cloud. This includes global services, such as **Domain Name System (DNS)**, **Content Delivery Network (CDN)**, **Web Application Firewalls (WAF)**, and **API Gateways**. These services provide amazing scalability and availability by serving some content from the edge and optimizing access to cloud regions and availability zones. They also help protect our systems by absorbing malicious traffic at the edge of the cloud before it reaches and impacts the regional cloud resources. In other words, it is important, for security and performance, to have all traffic pass through this perimeter.

We also need to provide authentication support, such as **OAuth 2.0** and **OpenID Connect (OIDC)**, for our boundary services. Each subsystem should provide social or enterprise identity federation for its specific user pool. **SAML 2.0** support for the corporate directory system should be readily available for employee user pools, similar to the SSO support mentioned earlier. We must also prescribe best practices for securing **JSON Web Tokens (JWTs)** on the presentation tier.

With all the traffic flowing through the secured perimeter, we need to monitor the system for threats, such as DDoS attacks and intrusion detection, and perform continuous penetration testing. This is a crosscutting concern that we can assign to a dedicated team with the necessary skills and experience. Cloud providers offer tools, such as AWS Security Hub, to facilitate the effort. And once again, the metrics and system events need to flow into the central monitoring system to provide holistic observability.

We will cover an approach to managing and rolling out these capabilities in the *Automating account creation* section shortly. One important thing to keep in mind is that the autonomous teams will need the ability to self-service provision their own perimeter resources, such as DNS zones, certificates, and CDN distributions, so that the central security group does not impede team lead times. The autonomous teams will own these resources, but the provisioning process will automatically include them in the central monitoring.

The bottom line is that teams do not have to choose between security and innovation. Serverless resources and a secured perimeter combine to form a safe environment that fosters innovation because teams can focus on their business domain.

The next part of the governance equation is shifting a portion of the testing effort all the way to the right, into production, so that we can continuously assert the health of the system.

Elevating TestOps

The role of QA is changing. Many traditional testing techniques impede innovation because they are optimized for predictable environments, large batch sizes, and long lead times. In today's dynamic environment, we cannot assume that we are building the right solution, because customers are fickle, competition is fierce, and our assumptions may be off base. We need testing techniques that enable a quick feedback loop, to give teams the confidence to experiment, learn, and adapt, all with zero downtime.

The new role for QA is to provide insights for governance and risk mitigation. For example, we may turn on a new feature for one division to see if it improves employee performance, while the previous version continues to support the other divisions. From a business perspective, we need to know if the experiment is achieving the business objectives, so that we can decide whether to pivot or forge ahead. From the team's perspective, we need to know if an experiment is having a negative impact on the existing features so that we can quickly focus our efforts on recovery and then learn from our mistakes.

We accomplish this by shifting a portion of the QA effort into production, where we monitor the signals that the system is emitting. This requires a combination of traditional QA and operations skills, hence the term **TestOps**. We discussed earlier, in the *Thinking about events first* section, how event-first thinking implicitly builds business analytics into the system because events are facts. These facts are work metrics that we can observe to gauge the success of an experiment and the health of the system. Traditional QA skills come to bear in helping to identify which work metrics reflect the business objectives and which indicate the health of the system's capabilities. Traditional operations skills come into play for collecting and alerting on these metrics.

We will also use our testing skills to implement a strategic set of synthetic transactions that continuously exercise the system by smoke testing critical usage scenarios to certify our regional canary deployments. We will leverage our QA and operations skills for chaos testing to proactively assert the resilience of the system during scenarios, such as regional failover, unexpected load increases, or external system degradation. All of this is part of a comprehensive and cohesive test engineering effort that stretches back into the continuous deployment pipelines to ensure the robustness of the continuously evolving system. We will go deeper into continuous testing in *Chapter 9, Choreographing Deployment and Delivery*.

Automating account creation

Autonomy is crucial for creating a flexible architecture. We have discussed the importance of autonomous teams, autonomous services, and even autonomous subsystems. However, in this section on governance, we have covered a range of crosscutting concerns, such as observability, tooling, security, auditing, and testing. We don't want teams to have to reinvent these wheels, but we also want to give teams the flexibility to innovate in these areas. As always, it is a balancing act, but at the very least every new team needs a jumpstart.

We are using cloud accounts as natural bulkheads for our autonomous subsystems. This means that we have more than just a few accounts to manage. For example, a typical account structure would include the following:

- A master billing account that all accounts roll up to

- A central account to collect audit logs

- An isolated disaster recovery account for backups

- A development account and production account per autonomous subsystem

Creating these accounts should *not* be a manual process. Our cloud accounts are part of our infrastructure, so we will follow the same *infrastructure-as-code* practices that we use for our services. I typically refer to this as *accounts-as-code* to help highlight the importance of governing our cloud accounts. For example, the security of our system is only as strong as the weakest link. We put a lot of effort into securing our services, but if there is no rigor in how we manage and secure our cloud accounts then the entire system is at risk. Thus, we need to leverage automation to govern the creation and maintenance of our accounts to help ensure we follow best practices.

Cloud providers are starting to provide specific capabilities to stamp our accounts. We will treat this process exactly like we handle services. I recommend creating a stack for each of the following:

- A stack for essential security configurations, such as enabling audit trails, creating administrator, developer, and read-only roles and permissions, requiring MFA and setting up SSO

- A stack that integrates the account with the SaaS observability tool so that it can ingest metrics and logs and perform needed actions

- A stack that integrates the SaaS CI/CD tool so that it has the minimum permissions necessary to initiate deployments

- One or more stacks that configure the auditing rules that will continuously assert the conformity of the account and the resources within

Dedicated teams with the appropriate knowledge and skills will handle the development of these crosscutting concerns. However, the owners of each autonomous subsystem must have control over when to apply changes to their accounts. They should also have the flexibility to override and/or enhance features as their circumstances dictate.
A good approach is for each subsystem to fork its own repository for each of the stacks mentioned here. This will give each team their own CI/CD pipelines and the flexibility to pull in changes when they are ready and to submit pull requests back with suggested enhancements. And of course, all of the same traceability and observability practices that we discuss throughout will apply to the governance of these stacks as well.

Summary

In this chapter, we learned how to define architectural boundaries that enable change. The key is understanding that people (that is, actors) are the source of change and then aligning our boundaries along these axes of change. We found that event-first thinking, with its focus on verbs and facts, naturally helps us with this alignment. We brought this all together to divide a system into autonomous subsystems, and these into autonomous services. We saw how we can create arbitrarily complex systems following this simple fractal pattern of autonomous components. Then, we dissected the anatomy of autonomous services and learned how to leverage observability and automation to govern without impeding innovation.

In the next chapter, we will start digging into the details of our architecture. We will learn how the microfrontend approach, along with other new techniques, helps to bring the seemingly endless churn at the presentation layer under control.

Section 2: Dissecting the Software Architecture Patterns

In this section, we dive deep into the details of the architectural patterns that enable teams to continuously deliver business value. We start with the frontend because it is the most visible part of the system and provides context to the other patterns. We then cover the foundational event and data patterns that support the entire architecture. Then we work our way back up through the autonomous service patterns. Along the way, we cover best practices for security, reliability, observability, performance, and so forth, in the context of the various patterns.

This section contains the following chapters:

- *Chapter 3, Taming the Presentation Tier*
- *Chapter 4, Trusting Facts and Eventual Consistency*
- *Chapter 5, Turning the Cloud into the Database*
- *Chapter 6, A Best Friend for the Frontend*
- *Chapter 7, Bridging Intersystem Gaps*
- *Chapter 8, Reacting to Events with More Events*

3
Taming the Presentation Tier

In *Chapter 2, Defining Boundaries and Letting Go*, we defined the architecture of a system by dividing it into a set of autonomous subsystems. These architectural boundaries create bulkheads that enable change by promoting autonomy. They give autonomous teams confidence to push the limits and continuously deliver business value because they know these fortified boundaries will help control the blast radius when things go wrong.

Now we turn our attention to the frontend user experience. Frontend architecture has been going through a revolution. Many of the new techniques are only at the beginning of the adoption curve. In this chapter, you will learn how to decompose the frontend into micro applications, to enable change and ensure autonomy. You will also learn how to secure the user experience and how to design for offline-first and regional failover.

In this chapter, we're going to cover the following main topics:

- Innovation on the presentation tier
- Breaking up the frontend monolith
- Dissecting micro frontends
- Designing for offline-first
- Securing the user experience
- Observing real user activity

Zigzagging through time

The presentation tier is a battleground. It always has been. It always will be. It is the most visible part of a system, so it elicits the most feedback and experiences the most churn. From a functional perspective, this is good, because it leads to innovations that help us zero in on the right solutions for users. From a technical perspective, this volatility is more of a mixed bag.

Today, a technical war rages over the use of the React framework versus the Angular framework. It is good to have choices and the competition drives technical innovation that benefits everyone. But it can also create a skills gap that impedes progress when team members move between projects that use different frameworks. We will provide some relief for this problem in the *Dissecting micro frontends* section, but I suspect we will never end the framework wars. However, debates over things such as client-side versus server-side rendering are more clean-cut. Let's see how.

Client-side versus server-side rendering

I started my career as a Visual Basic programmer in the client-server programming area. But I wrote my share of mainframe green screens as well. So, I had a feel for the differences in both the developer and the user experience of the different rendering approaches.

Everyone preferred the client-side rendering experience, but it had its problems, such as versioning and installation headaches and the limits of hardware and network performance at the time. So, when the World Wide Web emerged, rendering moved back to the server side. But the user experience suffered, and this drove the need for the Ajax innovation that moved some of the rendering back to the client side. We referred to this back and forth between client-side and server-side rendering as a **pendulum**.

So, when **Single-Page Applications (SPAs)** and **Angular 1** arrived, my initial reaction was, here we go again, the pendulum is swinging back to the client side, and we are going to experience a similar set of problems again. However, I had spent the last year wrangling with running server-side presentation tiers in the cloud, so I knew how costly and cumbersome it was to deliver a scalable solution.

This is when I realized that the pendulum wasn't just swinging back and forth; it was zigzagging through time. With each cycle, the context changed. Different options or variations on options would emerge that changed how we weighed the different decision variables. And this time around, we had the option to deploy the presentation tier to the edge of the cloud.

I knew everything was going to change the moment I realized that I could easily deploy the SPA artifacts to an AWS S3 bucket and serve them through AWS CloudFront, with no need to manage any servers. With little to no elbow grease and pennies on the dollar, I had a globally scalable and fault-tolerant solution. I didn't have to manage an elastic load balancer and multiple AWS EC2 instances across Availability Zones and pay for them by the hour, whether they were idle or not. We will see how to deploy an SPA to the edge of the cloud in the *Dissecting micro frontends* section.

I was sold. I had a powerful incentive to make the change. But the story wasn't complete.

Build-time versus runtime rendering

It's no surprise, but no sooner did we have SPAs rendering on the client side than the JavaScript community realized we also needed rendering on the server side as well. We needed isomorphic rendering that could render on the client side or the server side. Part of a screen could render on the server side and the rest could render later on the client side. The part that is rendered on the server side could re-render on the client side.

So, we would need to manage servers for the presentation tier after all. Or would we? Because other elements in the current context were continuing to change as well. Continuous deployment and GitOps practices were emerging. Our ability to observe the inner workings of the presentation tier was also improving and yielding insights that would drive us in a better direction.

As I managed and tuned the older server-side rendering applications I mentioned previously, I began to realize how inefficient they were. We had designed them to be extremely dynamic. The presentation tier logic allowed almost anything to change based on the current user's preferences, roles, and history. I watched the observability metrics roll in and it became clear that the vast majority of requests produced the same output. The requests came in and hit the servers, which hit the database and rendered the same results over and over again.

It made me think of the saying about the definition of insanity: doing the same thing over and over again and expecting a different result. This was a normal design pattern, but it was rooted in an era of long lead times and infrequent deployments. Now, the context had changed. We could deploy changes at any time, many times a day. We didn't need to make an application more complex and less efficient to accommodate change with data-driven logic. We could make a change, build it, and deploy it. This is when **Jamstack** (`https://jamstack.org`) emerged, along with tools such as **Gatsby** (`https://www.gatsbyjs.com`) and **Next.js** (`https://nextjs.org`).

The **Jam** in Jamstack stands for **JavaScript, API, and Markup**. It builds on the **GitOps** and continuous deployment practices that we cover in *Chapter 9, Choreographing Deployment and Delivery*, to create a lightweight content management system. It also leverages the power of server-side rendering at build time to deploy pre-rendered websites and SPAs that are super scalable, efficient, and cost-effective. We execute JavaScript on the client side to animate the rendering of any screen sections that do need to change dynamically. We make asynchronous calls to retrieve data that changes frequently. Also, when relatively static content does change, such as a news post, we use the likes of the **Markdown** markup language, to easily author the new content. Then our CI/CD pipelines build and deploy the change.

We can take this a step further and use our event-first architecture to react to business events and automate the rendering and deployment of a portion of an application, such as a micro application. With this approach, we can maximize efficiency by rendering content once, instead of over and over again. The application appears to be dynamic because it is. But we only render the content when it changes.

But there is more. Pre-rendering and deploying SPAs to the edge of the cloud has a positive impact on increasingly mobile and often disconnected users. This, in turn, has changed the equation of the web versus mobile decision.

Web versus mobile

Mobile devices and mobile applications have had a significant impact on end user expectations. Users expect to have access to their applications any time of day, from any location, with zero downtime. They understand that they may experience periods of poor connectivity, but they expect their applications to continue to function. These expectations have driven significant technical innovation. We will see some of this in the *Designing for offline-first* section.

There is technical debate over how to implement mobile applications. Should we write them using the native libraries of a specific device? Should we write responsive and **Progressive Web Applications** (**PWAs**)? Or should we follow a hybrid approach? This is another framework war that we cannot end. But the decision has a definite impact on the amount of work needed to support many different device types.

Building truly native mobile applications means we have to implement and maintain separate applications for Android and iOS. A hybrid approach only requires a single code base but may not provide users with the native feel that they want. For a consumer-facing application, it is important to have a presence in the app stores, but for enterprise applications the opposite is true. Meanwhile, as we will see in this chapter, SPAs have evolved into mobile-ready applications.

From a business value perspective, our job as architects is clear. We need to put a solution in place that enables us to shorten lead times and gather feedback from users as quickly as possible so that we can iterate to the best solution. Once we prove that an application has business value, then we can change the implementation if there are clear improvements.

Innovation is our goal. The presentation tier is the battleground where innovation plays out. We do not want to impede innovation by placing undue restrictions on the presentation tier because we cannot easily predict how users will interact with systems in the future. For example, voice and virtual reality add new dimensions to the equation as they mature and enter the mainstream.

But we do need to tame the presentation tier so that it does not impede itself. We need the ability to change the user experience, quickly and easily, as we learn and improve our understanding of what users need in their applications. So, we need an architecture for the frontend that enables change. Let's start by looking at ways to break up the frontend.

Breaking up the frontend monolith

Our goal is to create a software architecture that enables change. In *Chapter 2, Defining Boundaries and Letting Go*, we defined the architecture of a system by dividing it into a set of autonomous subsystems. In the remaining chapters, we dive into the details of decomposing subsystems into autonomous services. But first, we need to address the presentation layer.

We need to break up the frontend monolith, like the backend, to eliminate the friction that impedes innovation. We must decompose all the layers of the technical architecture to the same level of granularity. The frontend, the backend, and the database all need to work together as a cohesive unit. Then we can give autonomous teams control over a slice of the full stack so that they can move forward independently.

Before we get into the technical details, let's look at how we can functionally decompose the frontend into independent but seamless applications. This will allow us to easily extend the system as a whole, by adding new applications without modifying existing applications.

By subsystem

In *Chapter 2, Defining Boundaries and Letting Go*, we aligned the autonomous subsystem architecture with the actors, business units, business capabilities, and data life cycle of the system. For example, our *Food Delivery system* has separate subsystems for customers, drivers, and restaurants. Each subsystem caters to the needs of these different actors. There are similarities across these subsystems, such as they all have a sign-up process, but the details vary significantly.

Each subsystem should maintain its own frontend applications. A subsystem's frontend will have a main entry point for its users that provides access to all of its features. These features will be separately deployable frontend applications.

By user activity

Within a subsystem, we decompose the frontend into multiple applications along the lines of the activities the users perform. We call these micro applications or micro-apps. For example, the frontend for the customer subsystem of our Food Delivery system contains the following micro applications:

- The main entry point is a **Jamstack** application that provides static marketing material, sign-in and sign-up links, and navigation to start browsing restaurants and menus.

- Sign-in and sign-up are separate but related applications.

- Searching for and browsing restaurants and menus is another application.

- Adding items to the cart and the cart itself are separate micro applications.

- Checkout is another micro application and tracking the status of an order is another application.

- Managing a user's account is another set of micro applications for profile settings, order history, and so forth.

Each of these micro applications is separately deployable and likely owned by separate autonomous teams. We will see how to seamlessly stitch these applications together in the *Dissecting micro frontends* section. Each micro application has its own BFF service and database, which we cover in *Chapter 6, A Best Friend for the Frontend*, and in *Chapter 5, Turning the Cloud into the Database*. This last point is significant because it enables autonomous teams by giving them control over the full stack.

By device type

Today's users are on the move and interact with a system using multiple devices and device types. For example, you might order food from your phone when you are on your way home and then you track the order from a laptop or a tablet once you get home. Handling all the permutations can impact our ability to change a system quickly and easily.

Depending on the system, it may not make sense to support all activities on all device types. For example, a data entry-intensive activity may not be practical on a small phone. Or we might support the ability to perform part of an activity from a mobile device when the user is on the move and then complete the activity when the user is on a laptop. Some activities may only be available based on the type of device.

Up to a point, we can make an application responsive based on the type of device and automatically adjust the layout to accommodate the screen size. However, there are limits, and implementing a responsive screen may be counter-productive in some scenarios. In these cases, it may make sense to create separate applications for different device types. Then we direct the user to the appropriate application based on the current device type.

By version

In *Chapter 9, Choreographing Deployment and Delivery*, we discuss a versioning strategy to achieve zero-downtime deployments using the **Robustness** principle and feature flags. When we are making small, incremental changes to an application, we do not need to support multiple versions. However, feature flags can get messy, when we are making significant changes. In these cases, it is better to create a new version of an application and run both versions in parallel until the new version is complete. We use a special role as the single feature flag to limit access to the new version of the application.

Now, let's see how we can stitch all these micro applications together to create a seamless user experience.

Dissecting micro frontends

To achieve our goal of creating a software architecture that enables change, we need to give teams full control of the entire stack. As depicted in *Figure 3.1*, a single team should own a micro application, its BFF service, and the datastore. This reduces the need for inter-team communication, which adds dependencies on another team's schedule:

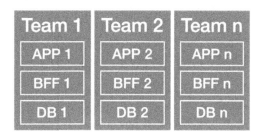

Figure 3.1 – Full-stack teams

These self-sufficient, full-stack, autonomous teams are able to move at their own pace, minimize lead time, and respond to user feedback at will, precisely because they are not dependent on other teams. We will learn more about them in the chapters ahead.

> **Note**
>
> In *Chapter 6, A Best Friend for the Frontend*, we will see how teams implement BFF services. In *Chapter 5, Turning the Cloud into the Database*, we will see how to decompose monolithic databases. Then, in *Chapter 4, Trusting Facts and Eventual Consistency*, we will see how these services communicate.

In this section, we look at how to create a micro frontend. The objective of a micro frontend is to divide the user experience into a set of independent micro applications, while also providing users with a seamless experience. As users move between different activities, it should not feel like they are jumping between applications. It should feel like a single application. As depicted in *Figure 3.2*, we may compose a single screen from many micro applications, but they will appear as a single application to the user:

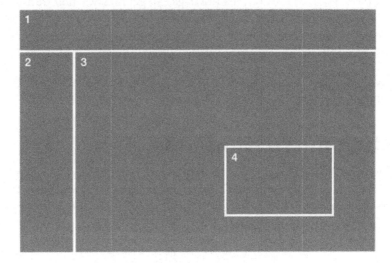

Figure 3.2 – Micro frontend

The preceding illustration shows the top (**1**) and left (**2**) navigation as separate micro applications. Another micro application (**3**) provides the contents of the page, which contains yet another micro application (**4**). As the user navigates through the subsystem, different micro applications provide the content of the different screens. But from the user's perspective, it is all one application.

The micro frontends approach provides the following three major benefits:

- **Isolates change**: Each micro application is independently deployable. Following the **Open-Closed principle**, we can deploy a new micro-app without changing existing applications. Following the **Single Responsibility principle**, each micro-app is responsible to a single actor, who drives change. When we do need to change and redeploy an existing micro-app, we have limited the scope of the impact to that one micro-app. In other words, micro applications are autonomous, and they enable autonomous teams.

- **Maximizes the potential for lazy loading**: Monolithic frontends are notorious for long load times and the problem grows more acute with each new feature added. **Code splitting** provides a workable solution to this problem, but micro-apps bring lazy loading to the forefront, instead of being an afterthought. An individual micro-app can and will leverage code splitting as well. This level of control is very important for mobile users.

- **Supports concurrent use of multiple frameworks and more importantly multiple framework versions**: Each micro-app can use a different framework, such as React or Angular. However, we should not abuse this capability. Each subsystem should standardize on a single framework. We should only utilize multiple frameworks as a migration path to the standard framework. This capability also enables the upgrading of a single framework, without requiring all micro applications to upgrade at once. This is significant, as there is constant innovation in these frameworks. New micro-apps can use the latest version and older apps can upgrade as they change.

There are many alternatives for implementing micro frontends. We can assemble them at build time or runtime, on the client side or the server side; we can link them together or we can programmatically connect them. We will look at an example throughout this chapter that utilizes the **single-spa** (`https://single-spa.js.org`) framework to programmatically stitch the micro frontend together on the client side at runtime. There is a `main` application that bootstraps the system, and each micro-app implements a well-defined life cycle so that the system can activate them and mount them at well-defined locations on the screen.

You can find a micro frontend template here: `https://github.com/jgilbert01/micro-frontend-template`.

Let's dig into the details of creating a micro frontend.

The main app

The presentation layer of each autonomous subsystem has a main entry point for gaining access to all of its features. However, the `main` application does not provide any specific features, other than bootstrapping the micro frontend environment. In essence, the `main` application owns the `index.html` file.

The main application has its own source code repository and its own CI/CD pipeline. The CI/CD pipeline performs the following duties:

- It creates the object store, such as an S3 bucket, that will hold all the resources of the various micro applications.

- It creates the **Content Delivery Network (CDN)**, such as an AWS CloudFront distribution, that will serve all the resources of the various micro applications from the edge of the cloud.

- It uploads the `index.html` file and a manifest file to the bucket. We will cover manifest files in the *Manifest deployer* section.

- It creates the domain name that we use to access the `index.html` file, such as with an AWS Route 53 record set.

The bootstrapping process starts when we access the `index.html` file.

The index file

The `index.html` file is lean and trim. It initializes the dynamic module loading system and kicks off the micro application registration process. This is how it appears:

```
<html>
<head>
 <title>My Main</title>
 <meta name="importmap-type" content="systemjs-importmap"/>
 <script type="systemjs-importmap" src="/importmap.json"/>
 <script src="https://cdn.../system.min.js" />
```

```
  <script src="https://cdn.../amd.min.js" />
  <script>System.import('@my/main');</script>
  <link ... href="//cdn.../semantic.min.css" />
</head>
<body />
</html>
```

The primary job of index.html is to load the /importmap.json data structure and initialize the SystemJS (https://github.com/systemjs/systemjs) module loader. Then it imports the @my/main micro application to kick off the registration process. Finally, it loads the global style sheet.

The importmap file

Lazy loading is one of the primary benefits of the micro frontend approach. We load each micro application just in time. This provides a more responsive user experience since we do not spend time loading applications that we do not use.

However, by default, JavaScript does not support dynamic module loading. Take the following import statements as an example:

```
import React from 'react';
import { useMountPoint } from '@my/shared';
```

Unless we specify otherwise, a bundler, such as **webpack**, will pull these dependencies into the bundle that it creates. This increases the size of the bundle and duplicates these dependencies across multiple micro applications.

Alternatively, we can tell the bundler to externalize specific dependencies. Now we need a mechanism to dynamically load these modules when our code imports them. This is where the importmap.json file and **SystemJS** come into play. Here is an example of an importmap file:

```
{
  "imports": {
    "@my/main": "/my-main/{commit-hash}/my-main.js",
    "@my/main/": "/my-main/{commit-hash}/",
    "@my/app1": "/my-app1/{commit-hash}/my-app1.js",
    "@my/app1/": "/my-app1/{commit-hash}/",
```

```
    "@my/shared": "/my-shared/{commit-hash}/my-shared.js",
    "@my/shared/": "/my-shared/{commit-hash}/",
    "react": "https://cdn.jsdelivr.net/...",
    "react-dom": "https://cdn.jsdelivr.net/...",
    "semantic-ui": "https://cdn.jsdelivr.net/...",
    "single-spa": "https://cdn.jsdelivr.net/...",
    }
}
```

This file does what its name implies. It maps the import names of modules to the path where they are located. SystemJS uses this file to import externalized modules. When we import the @my/main module, SystemJS will load it from our S3 bucket.

Note that there are two entries for each of our micro applications. We use the first entry to bootstrap a micro application without loading the entire module. Then we use the second entry when it is time to load a micro application.

We will cover the life cycle of a micro application in the *Micro-app activation* section. But first, we need to register the applications.

Micro-app registration

We need to register each micro application with the main application. The registration process begins when we import the main application at the bottom of the index.html file. The following code block shows the registration process:

```
import { registerApplication, start } from "single-spa";
...
fetch('/apps.json').then(res => res.json())
  .then((apps) => {
    const routes = constructRoutes(apps);
    const applications = constructApplications({
      routes,
      loadApp: ({ name }) => System.import(name),
    });
    const engine = constructLayoutEngine({ routes,
      applications });
    applications.forEach(registerApplication);
```

```
    engine.activate();
    start();
});
```

The main application retrieves and processes the `apps.json` manifest file. It constructs the routes and registers all the applications, and then it calls `start` to activate the system. It also defines a `loadApp` function for each application. This function will lazily load the entry file for a micro application. This is the first entry for the application in the `importmap` file. We will cover the entry file shortly in the *Micro-app* section. Here is an example of an `apps.json` file:

```json
{
  "routes": [
    {
      "type": "application",
      "name": "@my/nav"
    },
    {
      "type": "route",
      "path": "/things",
      "routes": [{
        "type": "application",
        "name": "@my/app1"
      }]
    },
    ...
]}
```

The single-spa layout engine defines the structure of the `apps.json` file. The file contains all the applications and their activation policies. For example, the `@my/app1` micro application will activate when a user accesses the `/things` route and the `@my/nav` micro application is always active. We will see how we use this information in the *Micro-app activation* section. We will cover the creation of this file in the *Manifest deployer* section.

Now, let's look at the resources of a micro-app.

Micro-app

In the *Breaking up the frontend monolith* section, we discussed various ways of decomposing the frontend into a set of micro applications. We also just covered dynamic module loading and application registration. Now let's look at what goes into a micro-app.

Each application has its own source code repository and its own CI/CD pipeline. The CI/CD pipeline performs the following duties:

- It tests all of the micro application's source code. We will cover testing in *Chapter 9, Choreographing Deployment and Delivery*.

- It builds the micro application's bundle with a bundler, such as **Webpack**.

- It uploads the bundle and a manifest file to the bucket created by the main application. We will cover manifest files in the *Manifest deployer* section.

The internals of a micro application are the same as for your chosen framework, such as React. The only difference is the entry point. A micro application has an entry file and a root component. Let's look at each in turn.

The entry file

Each micro application must have an entry file. We externalize this file from the rest of the micro application's bundle to maximize lazy loading. The main application will lazily load this file using the `loadApp` function that we defined in the *Micro-app registration* section. The following code block shows the core elements of the entry file:

```
import singleSpaReact from 'single-spa-react';
...
const lifecycles = singleSpaReact({
  ...
  loadRootComponent: () => import('./root.component.js'),
  domElementGetter: () => document
    .getElementById('container'),
  ...
});
export const bootstrap = lifecycles.bootstrap;
export const mount = lifecycles.mount;
export const unmount = lifecycles.unmount;
```

The entry file defines the following micro application life cycle functions:

- The `loadRootComponent` function lazily loads the micro application's bundle.
- The `bootstrap` function is called once to resolve the root component.
- The `domElementGetter` function returns the element where we want the root component mounted.
- The `mount` function renders the application in the location defined by `domElementGetter`.
- The `unmount` function removes the DOM elements that we rendered during `mount`.

We will see how we use these life cycle functions in the *Micro-app activation* section.

Root component

The actual functionality of a micro application starts in the root component. This is analogous to the `App` component in a typical React application, such as the `App` component generated by the *Create React App* utility. The following code block shows a basic root component:

```
import React from "react";
const Root = (props) => (<p>{props.name} is mounted!</p>);
export default Root;
```

This root component example is just the equivalent of `hello world` for micro applications. It displays the name of the micro application. The typical React root component will set up routing rules and initialize a Redux store. We will see a more elaborate example like this in the following *Micro-app activation* section.

Micro-app activation

For a typical monolithic SPA, the browser will load the entire code base when the user accesses the page. This process grows more and more time-consuming as the monolith grows larger. The micro frontend approach solves this problem by dividing the application into a set of lazily loaded micro applications. Then we *activate* a micro-app just in time.

Let's bring all this metadata and code together and see how we activate micro applications. We typically activate micro applications based on routes and we can manually activate them as well. But first, let's look at the full life cycle flow.

Micro-app life cycle

As we saw in the *Entry file* section, each micro application provides a set of life cycle methods that the micro frontend framework uses to bootstrap, mount, and unmount the application. The following steps outline the micro-app life cycle:

1. At startup, the main application registers each application in the apps.json manifest and starts the micro frontend framework.

2. Then the framework checks the *activation policy* of each application.

3. The first time an application activates, the framework loads the *entry file* to gain access to the application's life cycle functions. Then it calls the bootstrap life cycle function to load the *root component*.

4. Each time an application activates, the framework calls the mount life cycle function to attach the root component to the DOM as specified by the domElementGetter function.

5. When an application deactivates, the framework calls the unmount life cycle function to remove it from the DOM.

6. As the user navigates the systems, the framework checks all the activation policies and mounts and unmounts applications accordingly.

Some micro applications are always active. For example, a global navigation micro application may always be available to provide a main menu feature. Most micro applications will activate when the user selects these menus. Also, to a lesser degree, one micro application will manually activate another.

Route-based activation

In a SPA, routing is the practice of rendering different components as the URL changes. Frameworks hook into the browser history and location interfaces and render the appropriate components as the user navigates through the application. These routes represent different user activities. In the *Breaking up the frontend monolith* section, we identified that it is a best practice to create a separate micro application per user activity.

Routes are the most common way to activate micro applications. The micro frontend framework uses top-level routes to identify when to activate a specific micro application. Then the micro application uses sub-level routes to direct the rendering of its components. The following code block shows the root component of a micro application that defines sub-routes:

```
const Root = (props) => (
  <Router>
    <Things path="things" {...props} />
    <Thing path="things/:id" {...props} />
  </Router>
);
```

The micro frontend framework will activate this micro application based on the `/things` route, as defined in the `apps.json` file. Within this micro application, the `/things` route will render the `Things` component to browse things and the `/things/:id` route will render the `Thing` component to view a specific thing.

Now let's see how we can manually activate a micro application.

Manual activation

It is also possible to take full control and manually activate a micro application. We will typically do this when we want to embed one micro application within another micro application. For example, in our food delivery system, we embed the `add-to-cart` micro application inside the `view-menu-item` micro application.

The following code block shows manually activating another micro application:

```
<div>
  <Parcel
    config={() => System.import('@my/add-to-cart')}
    {...props, additionalProp } />
</div>
```

The `single-spa-react` library provides the `Parcel` component. We place this component in the location where we want to mount the micro application. This means that embedded micro applications do not need to declare the `domElementGetter` function. Then we configure a load function and specify the name of the micro application we want to load. We can also pass properties to the embedded micro application to initialize it with the proper information.

Now, let's see how we can dynamically associate micro applications to mount points.

Mount points

A micro application mounts to a specific dom element when it activates. We refer to this dom element as a **mount point**. A mount point represents a contract between the owner of the mount point and the micro applications that use the mount point. For example, the owner controls the location, width, and height of the dom element, and we must design a micro application to work within those parameters.

Navigation is a typical example of a mount point. For example, a left navigation menu will define links to activate micro applications based on routes and define a container dom element where the applications will mount. As another example, top-right navigation may open a sliding drawer and manually activate the specified micro application. In either case, we design the micro applications to make appropriate use of the given screen real estate.

For some systems, it may be reasonable to hardcode the navigation for a fixed set of micro applications. However, for a large application, we prefer to dynamically generate the navigation based on metadata. This allows us to add and remove micro applications without making changes to the navigation source code. The following code block shows an example of a dynamically rendered navigation component:

```
export const LeftNavMenuItems = () => {
  const { items } = useMountPoint('left-nav');
  return items.map((item) => <Menu.Item key={item.key}
        content={item.content} icon={item.icon}
        as={Link} to={item.to} />);
};


export const MainContainer = ({ children }) =>
  <div id='container'>{children}</div>;
```

The useMountPoint Hook retrieves a /mount-points.json file and returns the requested metadata. This component loops over the metadata and renders menus with links that will route to the micro applications. We also define the container element where we intend to mount the micro applications. Here is an example of a mount-points.json file that provides the metadata:

```
"mount-points": {
  "left-nav": [{
      "key": "thing",
      "content": "Things",
```

```
        "icon": "star",
        "to": "/things"
    }, ...]
  }
```

The mount point code dictates the contents of the metadata for a specific mount point. In this example, the mount point expects a unique key, the content and icon to display, and the route that the link will navigate to. When a user clicks on a menu link, the framework will then activate a micro application following the process that we outlined in the *Micro-app activation* section.

We can take mount points further and add conditional rules to further control navigation. For example, we may filter links based on the user's role or device type. We may disable menus based on the state of the domain entities. We would add these criteria to the metadata, such as a list of valid roles, user agents, or status flags. We will see an example of this in the *Securing the user experience* section.

Now let's see how `manifest-deployer` automates the process of bringing together all the metadata from our various manifest files.

Manifest deployer

As we have seen in the preceding section, we have three manifest files that allow us to dynamically create a micro frontend from a set of micro applications. These are the `importmap.json`, `apps.json`, and `mount-points.json` files. These files and the micro frontend framework allow us to independently deploy micro applications without modification to the other micro applications.

However, we do not want to risk manually updating these master manifest files as we add and change micro applications. Instead, each application defines its own manifest file that contains the fragments that we want to add to the main manifest files. Here is an example of an `mfe.json` manifest file:

```
{
  "orgName": "my",
  "projectName": "app1",
  "importmap": { ... },
  "apps": { ... },
  "mount-points": { ... }
}
```

The CI/CD pipeline for each micro application uploads its `mfe.json` manifest file to the S3 bucket. This in turn triggers the `manifest-deployer` service. This service builds the master manifest files from all the individual manifest files. The deployer service leverages the same stream processing framework we cover in *Chapter 4, Trusting Facts and Eventual Consistency*.

Now let's see how micro applications can communicate with each other.

Inter-application communication

Now that we have divided the system into micro applications, we need mechanisms that allow the applications to communicate with each other. For example, one application may launch another, or multiple applications on a screen may need to update together as the context changes.

In the *Breaking up the frontend monolith* section, we identified several best practices we can use to decompose a system into micro applications. We minimize the need for inter-application communication when we follow these best practices because each user activity is self-contained. If we find that two micro applications need to talk back and forth, then this may be an indication that we should merge them. But there are plenty of non-cyclic scenarios where one application interacts with another application.

One application can pass information into another application using route parameters. For example, one application may solely provide a search feature. From the search results list, we may want to launch various user activities. We would implement each of these user activities as a separate micro application. Then we would pass identifier information as a parameter so that the micro applications can retrieve the appropriate information as they see fit. The same is true for manually activating a micro application and passing properties.

We can also create micro applications that act as a shared library. They export functions and we import them dynamically using `importmap`. This ensures that only a single instance of the library exists. This allows us to cache common data within these modules and access it through the exported functions.

We can also use an event bus to exchange information with minimal coupling. For example, one application can register an event listener using `window.addEventListener('my-evt', ...)`. Then, other applications can send out information as their state changes using `window.dispatchEvent(...)`.

It is also possible to share state information across micro applications with libraries such as Redux, but this limits the independence of the micro applications. Each micro application should maintain its own state store. We should limit any shared or global storage to a very specific scope that lives in a shared micro application with a clearly defined and exported interface.

The micro frontend approach is a significant architectural improvement that brings the flexibility of independent deployments to the presentation layer. We have divided the system into multiple micro applications so that they can all change independently. This enables autonomous teams that have control over the full stack, so they can reduce lead times.

Now, let's take a deeper look at state management and how to design our micro applications to work offline, so that mobile users can work when disconnected.

Designing for offline-first

Today's users are on the move and they increasingly rely on mobile devices. You are likely reading this on a mobile device. If so, you likely downloaded the content to your device, so you can read it when you are offline. For static content, this is straightforward, and you knew up front that you wanted offline access.

For applications with dynamic content, the process of making the content available offline is more involved. Plus, it is more difficult to predict when connectivity will be unavailable. It is helpful to think of this problem in terms of the *CAP theorem*, which shows us that in the case of a system *partition* we have to choose between *consistency* and *availability*. We cannot have both.

Loss of connectivity is a perfect example of a system partition because the application can no longer retrieve and update the dynamic content. In this case, users favor availability over consistency. They want the application to continue working and for it to sort things out when the connection is reestablished. This means that mobile users are driving the need for *eventually consistent systems*.

We discuss eventual consistency in detail in *Chapter 4, Trusting Facts and Eventual Consistency*, and we cover related data patterns in *Chapter 5, Turning the Cloud into the Database*. In this section, we cover the concept of *session consistency* and extend it to support disconnected users. In other words, we will design the presentation tier to work *offline-first*. It will cache data locally and be fully functional when disconnected.

As a bonus, this also facilitates a *UI-first* development approach and accelerates the feedback loop, because it allows us to prototype a fully functioning application before we spend effort on creating the backend services.

Let's start by looking at how an application can be transparent with the user about the current status of the system. Then we will cover caching and live updates. Finally, we will see how offline-first enables smooth regional failover as well.

Transparency

Transparency is the first order of business for offline-first applications. We need to provide users with visibility into the status of the application so that they can make informed decisions. This can range from very basic indicators to more elaborate reconciliation features, based on the needs of the application and the experience of the users. A typical mobile email application provides an excellent frame of reference.

Status indicators

First and foremost, an application needs to provide the user with some sort of connectivity status indicator. This is in addition to the indicator provided by the device, because an application may only lose connectivity to its backend, such as during an outage. For example, an email application will indicate when it cannot reach a specific email account.

Next, it may be helpful to provide information about the cache, such as the version of the application code and the time of the most recent synchronization. In some cases, it may be useful to provide an as-of date (that is, a timestamp) for each record. The indicator should also show when synchronization is in progress. Again, an email app indicates when an account was last synchronized and when a sync is in progress, and, of course, the individual messages have timestamps.

Outbox

Things get more interesting when the user edits dynamic content offline. We need to queue the changes and push them to the backend when we have a connection. We need to make this clear to the users. They need to understand that their work is incomplete, and they may need to intervene in the worst case.

An outbox metaphor, such as in an email application, may be a good option. An application may already maintain status fields on the data, and this could be an additional intermediate status.

Inbox

Once we have a connection and synchronization is complete, there may be certain updates that are important to highlight for the user. For example, there may be changes that are related to the data that the user had in the outbox. This may just be informative, but in the worst case, the user may need to reconcile changes if there were any conflicts with changes performed by other users. In this case, it may be helpful to keep a visible list of all the changes we sent as well.

It is important to give users control. They can initiate a cache synchronization to increase their confidence in the data. Or they can initiate a synchronization when they know they are going offline. Let's see how the caching mechanism works.

Local cache

An offline-first application maintains a local cache on the client device to hold the application code and the content. Our objective is to provide the user with **session consistency**. In other words, we need to guarantee *read-your-writes* consistency. When offline, we cannot read the writes of other users, but we must retain and provide access to any changes made by the current user. Also, when we are online, we aim to keep the cache up to date and be transparent about its accuracy.

To achieve session consistency, we will maintain a read-through cache and a write-through cache. But first, we need to cache (that is, install) the application itself. So, let's start with installation.

Installation

Traditionally, we install an application by downloading it from an app store and allowing it to automatically update when changes are available. As we covered in the *Web versus mobile* section, this approach comes with some choices and dependencies we may wish to avoid.

The web, on the other hand, traditionally downloaded resources just in time, which meant that a web application was only available when online. Cache-control headers allow a browser to cache content to improve performance and minimize data transfer, but a browser will still produce errors on cached content when there is no connectivity.

A PWA is a newer alternative that strives to provide the benefits of both these approaches. A PWA is a normal web application that runs in the browser, but it progressively downloads and caches the application code and eventually runs the entire application from the downloaded code as though we installed it all initially.

A PWA has a `ServiceWorker` instance that operates in a separate thread and acts as a proxy for network requests. The service worker intercepts `fetch` requests and gives the application an opportunity to utilize the browser's cache API. A service worker also has a life cycle that we can hook into and use to install the application.

The following code block shows an example of installing a micro frontend:

```
self.addEventListener('install', (event) => {
  event.waitUntil(
    fetch('/importmap.json').then((response) => {
      caches.open('myapp').then((cache) => {
        return cache
          .addAll(response.json().imports.values());
      });
    })
  );
});
```

This example registers a listener for the `install` event. It leverages the `importmap.json` metadata file that we introduced in the *Dissecting micro frontends* section. The file contains a listing of the imports for all the micro applications. With one fell swoop, we can download and install the primary resources for all the micro applications.

A more elaborate implementation could leverage more metadata from the `apps.json` file and only install micro applications based on the user agent of the current device. This will avoid installing micro applications that the user would never use on the specific device.

Now let's see how we can use service workers to implement a read-through cache.

Read-through cache

So far, we have installed the application, but it doesn't do much without data. To gain access to data, we need to make remote calls to BFF services, which we cover in *Chapter 6, A Best Friend for the Frontend*. But we won't have access to these services when we are offline, so we need to maintain a read-through cache that stores data locally on the user's device.

A **read-through cache** intercepts remote calls and checks for a cached response before forwarding the request to the remote service. If we have a cached response, then we can return it. If we think the response is stale, then we may forward the request to retrieve the latest values and update the cache. If the remote call fails, because we are offline, then we can return the cached response, so the user can continue working.

The following code block shows an example of implementing a read-through cache with a service worker:

```
self.addEventListener('fetch', (event) => {
  event.respondWith(caches.open('myapp').then((cache) => {
    return cache.match(event.request).then((response) => {
      return response || fetch(event.request)
        .then((response) => {
          cache.put(event.request, response.clone());
          return response;
        });
    });
  }));
});
```

This example registers a listener for the fetch event, so that we can intercept all remote calls. It tests the cache for a match for the specific request. If there is no match, then it calls fetch to forward the request. Then we put a clone of the response in the cache and return the response.

This is a basic example, and we can define more elaborate caching policies. For example, we can control the caching logic based on the request content-type header. We can leverage the response cache-control header in a similar manner as the browser does to determine when data is stale. Or we define custom request headers to drive our caching policies.

To be fully prepared for offline mode, we also need to proactively fetch and cache certain types of data. For example, we can cache reference data that the UI needs to populate drop-down lists. Or we can cache the user's current assignments and work in progress. We can preload this data in the service worker's activate state, just like we installed the application code during the install state. Then, when the application makes a remote call for this data, we will get a cache match.

At this point, we have a working application, and users can use it to perform their duties whether they are online or offline. In a given session, a user will take actions and write data to the local cache. Our read-through cache must ensure *session consistency* by returning the results of these writes instead of reading through to the remote service.

Now let's see how we can implement a write-through cache that ensures all writes make it to their BFF service.

Write-through cache

Up to this point, we have cached the application code and pertinent data in local cache, so that an application works offline. If the application allows users to create or modify data, then we need to make remote calls to BFF services to persist the changes and produce events for downstream services. We will cover BFF services in *Chapter 6, A Best Friend for the Frontend*. But we won't have access to these services when we are offline, so we need to maintain a write-through cache that stores data locally on the user's device and pushes changes to remote services when a connection is available.

A **write-through cache** intercepts remote calls that update data and stores the data locally first, so that read requests will see the changes and maintain session consistency. Then it forwards the request to the remote service if the application is online. If the application is offline, then we queue the requests until a background process is able to push the changes through to the remote services. We can think of this as a client-side implementation of the **Database-First** variation of the **Event Sourcing** pattern that we cover in *Chapter 5, Turning the Cloud into the Database.*

The following code block shows an example of implementing the background process with a service worker:

```
navigator.serviceWorker.ready.then((swRegistration) => {
  return swRegistration.sync.register('sync-outbox');
});


self.addEventListener('sync', (event) => {
  if (event.tag == 'sync-outbox') {
    event.waitUntil(syncOutbox());
  }
});
```

First, this example registers the sync-outbox background process that detects connectivity and triggers a sync event. Then we register the syncOutbox listener for the sync event. The syncOutbox listener function pulls any outstanding requests from the outbox cache and executes them. Then it updates the status of the domain entities in the read cache with the results.

Other users may have updated the same content while the current user was offline. If the syncOutbox listener detects a conflict, then it can follow a given policy to resolve the conflict automatically. Or it could create a record in an inbox so that the user can decide how to reconcile and resolve the conflict.

Now that we have data cached locally, we need to keep it up to date with any changes. Let's see how we can utilize a live update service to keep data synchronized in near real time.

Live updates

We understand that cached data can become stale when an application goes offline. This is a compromise we are willing to make so that we can continue to work when we lose connectivity. Yet, we want to bring the cache up to date as quickly and as efficiently as possible. We can expire a cache after a time period, but this can allow the data to go stale in the meantime. We can query for updates over and over again, but this is inefficient. We need a better solution.

Instead, we will implement a live update solution that capitalizes on our event-first architecture. In *Chapter 4, Trusting Facts and Eventual Consistency*, we cover the core concepts of this architecture, and in *Chapter 5, Turning the Cloud into the Database*, we will see how autonomous services leverage events to implement the CQRS pattern and maintain their own living cache that continuously updates as data changes. In this section, we will extend events to the client side with a live update service.

Let's look at two alternative implementations of the live update service. First, we will look at the WebSocket implementation and then the long polling alternative.

WebSocket

Our system is composed of autonomous services. These services publish domain events to an event hub as their state changes. A micro application interacts with a specific set of domain entities and maintains them in a local cache. To keep this cache up to date, we want to subscribe to domain events, so that we can update the local cache in near real time when we are online. *Figure 3.3* depicts how we can implement this solution with WebSocket:

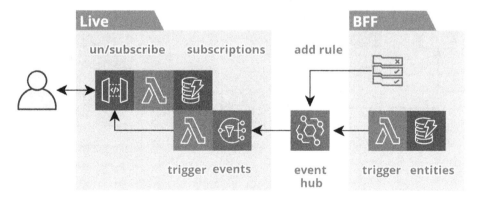

Figure 3.3 – Live updates – WebSocket

The **Live** update service defines an **events** topic, using AWS SNS. The **BFF** services for the various micro applications add rules to the **event hub** for the specific domain events they want to be routed to the **events** topic. A shared micro application initiates a connection with the **Live** update service to create the WebSocket for the user and the callback URL for the WebSocket is stored in the subscriptions database. Individual micro applications can add specific subscriptions to control the events the user will receive.

A `trigger` function reacts to events as they arrive on the `events` topic. The function looks up subscriptions in the database and forwards the events to the users' callback URLs. The shared library receives the events through the WebSocket on the client side and makes the events available to the micro applications through a window events listener, as we discussed in the *Inter-application communication* section.

From here, the individual micro applications take over. For example, a React-based micro application may leverage **Redux** for state management and persist the state to the local cache. The micro application's window events listener forwards the domain events to Redux and the micro application's reducers react to the events, causing the state of the cache to update and consequently update the screen with the new values.

Long polling

The WebSocket implementation works well when an application is online but does not directly support an application when it is offline. *Figure 3.4* depicts an alternative implementation that uses AWS SQS to buffer events when a user is offline:

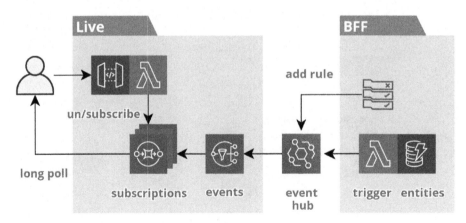

Figure 3.4 – Live updates – long polling

The right-hand side of *Figure 3.4* is identical to *Figure 3.3*. The difference starts after the **events** topic receives events. The shared micro application subscribes to the `Live` update service and creates a dedicated SQS queue for the current user and registers the queue with the **events** topic. Again, the micro applications can refine the subscriptions with their own filters.

The shared micro application performs the long polling for the user every 20 seconds. Any events that arrive on the queue during that interval will immediately flow through the connection in near real time. From here, the shared micro application makes the events available to the micro applications through window events listeners and the micro applications take over just like in the WebSocket implement.

When the user goes offline, the shared application stops polling. In the meantime, events collect for the users in their dedicated queues. When the connection is re-established, the long polling will resume, and the buffered events will flow in and update the cache.

Now let's look at how our offline-first approach also makes for a smooth transition during regional failover.

Regional failover

Designing the frontend to work smoothly offline and across multiple regions has a lot in common. Running a system across multiple regions is a running theme throughout this book. Each layer of the system plays its role.

In *Chapter 4*, *Trusting Facts and Eventual Consistency*, we cover the implications of multi-regional deployments on stream processing and why we rely on replication at the datastore level, instead of replicating streams. In *Chapter 5*, *Turning the Cloud into the Database*, we cover the different strategies for data replication. In *Chapter 6*, *A Best Friend for the Frontend*, we cover the regional health check and regional failover mechanisms used by BFF services. And in *Chapter 9*, *Choreographing Deployment and Delivery*, we examine how to leverage multiple regions for canary deployments.

In this chapter, we have seen how *session consistency* and *offline-first* mechanisms allow the presentation tier to continue working even when the application has lost its connection to the network. As it turns out, this behavior is exactly what we need to ensure a seamless transition during a regional disruption as well.

During a regional failure, the remote calls from the frontend to the BFF services will begin to fail. This will resemble intermittent connectivity and the session consistency provided by the local cache will act as a buffer. Meanwhile, the data from the user's previous transactions will replicate across the regions. Future requests will route to the next closest and healthy region. The frontend's background processes will detect connectivity and any pending updates will process in the new region.

Designing the frontend to work offline-first is no longer optional. Users expect their applications to work at all times. Fortunately, the added development effort comes with the added benefits of smooth regional failover and UI-first prototyping. Once we have the mechanisms in place for one micro application, all additional micro applications will benefit.

Now let's turn our attention to securing the user experience.

Securing the user experience

Security is a top priority and a common thread throughout this book. In *Chapter 2, Defining Boundaries and Letting Go*, we secure the perimeter of a system, in *Chapter 5, Turning the Cloud into the Database*, we encrypt data at rest, in *Chapter 6, A Best Friend for the Frontend*, we secure BFF services in depth, and in *Chapter 7, Bridging Intersystem Gaps*, we secure the interactions with external systems.

In this section, we look at the security of the presentation tier. First, we will provide authentication with **OpenID Connect (OIDC)**. Then we will add role-based authorization with conditional rendering and routing. Finally, we will pass the **JSON Web Token (JWT)** along on BFF calls to help secure the service side.

OpenID Connect

User authentication is the first step in securing the presentation tier. We need to identify the user so that we can determine what we will allow them to see and do. Traditionally, teams spent many cycles building an authentication system. Today, we can accelerate delivery by leveraging the OIDC specification and SaaS security providers.

OIDC is a simple identity layer on top of the **OAuth 2.0** specification. It defines the authentication flows and adds the identity token (that is, `idToken`). The identity token provides information about the user in the form of claims, such as the user's assigned groups or roles. `idToken` is represented as a JWT. We will use this information to secure the frontend and the backend.

The following code block shows an example of integrating an SaaS security SDK into the presentation tier:

```
import { useState, useEffect } from 'react'
import Auth from '@aws-amplify/auth'
Auth.configure({
  userPoolId: '...',
  redirectSignIn: window.location.origin,
  responseType: 'code'
  ...
});
export const useAuth = () => {
  const [state, setState] = useState({ isSignedIn: false,
    ... });
  useEffect(() => {
    Auth.currentAuthenticatedUser()
      .then((user) => setState({
        user, isSignedIn: true,
        groups: user.signInUserSession
          .idToken.payload['cognito:groups'],
        idToken: user.signInUserSession.idToken.jwtToken,
      }));
  }, []);
  const signIn = () => Auth.federatedSignIn();
  const signOut = () => Auth.signOut();
  const hasRole = (role) => state.groups?.includes(role);
  return { ...state, signIn, signOut, hasRole };
};
```

This specific example creates a custom React Hook called useAuth. The Hook hides the interface of the specific SaaS security provider from the rest of the system. In this case, we are integrating AWS Cognito using the AWS Amplify SDK. However, the rest of the system will interact with the interface returned by the Hook. This will allow the team to change the security provider more easily.

The Hook lives in the @my/shared micro application that contains the various utilities used across all the micro applications. It configures the SaaS SDK with the subsystem's information, such as the identifier for the specific user pool, where to redirect the user after the hosted login page completes, and which authentication flow to follow.

The Hook returns state information, such as `isSignedIn`, `idToken`, and `user`, along with wrapper functions, such as `signIn`, `signOut`, and `hasRole`. The custom Hook also creates a `useEffect` Hook that acts as a callback to handle the redirect from the hosted login screen and receive the user information. The following code block shows how to use the custom Hook to render sign-in and sign-out links:

```
import { useAuth } from '@my/shared';
export const SignInOut = () => {
  const { isSignedIn, signIn, signOut, user } = useAuth();
  return isSignedIn ?
    <SignOut user={user} signOut={signOut} /> :
    <SignIn signIn={signIn} />;
};
```

This component imports the `useAuth` Hook and calls it to retrieve the user state and the helper functions. It conditionally renders the `SignIn` and `SignOut` components based on the `isSignedIn` flag. It passes the `signIn` and `signOut` functions for the use of clicking on links. Once the user has signed in, the SDK handles the details of storing the user information and refreshing expired tokens.

Each autonomous subsystem should maintain its own user pool and security configuration, even if they use the same SaaS security provider. For example, our Food Delivery system has separate subsystems for customers, drivers, and restaurants. Each of these is a different pool of users, even though drivers and restaurant employees can also be customers. This gives each subsystem complete flexibility. For example, we probably want to allow social sign-in options for customers, but we may not want this for restaurant employees and drivers.

Now that we have the user's information, we can use it to control access.

Conditional rendering

The user experience should follow the principle of least privilege. In *Chapter 6, A Best Friend for the Frontend*, we will see how BFF services enforce the principle of least privilege. For a smooth user experience, the presentation tier should not present the user with menus and buttons that require higher authorization. We should conditionally render components based on the user's permissions. For example, we should not render save and delete buttons if the user has read-only access.

We have already seen conditional rendering based on the isSignedIn flag. The following code block shows role-based rendering:

```
import { useAuth } from '@my/shared';
export const SomeProtectedComponent = () => {
  const { hasRole } = useAuth();
  return hasRole('Admin') ? <div> ... <div/> : null;
};
```

This component uses the useAuth Hook to retrieve the hasRole function. Then it conditionally renders the content if the user has the Admin role. In this case, it renders nothing (that is, null) if the user does not have permission. In other cases, it may make sense to render alternate content.

We can also integrate role-based access into our mount points. The following code block revisits the mount points example from the *Dissecting micro frontends* section:

```
import { useAuth, useMountPoint } from '@my/shared';
export const LeftNavMenuItems = () => {
  const { hasRole } = useAuth();
  const { items } = useMountPoint('left-nav');
  return items
    .filter((item) => hasRole(item.role))
    .map((item) => <Menu.Item ... />);
};
```

In this example, we add a filter on the metadata for the mount point. The metadata defines the required role, and we pass it to the hasRole function. For each micro application, we include the required role in its manifest file as follows:

```
"mount-points": {
  "left-nav": [{ ..., "role": "Admin", ...}, ...]
}
```

In addition to conditionally rendering components, we must also control access to routes.

Protected routes

The user can manually enter a route into the browser's navigation bar to navigate to a page without clicking on a menu or button. For example, the user can bookmark a specific page. This will allow an unauthorized user to gain access to a page unless we secure the routes within each micro-app.

As we covered in the *Dissecting micro frontends* section, the micro frontends framework handles top-level routing and then delegates routing to the micro application. From here, the routing rules within a micro-app should use the `isSignedIn` flag and the `hasRole` function to control access to content. The following code block shows how to create a `ProtectedRoute` component that we can include in our shared library:

```
import React from 'react';
import { Route, Redirect } from 'react-router-dom';
import { useAuth } from './auth';
const ProtectedRoute = ({ component: Component, role,
    ...rest }) => {
  const { hasRole } = useAuth();
  return <Route {...rest} render={
      props => hasRole(role) ?
        <Component {...rest} {...props} /> :
        <Redirect to='/' />
    } />;
};
export default ProtectedRoute;
```

This specific example uses `react-router`. The `ProtectedRoute` component wraps the unprotected `Route` component to override its `render` property. The new `render` function asserts that the user has the required role. If the user has permission, then we render the requested page component; otherwise, we render the `Redirect` component to send the user to the home page.

Now that we have the conditional rendering and routing, we need to pass the user's information along when we invoke a BFF service.

Passing the JWT to BFF services

In *Chapter 6, A Best Friend for the Frontend*, we will cover the various responsibilities of BFF services and the important role they play in supporting micro applications. Many BFF services are only accessible to authorized users. To invoke a secured BFF service, the micro application must pass a JWT on each call to the service. The following code block shows an example of calling a secured BFF service:

```
import { useAuth } from '@my/shared';
const { idToken } = useAuth();
const { data, loading, error } = useFetch('/my/bff', {
  headers: { Authorization: `Bearer ${idToken}` }
});
```

First, the micro application retrieves idToken from the shared micro application that manages the information about the user's authenticated session. Then the application includes the token in the request using the Authorization header field.

It is important to note that we should not pass an ID token to third-party services. They will require an access token instead. We cover interactions with third-party services and the use of access tokens in *Chapter 7, Bridging Intersystem Gaps*.

A BFF service, on the other hand, specifically supports a given micro application and provides the service-side functionality of the application. Therefore, we need to pass idToken to a BFF, so that it can leverage the claims to perform assertions and filters, based on the user's entitlements. We cover the various topics related to securing BFF services, such as JWT authorizers, assertions, and filters, in *Chapter 6, A Best Friend for the Frontend*.

Now let's turn our attention to observing the performance of the frontend application logic.

Observing real user activity

Observability is an essential ingredient for understanding the performance of a system. We must be able to see the inner workings of every part of the system so that we can assess the health of the system and identify the root cause of any issues. Traditionally, we have focused on monitoring the backend services and servers. However, a significant portion of today's application logic executes on the frontend within a user's browser on their own devices.

Leveraging the processing power of the user's device allows us to spread out the load and dramatically improve the scalability of a system. However, it also makes it more difficult to monitor the behavior of the system, since we have to capture information from many devices. To address this problem, we need **Real User Monitoring** (**RUM**) and synthetic transactions.

RUM

RUM encompasses the set of tools we use to observe the performance of the frontend application logic. This includes sampling page load performance metrics, capturing errors and console logs, and sending this information to the central monitoring system. Then we correlate the frontend metrics with the backend metrics to create a full picture of the performance of the system across the entire technology stack.

Adding RUM to a web application is straight forward. The following code block provides an example of initializing a third-party RUM tool:

```
<script src="https://.../datadog-rum.js"
  type="text/javascript" />
<script>
  window.DD_RUM && window.DD_RUM.init({ ... })
</script>
```

This script simply loads and initializes the library with the necessary configuration settings. Add this to the `index.html` file of the main micro application that we covered in the *Dissecting micro frontends* section. Then, all the micro applications will benefit from RUM.

RUM provides more than just technical metrics. It also provides functional metrics, such as page view counts and the time spent on a specific page. This information can help evaluate the outcome of experiments. For example, it can help us answer questions such as whether or not more people are using the new page versus the old page.

But RUM only provides information when we have real users exercising the system. We also need a control group of users that continuously exercise the system. We will cover this set of synthetic users next.

Synthetics

In addition to monitoring real users, we also want to simulate a set of users. We can think of this group of users as a scientific control group that allows us to set a baseline for the expected performance. To establish this baseline, we automate a set of synthetic transactions and execute them continuously, such as every 5 to 30 minutes. These transactions and the category of tools we use to create them are referred to as **synthetics**.

These synthetic transactions execute in a real browser, so they will generate the RUM metrics that we will use as the baseline. We also execute these transactions from multiple global locations to introduce different latency and network conditions. They also provide metrics during periods when there are little to no real user transactions.

Synthetics are essentially smoke tests. They allow us to continuously assess the stability of the system. But these scripts can be time-consuming to write and maintain. So, we need to craft a strategic set of tests that provide the most bang for the buck.

At a bare minimum, we should implement an uptime check. This test simply loads the home page, checks for errors, and generates page load metrics. Going a bit further, we can navigate through the public pages. We should also test the sign-up and sign-in flows and then navigate through the protected pages. From here, we should also check the most essential transactions that the user cannot do without.

We will revisit synthetics in *Chapter 9, Choreographing Deployment and Delivery*, to see how they fit into the overall development life cycle.

Summary

In this chapter, you learned about many of the recent innovations in the presentation tier, such as SPAs, Jamstack, and deploying at the edge of the cloud. We learned how to decompose the presentation tier using the micro frontends approach to create autonomous micro applications that allow us to tame the presentation tier and easily extent the system by adding new applications instead of modifying existing applications.

We dug into the details and learned advanced state management techniques that allow us to create PWAs that work offline and smoothly support regional failover. We learned how to secure the frontend with OIDC and JWTs and how to monitor real user activity.

In the next chapter, we will cover eventually consistent systems and see how turning events into facts promotes autonomy and resilience. We will create an event hub, dissect the Event Sourcing pattern, and learn how to implement stream processors.

4
Trusting Facts and Eventual Consistency

In *Chapter 3, Taming the Presentation Tier*, we covered the *micro frontend* approach for decomposing and decoupling monolithic frontend applications. We also cover *Offline-first* and *Mobile-first* thinking and found that increasingly, mobile users are driving the necessity for *Event-first* thinking and eventually consistent systems.

Now we turn our attention to the asynchronous, inter-service communication patterns that form the foundation for an architecture that enables change. We will see how an *event hub* sits at the heart of each autonomous subsystem and creates an outbound bulkhead that protects upstream autonomous services from downstream outages. And we will see how the *event sourcing* pattern turns events into facts and gives teams the confidence to trust eventually consistent systems. These are the foundational elements that allow us to drive down lead times and accelerate the pace of innovation.

In this chapter, we're going to cover the following main topics:

- Living in an eventually consistent world
- Publishing to an event hub
- Dissecting the Event Sourcing pattern
- Processing event streams
- Designing for failure
- Optimizing throughput
- Observing throughput
- Accounting for regional failover

Living in an eventually consistent world

In *Chapter 1, Architecting for Innovation*, and *Chapter 2, Defining Boundaries and Letting Go*, we discussed the importance of event-first thinking and decomposing a system into an event-first topology of autonomous services and subsystems. And in *Chapter 5, Turning the Cloud into the Database*, we will turn our databases inside out and replicate derived data across the system. We do all this in an effort to create an architecture that enables change. We are fortifying the boundaries between services and minimizing the need for inter-team coordination so that autonomous teams can experiment, learn, and adapt more quickly.

But sooner than later, in any conversion about loosely coupled, event-driven systems, questions and concerns naturally arise regarding data consistency. These concerns stem from the days of information silos, long batch cycles, and spaghetti integrations that produced reconciliation nightmares. The relational database and real-time integrations were supposed to solve these data consistency problems, but instead, they produced highly coupled systems that are difficult to change and prone to cascading failures.

Data is an information system's most important asset. It must be accurate. But instead of controlling data too tightly, we want to embrace the fact that we live in an eventually consistent world. Long before there were information systems, the world was able to transact business. We simply need to mimic those traditional processes and make them work in near real time.

The typical coffee shop provides the perfect example. On a slow day, when you are the only customer, the coffee shop owner can take your order, prepare your coffee, receive your payment, and finally give you your coffee. Everything is nice and consistent. But on a typical busy morning, this single-threaded, sequential process will completely break down. The line of customers will stretch out the door. Potential customers will avoid the long line and unhappy customers will not return.

Instead, the typical busy coffee shop is governed by a well-designed and highly efficient eventually consistent business process. It is divided into stages, it is fault-tolerant, and it supports concurrency and parallelism. Let's dig deeper into this example.

Staging

The typical coffee shop business process is divided into a set of stages. You place your order with the cashier, and you receive a receipt, which states the *fact* that you paid for your order. Then you go and stand in the waiting area and you monitor the progress of your order. The cashier hands your order off to the next station and is now free to address the next customer. If you ordered multiple items, then your order fans out to multiple stations.

With everything running smoothly, your order works its way through the stations, and one by one you receive the items in your order. Meanwhile, other customers are moving through the same process, instead of waiting for your order to complete before theirs can start.

This process is an example of **Staged Event-Driven Architecture (SEDA)**. We have divided the process into a set of stages (that is, stations) and each stage has an input queue. The queues improve the rate of throughput by minimizing the need for one stage to wait on another. Upstream stages do not need to wait on downstream stages and downstream stages are never idle unless there is no work.

We will utilize SEDA at multiple levels. At the macro-level, the event hub provides the queues (that is, streams) and the autonomous services perform the work at the different stages of a process. We will cover the event hub shortly in the *Publishing to an event hub* section.

At the micro-level, the individual stream processor functions within the autonomous services will implement their own staged process flows. They will leverage **Asynchronous non-blocking I/O** to provide the queues that enable multi-tasking and **Functional Reactive Programming (FRP)** to define the stages of work. We will cover these topics in the *Processing event streams* and *Optimizing throughput* sections.

Cooperative

The notion of *cooperative programming* is also in play here, at both levels. The amount of work performed at each stage should be relatively similar. Otherwise, we are creating an unbalanced process flow, where a quick stage can overwhelm the next stage, or a slow stage can starve the next. There is no particular way to enforce this other than through intentional design and inter-team cooperation, hence the term *cooperative*.

Atomic

Each stage must also perform an atomic unit of work. In other words, each stage should update a single resource. This will allow us to maximize parallelism. It will also minimize waste when something goes wrong since we will not need to repeat successful stages. Ultimately, we will chain together a series of atomic actions (that is, stages) to achieve eventual consistency.

Consistency

Everyone is happy in our coffee shop example when everything is running smoothly. You have to wait for your order, but you have a receipt that states the *fact* that you have made your payment. You understand that you will *eventually* receive your coffee and the shop understands that it must fulfill your order or give you a refund.

All the participants agree on how the process works and understand that a little *inconsistency* produces the best outcome for all involved. The process works because we have transparency, facts, and a chain reaction.

Transparency

Transparency is essential in an eventually consistent system. Users need to understand the process, so they can set their expectations. And they need to know the state of the system so that they can make informed decisions.

In *Chapter 3*, *Taming the Presentation Tier*, we saw how increasingly, mobile users are driving the necessity for eventually consistent systems. Mobile devices lose connectivity, but users can continue working, even though the system is becoming inconsistent. Users understand this reality and the system provides them with visual cues into the current situation.

When a user is consuming data, the system needs to clearly show how old and potentially stale the data may be. If the user is producing data, then it needs to be clear when the data has been successfully submitted. This way, we know when we are working in offline mode and we understand that everything will eventually become consistent when we reconnect.

Facts

Facts are the lifeblood of an eventually consistent system. Each stage produces an event to record the fact that it completed an atomic unit of work. These facts are not ephemeral. We retain them indefinitely. They represent *data in motion*.

In total, these facts represent the current state of the system. Downstream services may be temporarily inconsistent, but the facts contain all the information needed to make them consistent. The system as a whole is not inconsistent; it just may have more work to complete.

We will see how to turn events into facts in the *Dissecting the Event Sourcing pattern* section.

Chain reaction

We achieve eventual consistency by chaining atomic actions together. Each atomic action produces a fact (that is, an event) and the next atomic action in the chain reacts and produces its own fact. This chain reaction continues until we achieve the desired result. The process is not haphazard. It does not happen by chance. We specifically design the chain reaction to ensure that the system becomes consistent.

We will cover different approaches for controlling a chain reaction, such as choreography and orchestration, along with compensation, in *Chapter 8, Reacting to Events with More Events*.

At any given point, we can review the facts, assess the current state of the system, and determine whether there is any outstanding work to complete. When everything is running smoothly, a chain reaction will happen in near real time. However, things will go wrong, and we have to be prepared.

Concurrency and partitions

In our coffee shop example, everything seems to be running smoothly. You have your breakfast sandwich, but they have lost your coffee. The crew knows how to handle this situation, so they insert a new coffee for you at the head of the queue. You have to wait a little longer than you planned, but you get your coffee. Meanwhile, they identify your original coffee. The name on the label was smudged. Now you get to choose. You can have the first coffee, the second, or both.

CAP theorem shows us that in the case of a system partition, we have to choose between *consistency* and *availability*. We cannot have both. Users clearly favor availability and expect us to ensure that everything eventually comes together cleanly. This is easy enough when no other users are operating on the same logical data. However, we have to account for *concurrency*. We have to consider what happens when users interact with the same logical data concurrently.

We have many opportunities for partitions in our systems. Offline mode is an obvious example. Downstream services experience a brief partition as upstream events make their way through chain reactions. And these partitions can be protracted under error conditions. Another example exists when we have two upstream services operating on separate instances of the same logic data.

Our missing coffee is an example of concurrency during a partition. A second person is producing a duplicate unit of work even though it turns out that another person is working on the original. In this case, duplicate output is better than no output. We just need to design the next stage to account for duplicates.

This scenario highlights the importance of *facts* in an eventually consistent system. Multiple users can simultaneously operate on different instances of the same logical data. But we record the result of each action as a fact, so we do not lose information.

One user's change does not necessarily have to overwrite the other. Downstream, we may design the data model to support both, weave them together, or drop one change or the other. Regardless, we retain the facts as an audit trail.

Inevitably, the facts speak for themselves. We will see how to turn events into facts in the *Dissecting the Event Sourcing pattern* section.

Order tolerance and idempotence

Our coffee shop is order-tolerant. Customers stand in line to place an order, but from that point on, the order in which work leaves the system will vary. Some items are easy to prepare and pass through the system quickly, while others take longer. Mistakes will happen, and items will be re-queued. And as we have seen, duplicates can enter the system. A customer waiting for multiple items can receive them in any order. The employees see the individual items as they pass through their stations and the customers sort out everything at the other end.

Many messaging systems provide **First-in, First-out** (**FIFO**) guarantees. When things are running smoothly, this can help improve the efficiency of the system. But, as our coffee shop example shows, we cannot rely on these guarantees. Messages may enter the system in the wrong order, others will fail and get re-queued, and multiple channels can work at different paces.

Our stream processors need to act like the customers in our coffee shop and sort things out as they receive events. We do this naturally as customers. We will see how to implement stream processors in general in this chapter. We will cover specific order tolerance and idempotence techniques in the *Implementing idempotence and order tolerance* section of *Chapter 5, Turning the Cloud into the Database*, and in the *Calculating event sourcing snapshots* section of *Chapter 8, Reacting to Events with More Events*.

Parallelism

A line begins to form as customers arrive at the coffee shop. If they arrive faster than we can serve them, then the line will overflow the shop and customers will avoid the line. We have already improved our throughput by dividing the process into stages and allowing different order items to fan out to different stages. But we can do better, a lot better, by adding another cashier and a second coffee station. This is classic queuing theory at work.

Let's say that customers are arriving at a rate (λ) of 40 per hour and on average it takes 1.2 minutes to service a customer for a rate (μ) of 50 customers per hour with a single queue. Following *Little's Law*, we can calculate that a customer can expect to wait (W) for 6 minutes using the equation $W=1/(\mu-\lambda)$. And we can also calculate that, on average, there will be 4 customers in line (L) using the equation $L=\lambda W$.

However, as the arrival rate increases and we are near the full utilization of our service rate, these numbers will jump significantly. For example, if the rate of customers increases to 48, then the length of the line will jump to 24 and customers will wait for 30 minutes.

In this case, we can open up the second queue (that is, cashier and coffee station) to increase our throughput. We will see both the wait time and the line drop down to approximately 1. A slight modification to our wait time formula bears this out: $W=1/(c\mu-\lambda)$, where c is the number of queues.

Of course, these equations are based on long-term averages, but in practice, the results can be quite astounding. Our eventual consistency systems are based on queues, which makes parallelism a natural fit. We will see the role that *asynchronous non-blocking I/O* and sharding play in the *Optimizing throughput* section.

The reality is that our systems live in an eventually consistent world. Some part of almost every system is eventually consistent. Mobile users need the ability to work in offline mode, which means they are eventually consistent. Integrations with legacy and external systems are eventually consistent and potentially even batch-oriented. Instead of imposing a strict consistency model on an eventually consistent world, it is better to embrace eventual consistency through and through. The impedance mismatch of switching between the different models actually slows us down and impedes innovation.

Let's see how this all fits together and we will start at the beginning with publishing events.

Publishing to an event hub

The ability to publish events is a fundamental capability of autonomous services. Upstream services publish events as their state changes and downstream services react to these events. This publish and subscribe paradigm decouples producers from consumers, but if we are not careful, we can inadvertently introduce coupling and complexity through the messaging infrastructure.

In *Chapter 2, Defining Boundaries and Letting Go*, we discussed the importance of creating an architecture of autonomous subsystems. Each subsystem is composed of a highly cohesive set of autonomous services. We have seen *Figure 4.1* before. It depicts how we can compose an event-first topology out of autonomous subsystems. This natural fractal pattern produces a system that is very easy to comprehend and reason about. We will see how to connect subsystems in *Chapter 7, Bridging Intersystem Gaps*:

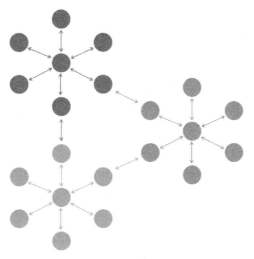

Figure 4.1 – Event-first topology

At the heart of each autonomous subsystem is an **event hub**. The event hub eliminates the mayhem that would ensue if we were to create a patchwork of topics and queues to connect the various services. Instead, *Figure 4.2* depicts how the event hub mediates between upstream producers and downstream consumers:

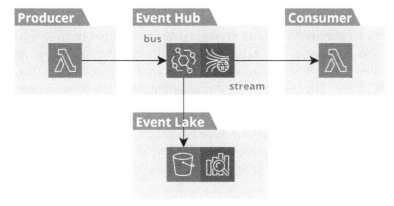

Figure 4.2 – Event hub

The general flow of events through the event hub proceeds as follows:

1. Upstream services publish domain events to the hub through a **bus**.

2. The bus routes events to one or more *channels*, such as a **stream**.

3. Downstream services consume events from the hub through a specific *channel*.

We also see that the **Event Lake** hooks into the **Event Hub** to consume all events. This is a crucial part of turning events into facts. We will cover this shortly in the *Dissecting the Event Sourcing pattern* section. First, let's look more closely at the event bus and the format and contents of domain events.

You can find an event hub template here: `https://github.com/jgilbert01/` `aws-lambda-stream/tree/master/templates/event-hub`.

Event bus

The event bus is the entry point into the event hub. It provides a level of indirection so that we do not couple producers to specific consumer channels. Producers only need to know about the bus. We will add rules to route events to specific consumer channels without impacting the producers.

The event bus also acts as the *outbound bulkhead* that protects upstream services from downstream failures and outages. The bus is a highly available, serverless service, such as AWS EventBridge or Azure Event Grid. An upstream service can publish an event to the bus and forget about it. It can trust that the bus will eventually deliver the event to all interested consumers, through the various channels (that is, streams).

Domain events

Domain events are the lifeblood of an event-first system. We use them to transmit information between services. An actor interacts with a service to perform an action on a domain model. The service produces a domain event to record the fact that the actor performed the action. Then we send the domain event from the producer service to all the consumer services via the event hub.

To support this flow of information, we need a standard event envelope, we need to include the domain model state in each event, and we need to consider the substitution of producers and consumers, both internally and externally.

Event envelope

The event envelope defines a standard set of fields that all events must contain. This allows the bus, any channel, and all consumers to handle any event. The bus relies on these fields to perform content-based routing to specific channels. Consumers utilize these fields to filter and dispatch events within their stream processing pipelines. And the event lake uses these fields to organize events for storage and retrieval.

Each domain event is a JSON object. The following code block defines the structure of the Event envelope:

```
interface Event {
  id: string;
  type: string;
  timestamp: number;
  partitionKey?: string;
  tags: { [key: string]: string | number };
  // <entity>: any;
  raw?: any;
  eem?: any;
}
```

The Event envelope defines the following fields:

- The id field contains the unique identifier for the event. This value must be deterministic. We cover this in the *Implementing idempotence and order tolerance* section of *Chapter 5, Turning the Cloud into the Database.*

- The type field indicates the type of the event and the expected payload. It will typically consist of a domain entity name and the action performed, such as thing-submitted, along with a namespace prefix for external domain events.

- The timestamp field contains the epoch value, in milliseconds, for when the actor performed the action that produced the event.

- The partitionKey field allocates events to shards for parallel processing. It typically contains a domain entity identifier or a correlation key, so stream processors can group related events. Otherwise, use a V4 random UUID to ensure even distribution across the shards. We will cover sharding in the *Optimizing throughput* section to come.

- The `tags` field contains general information, such as account, region, stage, source, function name, and pipeline.

- The `<entity>` field contains the event type-specific payload. The name of this field is usually the *lowerCamelCase* name of the domain entity type, such as `thing` for *Thing*. We will discuss the contents of this field next in the *Event carried state transfer* section.

- The `raw` field contains the raw data produced by the source of the event, in its native format. We include this data, when available, so the event lake can form a complete audit trail with no lost information. For example, an ESG service may not use all the external data, but it is available here if the requirements change. There are no backward compatibility guarantees for the structure of this data.

- Include the `eem` field when an event contains sensitive data. This field holds the envelope encryption metadata that permitted consumers can use to decrypt the values. We cover this in the *Redacting sensitive data* section of *Chapter 5, Turning the Cloud into the Database*.

The following JSON object provides an example of a `thing-submitted` domain event:

```
{
  id: 'ab3ba422-0a2f-11ea-8d71-362b9e155667',
  type: 'thing-submitted',
  timestamp: 1574100988321,
  partitionKey: 'edac237c-2523-41a2-84ee-2b1a3baeccce',
  tags: {
    source: that-bff-service-stg',
    functionname: 'that-bff-service-stg-trigger',
  }
  thing: {
    id: 'edac237c-2523-41a2-84ee-2b1a3baeccce',
    name: 'Thing One',
    description: 'This is thing one.'
  }
}
```

The `<entity>` field (that is, `thing`) carries the state to downstream services and represents the contract between producers and consumers. Now, let's look at this payload in more detail.

Event carried state transfer

Our domain events are more than just notifications. They represent the fact that something happened and they contain the data that provides the context of the event. Downstream services use this data to make decisions and to create materialized views. This is referred to as **event carried state transfer**. We already touched on this topic in the *Thinking about events first* section of *Chapter 2, Defining Boundaries and Letting Go*.

The `<entity>` field in the standard event envelope represents the payload of a specific event type. It contains a *snapshot* of all the relevant data that is available in the service when the actor performs the action that produces the event.

For example, two BFF services may provide different actors with the ability to work on different aspects of the same domain entity. Both services have a lean, read-only copy of the domain entity's summary information, but each is responsible for maintaining different subsections of the domain model.

When the BFFs publish events, they include the summary information for context, along with the detailed information they own. However, each does not need to maintain copies of each other's subdomain model and include it in the events. Instead, downstream services that need to will merge with the subdomains in their own materialized views to suit their needs. We will cover materialized views in detail in *Chapter 5, Turning the Cloud into the Database*.

Next, we need to ensure that we do not couple upstream services to downstream services through the contents of an event.

Substitution

We need the ability to change event producers without forcing consumers to change. In other words, a downstream service should be able to consume the same domain event regardless of what service produced it.

Over time, producers may change and, at any given time, there may be multiple sources producing the same domain event. This is the substitution principle that we introduced in *Chapter 2, Defining Boundaries and Letting Go*.

To support substitution, the `<entity>` field of a specific event type should conform to a standard canonical format for the specific domain entity. This format defines the contract between producers and consumers.

The contract does need to evolve, particularly in the early stages of development. To balance flexibility with stability, we will maintain internal and external domain events.

Internal versus external

In *Chapter 2, Defining Boundaries and Letting Go,* we discussed the benefits of creating separate event types for internal and external domain events. Internal domain events define the contracts within a subsystem, and external domain events define the contracts across subsystems.

We give strong backward compatibility guarantees to downstream subsystems for the external domain events. This allows teams to experiment and change the definition of the internal domain events more freely. We will see how ESG services create an anti-corruption layer by transforming between the internal and external domain events in *Chapter 7, Bridging Intersystem Gaps.* We will cover the versioning of domain events in the *Achieving zero-downtime* section of *Chapter 9, Choreographing Deployment and Delivery.*

Routing and channel topology

Routing is the purpose of the event hub. Routing helps decouple producers from consumers. Producers send events to the bus and it is responsible for routing them to the various consumer channels.

Many consumers may share a single channel, but a consumer generally subscribes to a single channel. The hub typically owns shared channels and the associated routing rules, whereas a service will own a dedicated channel and add its own routing rules to the bus.

The following `serverless.yml` fragment, from the event hub template, creates an AWS EventBridge routing rule to an AWS Kinesis stream:

```
Stream1EventRule:
  Type: AWS::Events::Rule
  Properties:
    EventPattern:
      detail:
        type: [ anything-but: fault ]
    Targets:
      - Arn:
          Fn::GetAtt: [ Stream1, Arn ]
        InputPath: $.detail
    ...
```

The `detail` field in the rule represents the event envelope and we use it to access the content of the event. `EventPattern` includes all event types, except for `fault` events. The rule passes the event envelope (that is, `$.detail`) to the stream via `InputPath`.

A subsystem may have many channels. There are a variety of things to consider when defining a topology of channels, such as isolation, message size, priority, volume, and the number of consumers.

It may be necessary to *isolate* specific channels. The event lake, which we will cover in the *Dissecting the Event Sourcing pattern* section, will maintain its own channel and routing rule to ensure that it consumes all events. In *Chapter 7, Bridging Intersystem Gaps*, we discuss the value of *isolating* external events in a separate ingress channel and using egress routing rules for connecting subsystems.

The *size* of events is important. The routing rule we defined in the preceding paragraphs weeds out fault events. This is an example of excluding a specific event type based on the potential message size. Channels have capacity limits and large events can impact the throughput of other events. These large events may warrant a dedicated channel. As an example, the fault monitor that we will cover in the *Designing for failure* section maintains its own channel for just fault events.

The *priority* of events is another consideration. We may define a high-priority channel for one or more event types to avoid competition with low-priority event types. A specific consumer may define a dedicated channel for a specific event type to ensure that there is no competition.

The *volume* of events is also a consideration. In the *Processing event streams* and the *Optimizing throughput* sections, we will discuss the value of multiplexing many event types through a single channel and filtering on the consumer side. However, some consumers may only require a small fraction of the events. So, it may make sense to have a separate channel for low-volume event types.

The *number of consumers* may also have an impact on throughput. More consumers on a single channel create competition for the read capacity and this can result in throttling. In this case, if we cannot add more capacity to the channel, then we can create duplicate channels and spread the consumers across the channels.

The routing rule we defined earlier acts as a default channel because it includes all events except for faults. I typically start with this single default channel and refine the rules and channels as the subsystem evolves and we learn the exact nature of its domain events and their consumers.

I also prefer to implement channels as streams. They help to turn events into facts and first-class citizens, as we will see in the *Dissecting the Event Sourcing pattern* section. And they provide many performance-related and resilience benefits, as we will see in the *Processing event streams*, *Designing for failure*, and *Optimizing throughput* sections.

Let's dig into the details.

Dissecting the Event Sourcing pattern

The *Event Sourcing* pattern provides the foundation for eventual consistency and the subsequent flexibility that allows us to create reactive and evolutionary systems. It essentially proposes turning events into facts, instead of just ephemeral messages. We accomplish this by retaining all events and storing them in perpetuity. The events serve as an audit trail of historical activity so that we do not lose information.

Unfortunately, the Event Sourcing pattern has a reputation for making systems more complex. This concern is not unfounded. However, with the right alterations, communicating by events and treating them as facts, actually produces systems that are more straightforward and flexible. A few examples will help make this clear. Let's look at an example without event sourcing, another one with what I refer to as *Traditional Event Sourcing*, and a third example with the altered form, which I refer to as *Systemwide Event Sourcing*.

Figure 4.3 depicts a BFF service that allows users to query their account balance and perform a command to update the balance, without using the event sourcing pattern:

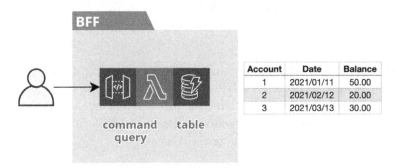

Figure 4.3 – Without event sourcing

The functionality is relatively easy and straightforward to implement. We store account balances as a single row per account. The command simply increments or decrements the balance and the query simply reads the latest state of the balance.

This is a simplistic example, but it highlights an important problem. We are losing information. We only retain the latest balance, so we are losing the history of the account. We are not recording the fact that the account holder performed a transaction to increase or decrease the balance.

Figure 4.4 depicts a BFF service that provides the same account balance functionality using the traditional event sourcing pattern:

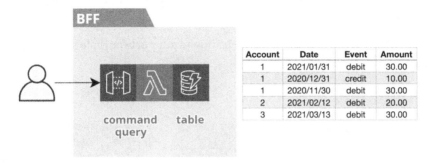

Account	Date	Event	Amount
1	2021/01/31	debit	30.00
1	2020/12/31	credit	10.00
1	2020/11/30	debit	30.00
2	2021/02/12	debit	20.00
3	2021/03/13	debit	30.00

Figure 4.4 – Traditional event sourcing

In this case, we do not lose information, because we are storing a separate record for each transaction. The command is still straightforward because it just writes a new record with the amount of the change and a credit or debit flag. But the query has become much more complex.

The query needs to read all the transactions for an account and calculate the balance on every request. This is not a big problem when there are only a few transactions. But as the number of transactions grows, the performance will suffer. Taking snapshots is a common solution to this performance issue, but snapshotting adds complexity because it adds a component to the design.

Now, let's look at how we can improve event sourcing.

Systemwide event sourcing

The first two examples have one thing in common; they each focus on supporting the usage scenarios of a single actor. This is great from the perspective of the *Single Responsibility Principle*. However, we also need to consider the system as a whole.

Going back to the *Living in an eventually consistent world* section, we saw that an eventually consistent system acts as a series of atomic stages that exchange facts. This simplifies the system as a whole because we design each stage to focus on a single task and then we string these building blocks together. Furthermore, a stage does not retain facts, it passes them along, so it can focus on performing its job.

With this in mind, we can alter the event sourcing pattern to take on a systemwide perspective. We can keep the simplicity of the first example but enhance it to share facts with downstream services. And we can simplify the second example by relieving it of the necessity to retain facts.

Figure 4.5 depicts two BFF services collaborating to support multiple stages in an eventually consistent system:

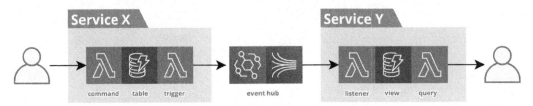

Figure 4.5 – Systemwide event sourcing

We saw a similar version of this diagram in *Chapter 1, Architecting for Innovation*, when we discussed the **Command, Publish, Consume, Query (CPCQ)** flow.

Service X implements the enhancement to our first example. The implementation of its **command** and query functionality remains straightforward because it only stores the latest balance. We simply add the **trigger** function to consume the changes from the table's CDC stream and send the facts to the **event hub**.

We will cover the details of the **trigger** function in the *Leveraging change data capture* section of *Chapter 5, Turning the Cloud into the Database*. We will also see how to retain facts in the remainder of this section. But so far, we have maintained the simplicity, focus, and atomic nature of **Service X** without losing information. And as we will see in the next chapter, the trigger enhancement is straightforward as well.

Now, **Service Y** and any other service can sit downstream and react to the facts that upstream services emit. We are gaining flexibility while also retaining information and simplicity. This is the **inversion of responsibility** that we covered in *Chapter 2, Defining Boundaries and Letting Go*. The addition of downstream stages is determined by the stages themselves. In other words, event sourcing is a key mechanism for creating an *architecture that enables change* because it allows us to change the system by adding services without modifying others.

We will see this example again, in the *Dissecting the CQRS pattern* section of *Chapter 5, Turning the Cloud into the Database*, where we will see how the event sourcing pattern dovetails with the CQRS pattern to complete the connection between upstream and downstream services.

Now, let's dig into the different ways that we can retain events and turn them into facts.

Event lake

The event lake is responsible for turning events into facts. It accomplishes this by capturing all events and storing them in perpetuity. It is the ultimate record of truth regarding the actions that have taken place within the system. It is a complete audit trail containing all the facts. At any time, we can dig into the event lake to find the truth about every single state change. In the *Turning the database inside out* section of *Chapter 5, Turning the Cloud into the Database*, we will see how the event lake acts as the *systemwide transaction log*.

We introduced the event lake in *Figure 4.2* in the *Publishing to an event hub* section. At the heart of each autonomous subsystem is an event hub and an event lake. The event lake maintains its own channels and adds its own routing rules to the event hub so that it receives all events published within the subsystem or consumed from upstream subsystems.

Perpetual storage

The durability of the events within the lake is of the utmost importance. For this reason, *object storage* is the best choice for persisting events in the lake. For example, AWS S3 provides 11 nines of durability, plus we can age events into long-term storage, such as AWS Glacier. We will also replicate the lake across regions and into a separate account for disaster recovery.

We organize the events in object storage based on their timestamp. We can browse events by year, month, and day, but we package multiple events into a single object for optimal throughput and storage. We can read the individual events with a command-line utility that we will cover in the *Replaying events* section. However, indexing the events gives us greater visibility into the event lake, as we will see shortly.

The security of events in the event lake is crucial. Maintaining a separate lake per subsystem helps to limit access on a least privileged basis. We also redact sensitive data in the lake using envelope encryption, as we will cover in *Chapter 5, Turning the Cloud into the Database*.

> **A note on terminology**
>
> In my previous books, I referred to the *event lake* as the *data lake*. Although an event lake is essentially a data lake, I prefer the new name because it helps highlight the autonomy of the individual event lakes owned by each autonomous subsystem. Each subsystem needs the liberty to replay events from its own event lake at will. Maintaining a single, centralized data lake limits a team's ability to respond quickly. That said, you will most likely create a subsystem dedicated to business analytics. The event lake of that subsystem will contain all the external domain events of all other subsystems and play the role of the corporate data lake.

You can find an event lake storage template here: `https://github.com/jgilbert01/aws-lambda-stream/tree/master/templates/event-lake-s3`. This template uses AWS Firehose as the channel to store events in S3.

Now, let's look at indexing the event lake so that we can easily search for events.

Indexing events

The event lake is a valuable source of information. Retaining events as facts in durable storage is crucial, but we also need the ability to easily find events of interest. For example, we can use the events for root cause analysis when we are investigating a defect or incident, and once we determine the root cause, we may need to find the right set of events to replay to repair one or more services.

Indexing events allows us to easily search for events on many dimensions. There are many alternatives for indexing events. Events are well suited for a time series database because they have a timestamp and various dimensions, such as type and tags. They are also well-suited for a search engine because they have rich, coarse-grained content.

Elasticsearch is uniquely suited for indexing this coarse-grained time series information. We can also think of the event lake as a log file and choose to index the events in an SaaS observability and log monitoring system. AWS Athena is another option when we store the lake in S3.

You can find an event lake indexing template here: `https://github.com/jgilbert01/aws-lambda-stream/tree/master/templates/event-lake-es`. This template uses AWS Firehose as the channel to index events in Elasticsearch.

Replaying events

Retaining facts in the event lake allows us to replay events. We might replay events to repair a broken service or to seed a new service or a new version of a service. For example, if a bug in a service causes it to miss some events, then we can replay the events after we deploy a fix. For a new service, we might replay the last several weeks or months of events to bring it up to date.

It is important to point out that we do not republish events because this would broadcast the events to all consumers. We send events to a specific listener function. This is the same listener function that is consuming from a channel, such as a stream. So, the replay utility needs to wrap the events in the format of the specific channel.

We do not need to filter down to the exact set of events when we replay events to a function. As we will see in the *Processing event streams* section, a `listener` function is a stream processor that already filters for the event types of interest. So, we can specify a date range and let the function weed out the unwanted events.

When we replay a range of events, the `listener` function will likely have already processed some of the events. So, there will certainly be duplicates and any missed events will now arrive out of order. This is one more reason why it is important to ensure that our listener functions are idempotent and order-tolerant. We cover these techniques in the *Implementing idempotence and order tolerance* section of *Chapter 5, Turning the Cloud into the Database*.

You can find the *aws-lambda-stream-cli* library here: (`https://github.com/ jgilbert01/aws-lambda-stream-cli`). This command-line utility works with the stream processor framework that we will cover in the *Processing event streams* section.

While the event lake is the record of truth and it enables us to replay events, we do not intend for autonomous services to access the event lake in real time. Instead, autonomous services interact with event streams and micro event stores. Let's look at these next.

Event streams

An event stream is a messaging channel that acts as a temporal event store for downstream consumers. We leverage streams for all **inter-service** communication channels. They act as the input queue for the various stages in our eventually consistent system.

Autonomous services *listen* for events on a stream so that they can react in near real time. From their perspective, a channel or stream is the source of events. In other words, streams provide temporal event sourcing to downstream services.

We will cover stream processing in detail in the remainder of this chapter and discover all the benefits that stream processing provides, such as batching, sharding, and backpressure. But first, we need to cover the benefits that event streams provide to upstream services by turning events into facts.

Temporal storage

Streams are different from other messaging channels because they also act as an append-only data store. Whereas most messaging channels treat events as ephemeral messages and discard them once acknowledged, a stream retains events for a prescribed period, such as days or weeks.

This creates a very different mental picture that is critical for creating eventually consistent systems. The simple notion of storing events turns them into facts. We start to treat events as first-class citizens. The results of all the atomic actions leading to eventual consistency (that is, the facts) become part of the data model. We no longer retain just the latest static image. The data becomes dynamic. It is in motion.

Persisting events gives us confidence that the data will flow to downstream services and the system will eventually become consistent. We can tune a given channel to hold events long enough to ensure that its consumers have the time they need to react. This frees upstream services from the responsibility of ensuring consistency. Instead, atomic actions and systemwide event sourcing greatly simplify upstream processing logic.

To implement systemwide event sourcing in an upstream service, we can execute either of the following two variations on the pattern: **stream-first** or **database-first**. Let's look at the stream-first variant next.

Stream-first event sourcing

Distributed transactions have fallen out of favor because the two-phase commit cycle does not scale. This is evident by the fact that many cloud-native services do not support distributed transactions. This means that we cannot reliably save data to more than one datastore at a time.

Instead, we create eventually consistent systems by stringing together a series of atomic stages. Each stage is *atomic* because it only updates a *single* datastore. But this means that we must choose between writing data to a database or emitting a fact to the event hub. We cannot do both as an atomic action.

This is where the stream-first and database-first variants of the event sourcing pattern come into play. We need to turn events into facts. A service can either send an event to the event hub first and trust that downstream services will react and store the data, or a service can store the data first and trust that its own trigger function will react and publish the event. We will cover the database-first variant in detail in the *Leveraging change data capture* section of *Chapter 5, Turning the Cloud into the Database*.

Here we will look at the stream-first variant. *Figure 4.6* depicts the stream-first variant of the event sourcing pattern:

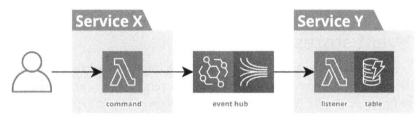

Figure 4.6 – Stream-first event sourcing

We have already seen that a stream is a temporal datastore. When a **command** sends an event to the **event hub**, we can be confident that the event hub will route it to one or more streams (that is, channels) for storage and consumption downstream. For example, in the *Routing and channel topology* section, we configured a stream as the default channel in the event hub. Downstream **listener** functions consume from these channels and store the data for use within their services.

Choosing between the stream-first and database-first variant largely depends on the capabilities of the database in use, plus the user's need to interact with the data immediately. If users need to interact with the data they create, then we will lean toward the database-first variant. However, the database-first variant requires a database that supports **change data capture** (**CDC**), such as DynamoDB streams.

In *Chapter 6, A Best Friend for the Frontend*, we will see that BFF services typically employ the database-first variant. However, if the database does not support CDC, then the commands of the BFF can use the stream-first variant and the BFF can consume its own events and persist the data.

In *Chapter 7, Bridging Intersystem Gaps*, and in *Chapter 8, Reacting to Events with More Events*, we will see that ESG services and Control services typically employ the stream-first variant because they are not user-facing.

> **A note on terminology**
>
> In my previous books, I referred to the stream-first variant as *event-first*.
> However, since that time, *event-first* has taken on a new and larger meaning,
> as we have discussed throughout this book. I also prefer the term *stream-first*
> because it is more congruent with the term *database-first*.

An event stream provides temporal storage of events and allows autonomous services to react to events as they happen in near real time. Some services also need access to older events. Let's now see how individual services can maintain their own micro event store.

Micro event stores

A micro event store contains a subset of facts that are important to a specific service. Whereas the event lake is responsible for storing all events and an event stream stores the most recent events, a service can define its own micro event store to provide dedicated access to a subset of events.

The service collects events of interest and correlates them in a micro event store, such as a DynamoDB table. This gives the service optimized access for retrieving these related events. It retains these facts only as long as necessary by setting a time to live on each record.

In *Chapter 5, Turning the Cloud into the Database*, we will see the role a micro event store can play in idempotence and order tolerance. In *Chapter 8, Reacting to Events with More Events*, we will see how we can use a micro event store to correlate events for complex event processing and business process orchestration. Plus, we will use a micro event store to calculate event sourcing snapshots.

Now, let's cover stream processors and learn how to implement listener and trigger functions.

Processing event streams

At first glance, stream processing might seem like it is some extreme paradigm shift. And truth be told, if you have to do it all from scratch, it is not for the fainthearted. For example, we need a process that consumes from a stream and invokes the business logic. And we need one of these for each shard. And we need logic to increase or decrease the number of these processes with the number of shards. And we need to restart these processes when they fall over. And we need to keep track of the offset so that we read from the right position on the next call.

This can add up to a decent cloud bill, not to mention all the development elbow grease required. Of course, we can implement this processing as a container sidecar. But serverless, function-as-a-service offerings, such as AWS Lambda, provide this capability for just the cost of invoking the functions to execute the business logic. It takes care of all the heavy lifting.

Still, stream processing is different, but in a good way. The difference starts with batch size, which leads us to functional reactive programming. This, in turn, opens a whole realm of possibilities, such as filtering, mapping, reducing, backpressure, and more.

You can find example stream processors here: `https://github.com/jgilbert01/aws-lambda-stream/tree/master/templates`.

Let's dive into creating a stream processor.

Batch size

The input signature of a function is one of the first things we must consider when we implement a service using function-as-a-service. The structure of the input events is dependent on the type of messaging channel feeding the function. For example, an AWS Lambda function consuming from an AWS Kinesis stream receives a batch of records like the following:

```
{
    "Records": [
        {
            "kinesis": {
                "partitionKey": "1",
                "sequenceNumber": "49590338...88898",
                "data": "SGVsbG8s...N0Lg==",
            },
            ...
        },
        {
            "kinesis": {
                "partitionKey": "1",
                "sequenceNumber": "49590338...5618",
```

```
                    "data": "VghpcyBp...zdC4=",
            },
            ...
        }
    ]
}
```

The `data` field of each record is `base64` encoded and contains the domain event in the format that we covered in the *Publishing to an event hub* section. The function will only receive one record if there is only a single record on the stream or up to the batch size limit specified for the function when there are many records in the stream. The following `serverless.yml` fragment, from the example service templates, creates a `listener` function and configures it to consume from the AWS Kinesis stream that we defined as the default channel in the event hub:

```yaml
functions:
  ...

  listener:
    handler: src/listener/index.handle
    events:
      - stream:
          type: kinesis
          arn: ${cf:event-hub-${opt:stage}.stream1Arn}
          batchSize: 100
```

We have control over `batchSize`. In this case, we set it to `100`. This is significant because it opens the opportunity for the many optimizations we will cover in this chapter, such as backpressure and asynchronous non-blocking I/O. This is the opposite of many traditional messaging channels that only allow us to process a single message at a time, even though they are batching and buffering at the lower level.

Batch size can also have a significant positive impact on the cost of serverless computing at high volumes because we pay for each innovation. Instead of paying for each message, the batch size acts as a factor to reduce the number of innovations. And when we apply the many optimizations, we also improve the efficiency of each innovation.

At a macro level, we have chosen to use streaming technology for our messaging channels. At a micro level, batch size allows us to slice up the data flowing through the macro-level streams and create micro-level streams within our stream processors. This, in turn, leads us to use a programming model that is best suited for processing streams, such as functional reactive programming.

Functional reactive programming

Stream processing is a natural fit for **Functional Reactive Programming** (**FRP**). The most obvious difference between FRP and imperative programming is the absence of loops. FRP is much more declarative. The following code block shows our `listener` function that consumes from the Kinesis stream:

```
import { fromKinesis, ... } from 'aws-lambda-stream';
export const handler = async (event) =>
  fromKinesis(event)
    .filter(onEventType)
    .map(toUpdateRequest)
    .through(update({ parallel: 4 }))
    .through(toPromise);
```

This example consumes events from a Kinesis stream and materializes the data in a DynamoDB table. The `fromKinesis` function understands the structure of the Kinesis records and turns the `event.Records` array into a micro-level stream of events. We declare the remaining steps to establish how we process the data as it flows through the processor.

A key thing to note is that the code we see here is only responsible for assembling the pipeline of steps the data will flow through. The final step, `toPromise` returns `Promise` from the `handler` function. Then, and only then, does the promise start consuming from the micro-level stream and the data starts flowing through the processing stages.

This is an important distinction. Each step pulls work from the previous step, instead of looping over the data and pushing it downstream. This will be very important when we talk about backpressure in the *Designing for failure* section. The promise will resolve once all the data has passed through all the stream steps or reject when we encounter an unhandled error.

This is an example of micro-level **Staged Event-Driven Architecture** (**SEDA**), as we covered in the *Living in an eventually consistent world* section. Each step represents a stage in the processing pipeline. Each stage has an input and output buffer provided by the low-level streaming library. Upstream stages can continue to pull work when downstream stages block. This will be very important when we talk about asynchronous non-blocking I/O in the *Optimizing throughput* section.

You can find the open source `aws-lambda-stream` library here, `https://github.com/jgilbert01/aws-lambda-stream`. This library provides a lightweight framework for creating stream processors. The underlying streaming library is **Highland.js** (`http://highlandjs.org`), which provides features such as filter, map, reduce, backpressure, batching, parallel processing, and more.

Immutability is another crucial aspect of FRP. The data we pass between the steps of the pipeline is immutable. This ensures that the various stages do not interfere with each other. Without immutability, it would be virtually impossible to reason about the current state of the data because we do not have explicit control over when each stage pulls the next unit of work as the events flow through the pipeline. This is where the concept of a unit of work comes into play.

Unit of work

To help achieve immutability, we pass **unit of work** (**uow**) objects through the pipeline. Think of a uow object as an immutable object that represents the scope of a set of variables passing through the stream. Your processor steps will adorn their outputs to the uow for use by downstream steps. We will see how to do this in the *Mapping* section.

The various streaming and messaging channels each have their own formats. We want to decouple the stream processor logic from the choice of these technologies. The first step of a stream processor transforms the incoming records, using the appropriate `from` function, such as `fromKinesis`, `fromDynamodb`, and `fromEventBridge`, to normalize the records into our standard event envelope format. The output is a stream of `UnitOfWork` objects.

The following code block defines the base structure of a `UnitOfWork`:

```
interface UnitOfWork {
  record: any;
  event?: Event;
  batch?: UnitOfWork[];
}
```

A unit of work starts with the following fields:

- The `record` field contains the original record from the messaging channel.
- The `event` field contains the standard event envelope that we extracted from the original record.

- The optional `batch` field contains an array of related units of work that should succeed or fail together. We will see how to use this field when we discuss batching and grouping in the *Optimizing throughput* section.

More so than ever, we do not use global variables in stream processors. The scoping provided by a unit of work is crucial when we leverage the various parallel processing and pipeline features of the stream processing framework.

Now, let's filter for events of interest.

Filtering and multiplexing

In the *Routing and channel topology* section, we addressed the many considerations that go into defining the messaging channels within an autonomous subsystem. Achieving an optimal topology can be a balancing act. Inevitability, we will need to multiplex different event types through the same channel, as we will see in the *Optimizing throughput* section. And it is reasonable to start with a single channel for all event types and then evolve.

Filtering decouples a stream processor from these decisions. It weeds out unwanted event types. We specify the event types of interest and the processor ignores any others. As the messaging channel topology evolves, we simply reassign the function to a different channel. We do not need to update the filters or any other logic in the stream processor.

The following code block defines the `onEventType` filter we are using in our example `listener` function. It uses a regular expression to match all event types for the `Thing` domain entity. In other words, this `listener` function will process all events where the value of the `type` field starts with `thing-`:

```
const onEventType = uow => uow.event.type.match(/thing-*/);
```

A `filter` function can be arbitrarily complex. It is helpful to create layers of filters. The first filter weeds out unwanted event types, and then the next filter dispatches events to different pipelines based on the content of the event. And then an individual pipeline may have its own filters. We will cover pipelines in the *Optimizing throughput* section. Ultimately, a filter guards downstream steps against irrelevant events so they can focus on their responsibilities.

Now, let's transform the events of interest into the desired format.

Mapping

Transforming data from one format to another is the primary job of a stream processor. It is not glamorous work, but it is nevertheless important. A `listener` function consumes upstream domain events and creates materialized views so that end user queries do not need to perform transformations over and over again. And a `trigger` function transforms local state changes into domain events for downstream consumption.

The following code block shows the basic form of a mapping step. `uow` must be immutable, so we return a new `uow` object by cloning the original `uow` object with the spread operator (...) and adorning the additional variables:

```
.map((uow) => ({
  ...uow,
  variableName: {
    // mapping logic here
  }
}))
```

The following code block defines the `toUpdateRequest` mapping function we are using in our example `listener` function. It is responsible for preparing the data for the *connector* step. It transforms the domain event into the required format and assigns it to the `updateRequest` variable that the downstream connector step expects:

```
import { updateExpression } from 'aws-lambda-stream';
const toUpdateRequest = (uow) => ({
  ...uow,
  updateRequest: {
    Key: {
      pk: uow.event.thing.id,
      sk: 'thing',
    },
    ...updateExpression({
      ...uow.event.thing,
      timestamp: uow.event.timestamp,
    }),
  }
});
```

A mapping function can be arbitrarily complex. In this case, we are preparing to update a materialized view in DynamoDB. There is plenty of opportunity for reusing utility functions, such as the `updateExpression` function, which transforms a plain old object into a DynamoDB update expression. We will cover the details of creating materialized views in *Chapter 5, Turning the Cloud into the Database*.

It is important to perform mapping in a separate upstream step from the connector step that will perform the asynchronous non-blocking I/O work. This is an example of cooperative programming, which helps maximize the potential for concurrent processing, while our connectors are awaiting a response from external resources.

Now, let's make those external requests.

Connectors

At the tail end of a stream processor, there is a sink step that records the output of processing a unit of work. This sink step might persist data in a materialized view, send an email, call an external service, or publish a new domain event. The possibilities are endless, but the pattern remains the same.

We wrap these calls in thin Connector classes so that we can easily create mocks for testing. We will dig deeper into model and connector classes in *Chapter 6, A Best Friend for the Frontend*. We wrap a connector with a utility function to integrate it into the streaming framework.

The following code block shows the reusable `update` function we are using in our example **listener** function. It wraps a connector for DynamoDB and calls the `updateItem` operation to write the data to a table. We will cover the details of creating materialized views in *Chapter 5, Turning the Cloud into the Database*:

```
import { update, ... } from 'aws-lambda-stream';
export const handler = async (event) =>
...
  .through(update({ parallel: 4 }))
  .through(toPromise);
```

These utility functions leverage *currying* to override default configuration settings, such as `batchSize` and the number of `parallel` executions. In this example, we are overriding the `parallel` configuration. We will cover the `batchSize` and `parallel` configurations in the *Optimizing throughput* section.

Here is another example in a `trigger` function. This stream processor consumes change events from a DynamoDB stream and uses the reusable `publish` function to send domain events to the event hub:

```
import { publish, ... } from 'aws-lambda-stream';
export const handler = async (event) =>
  fromDynamodb(event)
    .map(toEvent)
    .through(publish({ batchSize: 10 }))
    .through(toPromise);
```

It is important to note that the stream processors are performing atomic actions, as we discussed in the *Living in an eventually consistent world* section. Each is updating a single resource. Each unit of work constitutes a separate idempotent transaction against a single resource.

Before we move on to the topic of optimizing throughput, we first need to cover the all-important topic of designing for failure.

Designing for failure

Sooner or later, our stream processors will run into trouble. A target system may go down, poison events may start arriving, or someone may make an honest human error. It will happen and we must be prepared. We will cover monitoring and alerting in the *Observing throughput* section. In the meantime, we need to prepare for the worst and design our stream processors to be resilient and self-healing.

We will cover idempotence and order tolerance in *Chapter 5, Turning the Cloud into the Database*. In this section, we will look at backpressure, rate limiting, and poison events. And when we do get into trouble, we will emit fault events.

Backpressure and rate limiting

Backpressure is an important characteristic of stream processing. A stream processor should not overload its target resource. In the best case, the target will throw throttling errors and we will have low throughput, as the stream processor wastes time and resources. Or we could end up with no throughput if the processor function times out and creates an infinite retry loop. In the worst case, the stream processor could overwhelm the target system and cause an outage.

When we use imperative programming, such as looping over the records in a batch, we can easily overwhelm the target resource. The loop will process the records as fast as it can without regard for the throughput capacity of the target system. If we send too many requests, too fast, the target could overload.

Functional reactive programming, on the other hand, provides natural backpressure, because it is pull-oriented. In other words, a step only pulls the next unit of work after it has completed the current. This means a slow target resource will naturally push back, based solely on its own latency. The steps in the stream processor will proceed only as fast as the slowest step.

However, cloud-native resources, such as AWS DynamoDB, can process requests with an extremely hit throughput. These resources rely on throttling to restrict capacity. In this case, the natural backpressure is not enough. We will need to insert artificial backpressure.

The following code block introduces rate limiting to add backpressure:

```
export const handler = async (event) =>
    ...
    .rateLimit(2, 100) // 2 per 100ms
    .map(makeSomeAsyncCall)
    ...
```

The Highland.js `rateLimit` feature acts as a governor to slow the flow of work through the stream processor. In this example, we call the target no more than twice every 100 milliseconds. You will need to know the capacity limits of the specific resource to calculate the proper rate. You will also need to account for multiple shards and parallel calls, which we will cover in the *Optimizing throughput* section.

Poison events

Some errors are transient and self-healing. For example, network hiccups just need a simple retry. We will cover *timeouts and retries* in *Chapter 6, A Best Friend for the Frontend*. Or a transient error could be something more serious, such as an outage in the target system of a stream processor. In this case, the stream processor can let events queue and retry an entire batch until the target system recovers. We can combine this with the *circuit-breaker* pattern that we will cover in *Chapter 7, Bridging Intersystem Gaps*. And we will monitor the *iterator age*, which we will cover shortly in the *Observing throughput* section.

Poison events, on the other hand, are not recoverable. A poison event contains data that breaks the consuming stream processor. It may be a bug in the consuming or the producing stream processor. Regardless, the consuming stream processor will continue to retry the entire batch unless we take corrective action.

Let's say we have a batch of 100 events, and it has a poison event in the 60th position. If the processor does not properly handle the poison event, then it will retry the batch over and over again until the event expires from the stream. In the meantime, the first 59 events will update the target over and over again. This is one reason why we need to implement idempotent transactions. We cover idempotence in *Chapter 5, Turning the Cloud into the Database*. And our iterator age monitor will alert us to the problem so that we can react well before the events expire.

The cloud services we leverage may provide support for these scenarios. For example, AWS Lambda provides a *bisection* feature that provides some relief. This will cut the batch size in half before retrying. So, in this example, the first 50 events will retry and succeed. Then the next 25 will retry and the first 9 will succeed again, while the tenth will fail. Then it will retry a batch of 12 with the same result. And then a batch of 6 will succeed, but there are still 3 more good events to go before we narrow in on the poison event. So, the bisection continues until it reaches a batch size of 1 that contains the poison event.

From here, we can send the poison event to a **Dead Letter Queue** (**DLQ**) for special processing. But when there is one poison event, there are usually many. So, this process continues. Meanwhile, the additional latency is causing more and more good events to queue in the stream.

We can do better. We can make our stream processor logic more proactive by handling poison events and emitting *fault* events.

Fault events

Stream processors emit fault events when they encounter expected error conditions. A fault is an event type that contains an error and the corresponding event or events that caused the error. We will see in a moment how a stream processor emits fault events by throwing handled exceptions. Then we leverage the event hub and all its routing features as the *DLQ*, instead of creating and maintaining something special. The fault events flow into the event lake like any other. And downstream, a *fault monitor* service collects faults, meaning that we can resubmit the affected events after we address the root cause.

The following code block defines the structure of a fault event:

```
export const FAULT_EVENT_TYPE: string = 'fault';
interface FaultEvent extends Event {
  err: {
    name: string;
    message: string;
    stack: string;
  };
  uow: UnitOfWork;
}
```

A fault event has all the standard fields of the event envelope, the `type` field is set to `fault`, and it includes the following additional fields:

- The `err` field contains the error information, including the name, message, and stack trace.

- The `uow` field contains the unit of work with the state of the variables that were in scope when the error happened, plus the one or more events that were affected.

When a stream processor encounters an error, the error will skip over all the remaining steps until it is either handled or reaches the end of the stream. If it reaches the end of the stream, then all processing stops, and the function returns the error. At this point, the batch will retry, as we discussed in the *Poison events* section.

Instead, we want to write proactive code that handles poison events explicitly. We will set them aside as fault events, so good events can continue to flow. Then we can delegate the processing of fault events to other components.

The following code block provides an example of a mapping step with error handling logic:

```
.map((uow) => {
  try {
    return {
      // mapping logic here
    };
  } catch (err) {
    err.uow = uow;
```

```
    throw err;
  }
})
```

We wrap the logic in a `try...catch` block. The `catch` block adorns the troubled unit of work to the error and rethrows it. The presence of the `uow` field on the error acts as an indicator that we handled the error, and we want to emit a `fault` event. The following example uses a utility function to accomplish the same error handling:

```
import { faulty } from 'aws-lambda-stream';
.map(faulty((uow) => ({
  // mapping logic her
}))) 
```

It is a good practice to add a specific validation step at the beginning of a processor to assert that events contain all the required information. This step throws handled errors when data is invalid.

At the tail end of the stream processor, we add the following steps to emit fault events:

```
import { faults, flushFaults, ... } from 'aws-lambda-stream';
  ...
  .errors(faults)
  .through(flushFaults)
  .through(toPromise);
```

The `errors` method is a Highland.js feature for catching errors in a stream. The `faults` function checks `err` to see whether we handled it and adorned a `uow` object. If so, then it buffers a new fault event. We buffer the faults until the end in case an unhandled error occurs later in the batch. Finally, the `flushFaults` step emits all the buffered fault events.

Now good events can continue to flow, and we avoid a traffic jam. We also delegate fault processing to the fault monitor service and Resubmission command-line Utility.

Resubmission

Our stream processors are now proactively handling poison events and producing fault events so that good events keep flowing. In the *Observing throughput* section, we discuss alerting on fault events so that we can jump into action and resolve the problem quickly. In the meantime, we need to collect fault events so that we can resubmit the affected events once we resolve the problem.

A fault monitor service consumes all fault events from the event bus and stores them in object storage. This is very similar to the event lake, but it makes it easier to access the faults for resubmission. You can find a fault monitor template here: `https://github.com/jgilbert01/aws-lambda-stream/tree/master/templates/event-fault-monitor`. This template uses AWS Firehose as the channel to store fault events in S3.

Once we address the root cause of a fault, we can resubmit the original event back to the stream processor that raised the fault to ensure that we successfully process all the events. The fault event contains the original event in the unit of work along with the name of the function. So, a command-line utility can read the fault event from the bucket and invoke the specific function with the original event.

You can find the `aws-lambda-stream-cli` library here: `https://github.com/jgilbert01/aws-lambda-stream-cli`. This command-line utility works with the stream processor framework that we are using in this chapter.

It is important to recognize that we are now processing these events out of order since we needed to set them aside. This is one more reason why it is necessary to ensure that our stream processing logic is order-tolerant. We will cover order tolerance in *Chapter 5, Turning the Cloud into the Database.*

Now, let's look at how we can optimize our stream processor logic to optimize throughput.

Optimizing throughput

Throughput is of the utmost importance for a stream processor. Is a specific stream processor keeping pace with the rate of incoming events or is it falling behind? Is the processor overworked or is it spending too much time waiting? Are we putting too much load on the target resource? There are many ways we can optimize throughput to ensure that we are neither overloading nor wasting resources.

In the *Living in an eventually consistent world* section, we introduced *Staged Event-Driven Architecture (SEDA)* and *Little's Law* and discussed their overall impact on eventually consistent systems. Now it is time to look at these again from the perspective of individual stream processors. Let's see how we can divide individual stream processors into stages and implement parallelism to optimize throughput.

Batch size

Batch size is one of the main parameters we have for adjusting the performance of a stream processor. It controls how much work we feed to a processor on each invocation. Should we give it more work and let it run longer or give it less work and invoke it more often? How does this impact the cost of the stream processor?

As you define and evolve your messaging channel topology, you will need to know the expected volume of traffic for each channel. For each stream processor, you will need to understand the characteristics of the target resource.

From here, you will need to experiment with different batch sizes. As you improve the efficiency of a processor you may be able to increase the batch size. If you are multiplexing many event types through a single channel, then a higher batch size helps to ensure that your processor has work to perform on each invocation. As you change the number of shards, you may also want to change the batch size. And as you increase the batch size, you may also need to increase the function timeout.

Reaching the optimal messaging channel topology and stream processor batch sizes is an iterative balancing act. Keep in mind that the optimal solution also accounts for cost. For example, we could have a channel for each processor, which may optimize the processors at the expense of channel cost and maintenance complexity.

It's a balancing act. I like to start with a single channel per subsystem and a default batch size of 100. Then I analyze the iterator age metrics and the invocation metrics as I dial in the best configuration. We will cover iterator age shortly in the *Observing throughput* section.

Now, let's make sure we are not wasting time waiting on blocked calls when we could be making progress on other elements in a batch.

Asynchronous non-blocking I/O

We introduced **SEDA** in the *Living in an eventually consistent world* section. At the macro level, a stream processor represents a stage in an eventually consistent process flow. At the micro level, a stream processor implements its own staged process flow.

In **Functional Reactive Programming** (**FRP**), we define a series of steps (that is, stages) that the data flows through. The processor pulls data through these steps instead of pushing it. Down inside the FRP mechanisms, each step maintains a buffer (that is, an in-memory queue). When a step completes work, it places the output in the buffer and then it pulls the next unit of work from the preceding step.

To optimize throughput, we need to keep these steps busy. We do not want to starve downstream steps and we do not want to make the output of upstream steps wait. This is where *asynchronous non-blocking I/O* plays a very important role.

The steps in a stream processor that make an external call (that is, I/O) are typically the most time-consuming. We do not want to waste time blocking these calls. We want to keep the other steps busy while we wait for a response. We want upstream steps to continue working on the batch and making preparations for more external calls and we want downstream steps to continue their work.

The following code allows up to eight `parallel` calls to the preceding asynchronous step:

```
export const handler = async (event) =>

    ...
    .map(makeSomeAsyncCall)
    .parallel(8)
    ...
```

While it waits for a response, the Highland.js `parallel` feature continues to pull work through the upstream steps until it has reached the specified number of calls. For example, an upstream mapping step can prepare the input for the next request, so that we can immediately make another call when we receive a response to a previous call.

Asynchronous non-blocking I/O is probably the most important feature for optimizing throughput. This is usually the first parameter I tweak when tuning a stream processor. The command-line utility we covered in the *Replaying events* section serves as an excellent example.

I was using an early iteration of the utility to replay a year's worth of events from an event lake to seed a new service. It was taking several hours to process just a month's worth of events. It turned out that I was not leveraging the `parallel` feature on all the calls to S3. So, I bumped the setting up to 16 parallel calls and performance jumped to just 5 minutes. In retrospect, following *Little's Law*, this makes perfect sense.

Now, let's leverage pipelines to further ensure that we are keeping our processors busy.

Pipelines and multiplexing

In the *Routing and channel topology* section, we covered the many considerations that go into defining the messaging channels within an autonomous subsystem. To achieve an optimal topology, we inevitably need to *multiplex* different event types through the same channel. This actually works to our advantage because it helps us to keep our processors busy while they wait on asynchronous calls.

Let's consider our coffee shop again as an example. There are many items on the menu. However, it does not make sense to have a separate station for each item on the menu. Many stations would sit idle, much of the time. Instead, a single station can prepare multiple items, provided they all follow a similar processing flow.

The same holds true for our autonomous services. Each service is responsible to a single actor, but each needs to react to multiple event types in support of its functionality. Yet, it is not optimal to maintain a separate channel and function per event type. So, we need a way to maintain good clean separation while processing multiple event types in the same stream processor.

Pipelines provide us with the mechanism to achieve this clean separation by dividing the processing logic into separate flows. We *fork* the master stream into many pipelines and merge the pipelines at the tail end. Each pipeline defines a set of related steps that apply to a specific event type and content.

The following code block shows our original stream processor, from the *Processing event streams* section, implemented as a pipeline:

```
const pipeline1 = (options) => // initialize
  (stream) => stream            // assemble
    .filter(onEventType)
    .map(toUpdateRequest)
    .through(update({ parallel: 4, ...options }));
...
export default pipeline1;
```

A pipeline is a curried function with the following functions:

1. The first function call will initialize the pipeline with the `options` configuration.

2. The second call receives a forked `stream`, so we can assemble the steps of the pipeline.

A pipeline typically starts with one or more filter steps that dictate which event types apply to the pipeline and will flow through the remaining steps. We implement each pipeline in its own module file, to create clean separation, and so we can test them independently. Note that we have also decoupled the pipeline from the channel technology decision because we are now performing the `fromKinesis` call elsewhere.

Next, we need to assemble a set of pipelines into a stream processor. The following code block shows our original `listener` function, from the *Processing event streams* section, implemented using pipelines:

```
import { initialize, defaultOptions, ... }
  from 'aws-lambda-stream';
import pipeline1 from './pipeline1';
import pipeline2 from './pipeline2';
const PIPELINES = { pipeline1, pipeline2 };
const OPTIONS = { ...defaultOptions, ... };
export const handler = async (event) =>
  initialize(PIPELINES, OPTIONS)
    .assemble(fromKinesis(event))
    .through(toPromise);
```

The `handler` code for a `listener` or `trigger` function is now mostly boilerplate. Here are the steps it takes to prepare a function to process a batch of events:

1. First, we import the pipelines and group them in the `PIPELINES` object.

2. Then we initialize the pipelines with any `OPTIONS` instance.

3. Then we create the master stream with the appropriate `from` function, such as `fromKinesis`.

4. Next, we assemble all the pipelines. The `assemble` function forks a stream for each pipeline and passes it to the curried function, so the pipeline can assemble its steps. At the tail end, the assemble functions merge all the streams and add the fault handling steps that we covered in the *Designing for failure* section.

5. And finally, we use the `toPromise` function to start the flow of events through the processing pipelines.

From here, the pipelines take control and perform their work. If one pipeline is waiting on asynchronous calls, then the other pipelines will continue to pull work until they need to wait. This cooperative programming approach helps us to minimize the amount of time a stream process spends doing nothing but waiting. The processing concludes when all the units of work have flowed through all the pipelines.

You can find the library for the stream processing framework here: `https://github.com/jgilbert01/aws-lambda-stream`.

Now, let's create reusable pipelines.

Pipeline patterns

It is important to assemble a cohesive set of pipelines into a single function. Throughout the remaining chapters, we will see how to use pipelines in autonomous services to create `listener` and `trigger` functions for BFF, ESG, and Control services.

As we build autonomous services, it becomes clear that we have repeatable pipeline patterns that we use over and over again, with consistent differences. For example, a `listener` function in a BFF service is responsible for consuming domain events and creating the materialized views used in queries. All the pipelines follow the same steps. They filter for specific event types, map the data to an update request, and save the data in the datastore. Only the details of the filter and map steps vary between the pipelines.

We can package these patterns into reusable pipelines and configure them with rules. The following code block shows our original stream processor, from the *Processing event streams* section, implemented with a reusable pipeline pattern:

```
import { materialize } from 'aws-lambda-stream';
import { toThingUpdateRequest } from './model';
...
const RULES = [
  {
    id: 'p1',
    pattern: materialize,
    eventType: /thing-*/,
    toUpdateRequest: toThingUpdateRequest,
  },
  {
    id: 'p2',
    pattern: materialize,
```

```
      eventType: 'something-else',
      toUpdateRequest: (uow) => ({ ...uow, ... }),
   },
   ...
];
export default RULES;
```

In this code block, we define a set of rules that we will use to initialize multiple reusable pipelines. Each rule declares a set of properties:

- The id field contains a unique name for the pipeline instance.

- The pattern field points to the function that implements the pipeline pattern. In this case, we are using the materialize pipeline function provided by the library.

- The eventType fields contain a regex, string, or array of strings used to filter on the event type.

- The toUpdateRequest field is specific to the materialize pattern. This field points to the mapping function that the pipeline will call in the mapping step to format a DynamoDB update item request. You can define the function inline, but it is best to implement and unit test them separately.

Each rule requires an id, pattern, and eventType field, and all remaining fields are specific to the pattern. We can think of the rules as pipeline-specific configuration options. We merge each rule with the global configuration options when we initialize the pipeline.

The following code block shows how we change the listener function to initialize the pipelines from the rules:

```
import { initializeFrom, ... } from 'aws-lambda-stream';
...
import RULES from './rules;
const PIPELINES = {
   ...initializeFrom(RULES),
  pipeline2,
};
```

The initializeFrom function iterates over the rules and prepares a pipeline instance for each using the pipeline function specified in the pattern field. Note that we can initialize one-off pipelines alongside rule-driven pipelines.

In addition to the `materialize` pattern, the stream processing framework includes a `cdc` pattern that we will use in *Chapter 5, Turning the Cloud into the Database*, to create `trigger` functions. In *Chapter 8, Reacting to Events with More Events*, we will use the `collect`, `correlate`, and `evaluate` pipeline patterns to implement Control services. You will find pipeline patterns in your own system and you can package them into shared libraries.

Now, let's add parallel instances of stream processors.

Sharding

We introduced *Little's Law* in the *Living in an eventually consistent world* section. Little's Law shows us that work spends more time in a system as the system nears full capacity. Ultimately, the system will fall behind when the arrival rate exceeds the service rate. The law also shows us that parallelism has a significant impact on the amount of time spent in the system.

This is where sharding comes into play with stream processing. Sharding essentially divides one input channel (that is, stream) into multiple output channels (that is, shards). A separate instance of a stream processor consumes from each shard, which increases the parallelism and throughput of the system.

The `partitionKey` field in the event envelope plays an important role in sharding. A hashing algorithm on the partition key value determines which shard an event will flow through. The distribution of the partition keys dictates how well we utilize all the shards. For example, if we were to use the date for the partition key, then, on any given day, all events would flow through a single shard. We commonly referred to this problem as a **hot shard**.

We should lean toward using a domain entity identifier for the partition key. These identifiers usually contain a V4 random UUID, which helps to ensure an even distribution across the shards. This also ensures that all events for a single domain entity instance will flow through the same shard.

Now, let's see how we can group these related events to gain efficiencies and further improve throughput.

Batching and grouping

Batching and grouping are similar because they reduce the number of calls a processor makes to the target resource. This reduces the amount of time a processor spends waiting on network latency and it also reduces the amount of work the target needs to perform. In the case of grouping, it can significantly reduce the load on the target.

In the *Processing event streams* section, we introduced the concept of a **unit of work**. A unit of work should succeed or fail together. In the *Designing for failure* section, we also attached the unit of work to a *fault* event, so that we could resubmit the unit of work. In general, each incoming event represents one unit of work.

Now we are looking to optimize throughput by collecting multiple events into a single unit of work. This is where we make use of the optional batch field that we specified in the UnitOfWork interface. When we batch and group, we are gathering events into a larger unit of work. We retain the individual units in this batch field to support fault handling and resubmitting all the individual units of work.

Batching

Before we can implement batching, we first need to determine whether the target resource supports it. Many services, such as AWS Kinesis and DynamoDB, provide both a batch and a non-batch interface. Next, we need to determine the limits on the batch size.

From here, it is straightforward to implement batching in functional reactive programming. We add a step that collects units of work. When it reaches the limit, then the step makes the batch available for the next step to perform the call to the target resource.

The following code block creates a batch with a maximum size of 10:

```
import { toBatchUow, ... } from 'aws-lambda-stream';
export const handler = async (event) =>
   ...
   .batch(10)
   .map(toBatchUow)
   .map(makeSomeAsyncCall)
   .parallel(4)
   ...
```

The Highland.js `batch` feature collects the batch, and the `toBatchUow` utility function formats the batch unit of work so that we can easily raise a fault for the entire batch. We can combine batching with the `parallel` feature to help ensure that the processor does not wait on these calls.

It is important to determine whether or not the API treats the batch as a single transaction or whether the individual entries in the batch can fail independently. If they can fail independently, then we need additional logic to resubmit the failed entries. This logic can be tedious, so it may be best to determine whether batching delivers sufficient improvements first.

Grouping

Multiplex different types of events through a channel allows us to group related events together and reduce the number of calls we make against the target resource. For example, we could group events based on common property, such as an account number, and just use the last event as input to the call.

The following code block creates a group based on the partition key:

```
import { toGroupUow, ... } from 'aws-lambda-stream';
export const handler = async (event) =>

    ...

    .group(uow => uow.event.partitionKey)
    .flatMap(toGroupUows)
    .map(makeSomeAsyncCall)
    .parallel(4)

    ...
```

The Highland.js `group` feature reduces the data into groups based on a field value and the `toGroupUows` utility function formats each group as a unit of work so that we can easily raise a fault for the entire group. Again, we can combine grouping with the `parallel` feature to help ensure that the processor does not wait on these calls.

We now have a set of techniques that help us optimize the throughput of our stream processors to ensure that they are not falling behind, wasting resources, or performing unnecessary work. Now let's see how we can observe the throughput of our stream processors so that we can identify when optimization is necessary.

Observing throughput

Observability is essential for optimizing the throughput of our stream processors and our messaging channel topology. It helps us to understand the normal ebb and flow of events and to identify bottlenecks. It allows us to monitor the health of the system and react accordingly. Let's look at the important role domain events play as work metrics and how we can leverage the iterator age metric and alert on fault events.

Work metrics

In *Chapter 2, Defining Boundaries and Letting Go*, we discussed the importance of work metrics. These metrics identify the behavior of the system from the perspective of the end user. They represent the user visible output of the system.

Domain events are work metrics. They are the output of the system. They state the facts about the work the system has completed. We can perform valuable business analytics based on domain events. And we can leverage domain events to monitor the health of the system.

As work metrics, we want to perform anomaly detection on our domain events. We want to monitor the rate at which we emit the various event types and alert on any deviations from the norm. Over time, we will hone in on the main event types that act as the key performance indicators of the health of the system. When we detect an anomaly in these domain events, we will know that it is time to take action and address the issue before it seriously impacts end users.

We will see how anomaly detection fits into the overall product delivery life cycle and continuous testing strategy in *Chapter 9, Choreographing Deployment and Delivery*. But first, we need to turn events into metrics by sending them to the monitoring system. Then we can set up anomaly detection algorithms, like those provided by AWS CloudWatch and Datadog, to alert us to variations in these metrics.

To send events to the monitoring system, we create a service with a stream processor just like we have discussed in this chapter. This stream processor consumes all events and writes out a count metric for each event. Exactly how we write out the metrics depends on the specific monitoring system. But in general, we want to create a count metric named `domain.event` with a standard set of tags. The most important is the `type` tag, which contains the value from the `event.type` field. The other tags help us understand the origins of the events, such as `account`, `region`, `stage`, `source`, `functionname`, and `pipeline`. It is also helpful to create a similar metric named `domain.event.size` with the same tags so that we can gain an understanding of the size of our event payloads.

You can find a service template for collecting event metrics here: `https://github.com/jgilbert01/aws-lambda-stream/tree/master/templates/event-metrics`.

Iterator age

Iterator age is an extremely important resource metric. Each stream processor function has an iterator metric. These metrics tell us how long an event is waiting in a channel for a specific stream processor. They can alert us to immediate or looming issues, and they help us to tune throughput.

If an iterator age is unusually high, then it is an indicator that there may be an unexpected error in the stream processor, such as a poison event. We need to alert on these metrics so that we can jump into action and resolve the problem before it is too late. We should send out a warning when an iterator age reaches 30 minutes. At this point, it is probably not a transient spike in volume.

The logs will usually show us the source of the error, and then we can deploy a fix and the stream processor should recover. If the fix is more involved, then we can deploy a quick fix to raise a fault event, as we covered in the *Designing for failure* section. This will buy us time and allow good events to continue flowing.

When we deploy a fix, we may need to make additional changes to help the stream processor catch up. For example, we may need to increase the batch size and the timeout, and we may need to temporarily increase the number of parallel function instances.

However, a high iterator age is not always the result of an error. It may be an indicator that we need to evolve our messaging channel topology. For example, we may have too many consumers competing for the resources of a single channel. In this case, we may need to split out multiple channels and adjust the routing rules. Or we may have more volume than expected and we need to add shards to a channel to increase the number of parallel stream processors.

In general, we use the iterator age metric to help us tune the throughput of a stream processor and the system as a whole. All the techniques we covered in the *Optimizing throughput* section come to bear. The iterator age helps us gauge the utilization and saturation of a specific stream processor as we dial in the best settings.

Of course, the iterator age will not increase when we handle expected errors and throw fault events, so let's see how to monitor for fault events.

Fault events

We introduced fault events in the *Designing for failure* section. Our stream processors set aside poison events by raising fault events so that good events can continue to flow. We have a fault monitor service that collects fault events, and we have a command-line utility that allows us to resubmit fault events.

Now it is time to react to fault events. We need to alert on fault events so that the team can jump into action and resolve the problem. The alert should include the *error message, stack trace,* and *tags* so that the team does not need to dig for this information. We also need to limit the number of alerts because we often receive many of the same fault events.

It is a good practice to automatically create a ticket in the issue tracking system based on these alerts. The solution may require a fix to the producer of the poison events. But it often requires at least a temporary fix to the specific consumer so that we can resubmit the affected events and process them successfully. Either way, fault events indicate that the team has work to do.

Observing domain events gives us a window into the overall health of the system. Monitoring iterator age and alerting on fault events helps us to optimize and fix our stream processors. But some issues, such as a regional outage, are beyond our control. Now, let's turn our attention to the multi-regional considerations for stream processing.

Accounting for regional failover

It is not a matter of if, but when, a given cloud provider will experience a news-worthy regional disruption. In my experience, this happens about every 2-3 years. Another major event occurred just 2 months before I started writing this chapter. It was a little overdue, but it happened nonetheless. It is inevitable.

Designing a system to run across multiple regions may seem daunting at first, but it is crucial because we rely on a cloud provider's serverless features as our platform. Fortunately, deploying serverless features in multiple regions is neither difficult nor expensive. In *Chapter 9, Choreographing Deployment and Delivery*, we will see how to deploy to multiple regions and leverage one region for canary deployments.

And, as it turns out, multi-regional deployments are not daunting. We are already designing for regional failover because we are designing for eventual consistency. And eventual consistency extends cleanly to support multiple regions.

Let's now look at protracted eventual consistency and regional messaging channels.

Protracted eventual consistency

It is difficult to run traditional systems across multiple regions because they depend on strong consistency, which does not exist across regions. The problem gets worse during a regional failover because many of our assumptions no longer hold. We simply didn't see a need to handle these edge conditions. So now we are stuck running in a primary region and taking an outage when we need to switch over to the secondary region.

Conversely, the resilience of eventual consistency shines through during a regional failover. We can start by thinking of a regional failover as just a period of protracted eventual consistency. It may take a little longer for the system to become consistent, but it will become consistent.

In the meantime, we have already built transparency into the system. In *Chapter 3, Taming the Presentation Tier*, we designed the presentation tier to leverage session consistency and support offline mode. This is a superset of the presentation tier functionality we need for regional failover.

In this chapter, we have learned to trust facts and understand how they support the concurrency that we may encounter during failover. We account for idempotence, order tolerance, and backpressure. Sooner or later, the chain reaction will update a datastore and replicate across regions, as we will cover in *Chapter 5, Turning the Cloud into the Database*.

We have all the pieces in place. Now we need to test them and work out the kinks. This is a great candidate for chaos testing. We can simulate a regional failure and watch the data flow.

Regional messaging channels

We must avoid the temptation to replicate messaging channels across regions. Replicating events across regions adds unnecessary cost and complexity. It adds cost because we are processing every event in every region. It adds complexity because we have to reason about the consequences of all this duplicate work and what happens when a region is down and it does not do the work. For example, do we also add datastore replication and address the complexity of replicating data in every direction all the time?

No, I recommend against replicating at the messaging channel level. It is just too difficult to reason about. It is better to replicate at the datastore level so that data is only ever replicating in one direction at a time. By all comparisons, protracted eventual consistency is much easier to reconcile when things go wrong. We can simply replay the events in the affected region and allow idempotence and order tolerance logic to sort things out.

Using a global messaging bus, on the other hand, is OK provided it is routing messages to only one region at a time and not routing to unhealthy regions. For example, when a stream processing in the East region publishes an event, the global bus should route the event to channels in the East region, unless it thinks that East is unhealthy. This avoids the latency of routing to a different region and then replicating the data back to the original region.

However, global messaging buses are not common at present. But this is, in effect, what we are already doing. In *Chapter 6*, *A Best Friend for the Frontend*, we cover the regional health check and regional failover mechanisms that we leverage for BFF services. We route user requests to the closest healthy region. The BFF emits events in that region and the chain reaction continues in that region. All data replicates from that region to the others.

When the user requests failover to another region, then the new chain reactions will proceed in that region. A global bus will help any chain reactions that are inflight in the unhealthy region. Without one, they will continue in that region. They may proceed more slowly depending on the reason for the failover, but this is where protracted eventual consistency comes into play.

Under normal conditions, the chain reactions of an eventually consistent system happen in near real time. But we have designed our autonomous services to continue to operate even when related services are down. Plus, we have designed our presentation tier to work offline. So, the protracted eventual consistency of a regional failure is just another scenario of everything we have already accounted for.

Summary

In this chapter, we learned that modern systems need to operate in an eventually consistent world and that eventual consistency is based on transparency, facts, and a well-crafted chain reaction. You learned how to increase team confidence by using an event hub to create an outbound bulkhead between upstream and downstream services and how the event sourcing pattern turns events into facts by saving them in perpetuity in an event lake.

We dug into the details and we learned how to implement fault-tolerant stream processors and how to observe and optimize a subsystem's messaging channel topology. You learned how to optimize throughput with techniques such as multiplexing, pipelining, asynchronous non-blocking I/O, and sharding. And you learned that regional failover is just a case of protracted eventual consistency.

In the next chapter, we will cover the **Command Query Responsibility Segregation (CQRS)** pattern and see how it helps us fight data gravity by implementing a data life cycle architecture that turns the database inside out and creates inbound bulkheads between downstream and upstream services. We will look at techniques for creating idempotent and order-tolerant stream processors, how to create lean and high-performance data models, and how we can leverage change data capture. Plus, we will cover regional data replication and how to secure sensitive data.

5
Turning the Cloud into the Database

In *Chapter 4, Trusting Facts and Eventual Consistency*, we covered the event hub and event sourcing patterns and learned how they create an outbound bulkhead that protects upstream services from downstream outages. Now we turn our attention to data architecture and how to reshape it to create inbound bulkheads that protect downstream services from upstream outages. Together, these bulkheads fortify the boundaries of autonomous services and give teams the confidence to forge ahead with changes, knowing that the boundaries will help control the blast radius when things go wrong.

In this chapter, we're going to cover the following main topics:

- Escaping data's gravity
- Embracing the data life cycle
- Turning the database inside out
- Dissecting the CQRS pattern
- Keeping data lean
- Implementing idempotence and order tolerance
- Modeling data for operational performance

- Leveraging change data capture
- Replicating across regions
- Observing resource metrics
- Redacting sensitive data

Escaping data's gravity

In *Chapter 1, Architecting for Innovation*, we saw that the role of architecture is to enable change so that teams can continuously experiment and discover the best solutions for their users. When we think about architecture, we tend to focus on how we organize and arrange the source code. However, a system's data is arguably its most valuable asset and simultaneously its biggest barrier to change. This is because data has gravity. As a system grows and evolves, so too does its data and its data's structure. We must spend as much or more effort on how we organize and arrange our data so that it does not succumb to similar forces as source code and become brittle, inflexible, and impossible to maintain.

When these deficiencies are combined with the sheer volume of data, the weight of our data becomes an intractable force that prevents teams from moving forward. This impact on a system's ability to grow and evolve is a measure of the data's gravity. To fight data gravity and ultimately escape its pull, we must first understand the forces that so negatively impact our ability to change a system's data architecture.

Let's take a look at how competing demands, insufficient capacity, and intractable volumes influence a system's data gravity.

Competing demands

In *Chapter 3, Taming the Presentation Tier*, we saw how the presentation tier has acted like a pendulum, oscillating back and forth between client-side and server-side rendering. There is a pendulum in motion at the data tier as well, but it is moving much more slowly between granular and monolithic datastores. In *Chapter 1, Architecting for Innovation*, we saw how the isolation of information silos drove our industry toward monolithic architecture. However, monolithic databases have proven to be equally deficient, because the force of their data gravity impedes innovation.

In *Chapter 2, Defining Boundaries and Letting Go*, we found that people (that is, actors) are the driving force behind change. The **Single Responsibility Principle** (**SRP**) tells us that each module must be responsible to one and only one actor. But we tend to ignore this principle at the data tier in monolithic databases. In fact, we encourage the reuse of database tables.

This is similar to the topic of whether the presentation tier should live on the client side or the server side. It takes a lot of discipline not to couple business logic with presentation logic when the code resides in the same repository. The same holds true for monolithic databases, because all the tables are easily accessible by all modules using the same database.

Furthermore, relation modeling teaches us to normalize database schemas to the third degree (that is, third normal form) so that there is no duplicate data. This has helped foster the belief that all duplication of data is bad. In other words, it incentivizes the sharing of tables between modules.

Each module that accesses a shared table likely represents a different actor. Each places competing demands on the structure of the database schema. Over time, the schema grows and contorts to accommodate the different requirements. This results in hidden dependencies between the modules. A misunderstanding of these hidden dependencies can lead to mistakes that cause system outages.

Ultimately, these competing demands reduce team confidence, and the force of data gravity starts to grow as we resist making changes.

Insufficient capacity

It's a classic story. You put an application into production, and it performs great for months. Then, one day, it just slows down. After wracking your brain for days, you learn that your application is no longer the sole owner of the database infrastructure. There are now a dozen or so applications competing for the same limited database resources.

This scenario is typical, because owning and operating a database, with all the safeguards in place, is not easy. Our data is our most important asset, and we must protect it. But hardening a database for security and redundancy takes skill, and database administrators are overworked. So, there is a disincentive for running more and more databases. Instead, we make a single database support more and more applications and we add more and more vertical and horizontal capacity. It never seems to be enough. There is always insufficient capacity, so we keep adding more and more.

But now we have created a monstrosity. The database infrastructure has become incredibly complex. Only a select few database administrators are entrusted with making significant changes. Redundancy is baked into the system, but making changes is perceived as high risk because the wrong mistake could cause an outage for all the applications. So we resist change, and the force of data gravity grows stronger.

Intractable volumes

Having lots of data is generally a good thing. The problem is when and where we use it. Our monolithic databases tend to collect data and never let it go, just in case we need it. Meanwhile, the applications that create and use the data need to evolve to support new requirements. This inevitably impacts the data schemas, so the old data must be converted. As the volume of data grows, the conversion effort becomes more difficult and time consuming.

But the applications no longer use much of this data, so why bother converting it? More than likely, the competing demands for the data have created so many interdependencies that we cannot archive the old data. So, it has to stay where it is and as the data grows, it becomes more and more difficult to govern and manipulate. It becomes intractable. It's a compounding effect. We can't archive it, so we must add more capacity. It's difficult to convert, so we resist change. And the force of data gravity grows ever stronger.

The bottom line is that monolithic databases have no bulkheads. There is no real data autonomy. Sooner or later, data's gravity will cause a system to implode or, worse yet, cause innovation to grind to a halt. We need to escape data's gravity by defining fortified boundaries and splitting up the data.

This is what cloud-native is really all about: leveraging the power of the cloud and turning the cloud into the database. Data life cycle architecture and turning the database inside out are two complimentary approaches to breaking up monolithic databases. Let's start by looking at how we use data over its life cycle.

Embracing data life cycle

We need to break up monolithic databases to ensure that our data's gravity does not impede innovation. A natural inclination is to divide a database into sets of related tables and wrap each of these new databases with a data access service. However, this approach is an anti-pattern, as it does not address the problem of competing demands. It just moves data gravity to a service layer and breaks one big problem into multiple smaller problems. It will delay the onset of the force of data gravity, but each database will eventually succumb. We need a better approach.

In *Chapter 2, Defining Boundaries and Letting Go*, we covered multiple approaches for discovering the boundaries between autonomous subsystems and we introduced a set of autonomous service patterns for decomposing a subsystem into services. For breaking up monolithic databases, the most applicable of these approaches and patterns are the data life cycle architecture and the **Backend for Frontend (BFF)** pattern.

Data Life Cycle Architecture (DLC) recognizes that over the life of a piece of data, different actors interact with the data at different phases in its life cycle. These actors are the sources of the competing demands on data. Following the SRP, DLC recommends breaking the database up along the phases of the data life cycle. This approach entails dividing a database along an entirely different dimension than you would expect, but it is not unprecedented. This is akin to the traditional approach of separating an **Online Transaction Processing (OLTP)** database from an **Online Analytical Processing (OLAP)** database. We are just applying this approach at a much more granular level.

In addition to functional differences, these actors have different access patterns and storage requirements. This is the perfect opportunity to apply the polyglot persistence practice by picking the right database technology for each phase of the data life cycle. We will see which database technologies fit the different phases best.

In *Chapter 2, Defining Boundaries and Letting Go,* we used the Event Storming technique to help us discover the event types that a system will emit, the relative order of those events, and the actors who produce them. During this process, we also identify the domain aggregate (that is, the data) that is in play when the events are produced. Using this technique, we naturally discover the phases of the data's life cycle, because it identifies the order in which the different actors interact with the domain aggregates.

Generally speaking, we will implement a BFF service for each actor, domain aggregate, and life cycle phase combination. Each of these autonomous services will own its slice in time of the data and use the database technology that best suits the access patterns:

Figure 5.1 – Data life cycle phases

As depicted in *Figure 5.1*, we can classify data life cycle into four phases: create, use, analyze, and archive. Let's take a look at each of these phases in turn.

Create phase

We are surrounded by and interact with data on a daily basis. This data originates from a variety of sources. We create much of the data manually, but a lot of it is generated, and from a system's perspective, data is often just received from an external source. There are many examples of data creation in our hypothetical food delivery system.

Restaurants create their menus manually and the delivery system receives the menu data through an ingress interface. Customers browse the menus, and the delivery system generates click-stream data to track customer activity. Customers manually create orders, and the delivery system sends orders to restaurants through an egress interface. The delivery system generates delivery assignments and the drivers manually accept the assignments. Restaurants generate order status data as they fulfill orders and drivers generate delivery status data as they carry out a delivery.

In the create phase of the data life cycle, we want to use datastores and data formats that are optimized for writing. For generated and integrated data, we can simply write events to a stream, such as AWS Kinesis. This is the stream-first variation of the Event Sourcing pattern that we covered in *Chapter 4, Trusting Facts and Eventual Consistency*.

For manual data entry, we should use a normalized data format, so that users do not need to enter duplicate data. Key-value, document, and relational databases, such as *AWS DynamoDB* and *AWS Aurora*, are well suited for data entry. It is important that the selected database provides a **Change Data Capture** (**CDC**) feature, so that we can implement the database-first variation of the Event Sourcing pattern. We will cover this shortly in the *Leveraging change data capture* section.

Another important characteristic of data creation is the rate at which we create it. We create some data infrequently, such as reference data or master data, whereas we produce transactional data continuously. We can refer to these as slow data and fast data, respectively. We will cover the implications of slow data in the *Soft deletes* section. We will see how to control the volume of fast data in the *Keeping data lean* section.

Upstream services create data and produce domain events so that downstream services can react to the data in the use phase of the data life cycle. Let's move on to the use phase.

Use phase

We create all data for a purpose. But the actors who create the data and those that use it are almost always different. The different actors have different requirements, so we want to separate these concerns into different autonomous services. We will let upstream services create the data and let an unlimited number of downstream services use the data in a format that best suits their needs.

For example, in our hypothetical food delivery system, restaurants create their menus and customers use the menus of many restaurants. But the access patterns and performance requirements are completely different. The way customers create orders and how drivers and restaurants use orders are very different. In fact, the way drivers and restaurants use orders are very different from each other. And the way customers track the status of their current orders and view the history of their previous orders are each different access patterns.

We traditionally refer to the databases that we use for these scenarios as OLTP databases or operational datastores. It is important to note that their access patterns are not ad hoc. We explicitly define these datastores to allow the actors to perform their tasks efficiently. We want to take full advantage of this characteristic and optimize these operational datastores for their specific scenarios. In the *Dissecting the CQRS pattern* section, we will see how to create materialized views that prejoin data for fast access, and in the *Keeping data lean* section, we will cover techniques for trimming the fat from these databases.

Key-value stores, search engines, and object storage are a great fit for these operational datastores. Examples of NoSQL services in these categories include AWS DynamoDB, Elasticsearch, and AWS S3. We will see examples of DynamoDB in the *Modeling data for operational performance* section, and we will see an example of using Elasticsearch in combination with S3 in *Chapter 6, A Best Friend for the Frontend*. These usage scenarios can also benefit from caching at the edge with CDN services such as AWS CloudFront. In very high-performance scenarios, a durable cache such as AWS **DynamoDB Accelerator (DAX)** may be warranted.

The create and use phases of the data life cycle are very interrelated because each autonomous service can use data created by upstream services and create more data for use in downstream services. But it is very important to draw a line between these phases and the analyze phase, because analytics access patterns are very different from operational access patterns. Let's move on to the analyze phase.

Analyze phase

All upstream data creation leads to the analyze phase. In *Chapter 2, Defining Boundaries and Letting Go*, we discussed how first-ever systems implicitly build business analytics and observability into a system because events represent facts and analytics deals in facts. There are many potential uses of analytics in our hypothetical food delivery system.

The delivery system tracks customer activity so that it can better target customers and drive up sales conversion. Restaurants need statistics so that they can gauge whether or not their partnership with the delivery service is producing positive results. Delivery statistics can help identify drivers that need more training. We can derive all this actionable information from the events generated by the system.

All the traditional analytics techniques and technologies are still applicable. For example, data marts and data warehouses can consume upstream events and use them to populate the fact tables in their star schemas. We traditionally leverage columnar databases for this purpose, such as AWS Redshift. These are relational databases that store data on disk organized by column instead of by row. This is because the large amount of data makes it impractical to create indices on tables. Storing data by column effectively creates an index per column. Time series databases, such as InfluxDB and AWS Timestream, and search engines, such as Elasticsearch, are alternatives to using relational databases for analytics.

One of the most significant advancements in the analyze phase of the data life cycle is the event lake. The event lake consumes all events and stores these facts in perpetuity. This allows us to defer commitment on how we want to utilize analytics technology. For example, teams can experiment with different hypotheses by replaying historic events from the lake into a datastore and validating whether or not the approach produces accurate forecasts. It also supports creating data marts on demand and tearing them down afterward to reduce cost. We covered event lakes in *Chapter 4, Trusting Facts and Eventual Consistency*.

Another significant advancement is in actionable analytics with big data and machine learning. Services consume events of interest and use them to train machine learning models. The models are then *used* by downstream services to identify conditions, such as in anomaly detection, and control the behavior of the system. We will cover additional details in the *Leveraging ML for control flow* section of *Chapter 8, Reacting to Events with More Events*.

Ultimately, the analyze phase plays an important role in driving innovation because it provides the insights that help organizations learn and adapt. But it is important to recognize that analytics services support different demands and need their own datastores.

Now, let's move on to the archive phase.

Archive phase

Sooner or later, the cost of keeping a piece of data readily available will become more expensive than the value it provides. As we saw in the *Intractable volumes* section, keeping data too long increases the force of data gravity, which inevitably impedes innovation. The solution is to archive data and keep operational data lean, but these are separate concerns that need to be handled independently to avoid adding complexity.

In the *Keeping data lean* section, we cover the time-to-live technique. This is a simple technique where each service decides how long it needs to use a piece of data. After that time, the database deletes the row so that the datastore can maintain a predictable and manageable size. These services do not concern themselves with the requirements of archiving because archiving requirements apply to different actors.

Instead, we create downstream archiving services that consume events and proactively archive data. In other words, we create the archives continuously as we create the data. This frees the operational services to delete data at will. The archiving services handle the records management requirements regarding what data we need to retain and for how long.

Object storage, such as AWS S3, is a great fit for archiving. As the data ages, it can transition to long-term storage, such as AWS Glacier. These archives are typically organized by actor and date. In our hypothetical food delivery system, we would organize the archive around restaurants, drivers, and customers. The archive would collect all the events and any documents.

An archive will likely support re-hydrating data, so that upstream services can reconstitute the data they have deleted. For example, in a case management system, we could reopen a closed case. An upstream service could produce a `case-reopened` domain event and the archive service would produce `re-sync` events once it retrieves the cold data, similar to the approach discussed in the *Soft deletes* section.

Creating a data architecture that decomposes a monolithic database along the phases of the data life cycle addresses the problem of competing demands. However, there is an ever-present concern around the amount of duplicate data the approach creates and the ability to keep it synchronized. It's an understandable concern, but there is relatively little duplication as compared to what traditional databases actually do. Let's look at what a database does inside so that we can turn the database inside out and ultimately turn the cloud into the database.

Turning the database inside out

When I built my first cloud-native e-commerce system, I knew I had to break out of the relational database mold. It was reasonable to expect that I could use AWS RDS MySQL for the back-office users who would maintain the product catalog, but I would need something different to support the expected volume of customers reading from the catalog. I was already using Amazon S3 and Amazon CloudFront to serve SPA applications, with no concern for supporting any load volume. So why couldn't I do the same thing for the catalog data?

The catalog data was public, and it was static. Offers didn't change; they just expired and were replaced by new offers. I could put the images and offer JSON data into an S3 bucket with a path structure that supported good RESTful URLs, such as `/merchants/123/offers/987/images/abc`, and set the `cache-control` property on the objects so that CloudFront would serve the requests more often than not. I combined this with Amazon CloudSearch to index the catalog and I had a solution that I was confident would scale with the user base and would be reasonable to operate.

The only remaining piece of the puzzle was synchronizing the catalog data from RDS to S3 and CloudSearch. Thanks to my experience with **Enterprise Application Integration (EAI)**, this was already a familiar problem. I just had to select the right cloud-native tools. Amazon Kinesis and AWS Lambda proved to be a perfect fit.

I didn't realize it at the time but I was implementing the Event Sourcing and CQRS patterns. Along the way, I came across Martin Kleppmann's excellent article, Turning the database inside out with Apache Samza (`https://www.confluent.io/blog/turning-the-database-inside-out-with-apache-samza`). This article put a fine point on what I was doing and helped solidify the approach for breaking away from monolithic databases, maximizing scale and flexibility, and keeping all the pieces working in harmony.

This last point is the real crux of the matter. We are accustomed to relying on the database to do a lot of the heavy lifting for us. But we no longer have one homogeneous database at the core of our systems. We now have many, heterogeneous databases, and it is incumbent on us to make them all work together. This, understandably, seems like a daunting challenge. But, other than query optimization, databases really aren't that magical.

When we think of a database, the first thing we typically think about is tables. After that, we think about executing queries against those tables. But this doesn't really scratch the surface of everything a database is actually doing for us under the hood. Yet, when we look inside, it turns out that the thing we are most concerned about, data synchronization, is not that daunting. And overcoming this obstacle is what leads to fully escaping data's gravity. So, let's look inside, at the transaction log, and see how a database manages derived data.

The transaction log

At the heart of the database is the transaction log. It is the source of truth for information about every insert, update, and delete statement that has been executed against a database. For example, when we execute an update statement against a specific table, the database finds the desired record, applies the changes, and then stores the previous state and the new state in the transaction log. In other words, the transaction log records all of the state-change events that occur within the database.

However, our modern systems now have many databases, which means that we have many transaction logs, but none of them provides a definitive source of truth about the state of the entire system. The solution is the event hub and event lake, as we covered in *Chapter 4, Trusting Facts and Eventual Consistency*. This is exactly what they accomplish. They provide the source of truth for information about every command that the autonomous services have performed within the system. Now, let's look deeper into what a database does with its transaction log, so we can understand what we can do with a systemwide stream of events.

Derived data

The transaction log is the heart of the database because it is used to push data out to the other parts of the database. These other parts of the database are the derived copies of the data, such as indices, materialized views, and replicated instances of the database. It's easy to overlook just how much derived data there is in a typical database, because the database manages and synchronizes these copies for us. But all this work the database is doing can have a steep cost.

The database uses the log to replicate the database to other database instances for failover and to create more copies in the form of read replicas that support more and more readers. It maintains indices, which are copies of the data arranged on disk in different sort orders to support faster reads. It calculates materialized views, and each is yet another copy of the data that contains the precalculated results of a query that is too expensive to execute over and over again in real time.

All of this work is not too much of a burden for a small, focused database with a predictable load. However, as we add more and more tables, indices, and materialized views to the database, and more and more consumers of the data, then all this competition for scarce resources adds up and drives down performance for end users.

The inevitable consequence is that applications add their own read-through cache to shield their users from this competition with other applications. This is yet another derived copy of the data. However, this time the copy is not managed by the database but by the application developers. The developers have to map the data to the desired format, handle cache misses, and account for stale reads. This additional code and infrastructure add to the complexity and cost of the applications. And the pull of the data's gravity continues to grow.

This is the way we have built applications for decades. But what if we stop and instead turn the database inside out? What if we create a unified transaction log across the databases? What if we take all the indices and materialized views and move them into the datastores of the services that use them? What if we can eliminate the need for applications to maintain their own read-through cache? What if we can stop centrally managing a one-size-fits-all read replication strategy? What if we can eliminate the single point of failure within the system and build bulkheads between the services? What if we could choose a different database technology on a query-by-query basis? What if we could spread the load of all this processing across the cloud?

What would this look like? We already have an event hub and event lake, which act as the systemwide transaction log. Now let's take a look at how a systemwide view of the CQRS pattern enables us to turn the cloud into the database.

Dissecting the CQRS pattern

The **Command Query Responsibility Segregation (CQRS)** pattern provides the foundation for turning our monolithic databases inside out and escaping data's gravity. It proposes the use of two different domain models, a write-optimized command model and a read-optimized query model. Separating these two concerns allows each to change and evolve independently and enables the creation of systems that are more responsive, resilient, and elastic.

Unfortunately, the CQRS pattern has a reputation for making systems more complex. This concern is not unfounded, however; with the right alterations, this segregation produces systems that are actually more straightforward and flexible. A few examples will help make this clear. Let's look at an example without CQRS, one with what I refer to as traditional CQRS, and a third example with the altered form that I refer to as systemwide CQRS.

Figure 5.2 depicts a BFF service that provides read and write capabilities to the end user without using separate domain models:

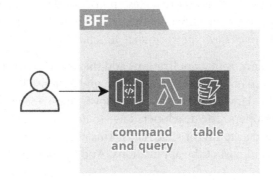

Figure 5.2 – Without CQRS

This results in a straightforward development experience for the vast majority of use cases, which only have **Create, Read, Update, and Delete (CRUD)** requirements. We can easily implement this with a single table and a single RESTful command and query service using HTTP PUT, GET, and DELETE methods.

Figure 5.3 depicts a BFF service that provides read and write capabilities to the end user using separate domain models:

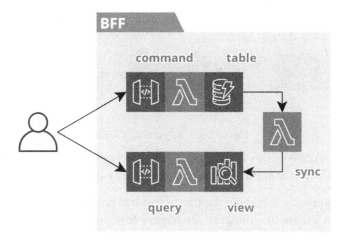

Figure 5.3 – Traditional CQRS

This is obviously more difficult to implement because there are more pieces. There is a **table** used by the command function, a **view** used by the query function, and a sync function to synchronize the data from the table to the view. If there is a distinct benefit to separating the domain models, such as using polyglot persistence, then it may be worth spending the extra effort. For example, in this case, we implement the view with a search engine that can support more expressive queries.

Now, let's look at how we can improve CQRS.

Systemwide CQRS

One important thing to notice in these first two examples is that they each focus on supporting the usage scenarios of a single actor. This is great from the perspective of the SRP. However, we also need to consider the system as a whole.

Going back to the *Embracing data life cycle* section, we saw that over the course of the data life cycle, different actors use the same logical data with different access and storage requirements. We proposed using the data life cycle phases to define the boundaries between different datastores. In the *Turning the database inside out* section, we saw how these competing demands result in the creation of derived data, such as materialized views and indices, and proposed moving them within the boundaries of the services that use them. As a consequence, the CQRS pattern must take on a much more strategic role when we adopt this holistic perspective.

Figure 5.4 depicts two BFF services collaborating to support multiple actors in different life cycle phases:

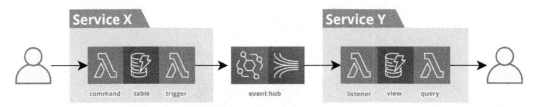

Figure 5.4 – Systemwide CQRS

We saw a similar version of this diagram in *Chapter 1*, *Architecting for Innovation*, when we discussed the **Command**, **Publish**, **Consume**, **Query** (**CPCQ**) flow.

Service X sits upstream, supporting the first actor, and provides a **command** function that *creates* data in a **table** that it owns. The **trigger** function produces a domain event to the **event hub**, which provides the systemwide transaction log that we discussed in the *Turning the database inside out* section. We will discuss this trigger mechanism in detail later, in the *Leveraging change data capture* section.

Service Y sits downstream, supporting the next actor, and provides a **listener** function that consumes events and materializes the needed data in a **view** that we specifically designed to support the access scenarios of this downstream actor. Furthermore, the **query** function and **view** provide the downstream actor with dedicated resources for *using* the data, to help ensure a responsive and resilient user experience.

This last example shows how the CQRS pattern is a key mechanism for creating an architecture that enables change. We employ it to create derived data that supports one and only one actor, so that we can turn our monolithic databases inside out and fight data's gravity. Along with these materialized views come the benefits of inbound bulkheads, live cache, and capacity allocation per query. Let's dig into each of these, starting with a look at how to create materialized views.

Materialized views

The primary job of a materialized view is to improve the responsiveness of the user experience. We accomplish this by choosing the most appropriate type of database, creating proper indices, and then pre-calculating joins and storing the data in the format needed by the specific consumer. There is no reason to calculate the join over and over again. We can do it once when we receive the data, so that the consumer does not pay the price on every request. This also reduces the cost of our serverless solution, since the price is based on execution time.

We have already seen how upstream services produce events, in *Chapter 4, Trusting Facts and Eventual Consistency*, using the stream-first variation of the Event Sourcing pattern, and we will look into the database-first variation of the pattern shortly in the *Leveraging change data capture* section. Now, let's look at how downstream services implement the CQRS pattern to create their materialized views.

The following stream processing example builds on the concept of pipeline patterns, which we covered in *Chapter 4, Trusting Facts and Eventual Consistency*:

```javascript
import { materialize, updateExpression } from
      'aws-lambda-stream';
const RULES = [{
  id: 'm1',
  pattern: materialize,
  eventType: /thing-(created|updated)/,
  toUpdateRequest: (uow) => ({
    Key: {
      pk: uow.event.thing.id,
      sk: 'thing',
    },
    ...updateExpression({
      name: uow.event.thing.name,
      description: uow.event.thing.description,
    }),
  }),
}, {
  id: 'm2',
  pattern: materialize,
  eventType: 'thing-submitted',
  toUpdateRequest: (uow) => ({
    Key: {
      pk: uow.event.thing.id,
      sk: 'thing',
    },
    ...updateExpression({
      status: uow.event.thing.status,
    }),
  }),
}];
```

This example is joining the data from three different types of domain events into a single record in the datastore. Here are the typical steps for creating a materialized view:

1. Filter for the desired events.

2. Map the data in the event to the needed format.

3. Save the data to the datastore.

These steps are so typical that it makes sense to wrap them in a reusable pipeline pattern. This example uses a `materialize` pipeline pattern that works with Amazon DynamoDB. Similar pipeline patterns are available for Amazon S3 and Elasticsearch. And of course, you can create your own or implement CQRS in your favorite language and framework.

> **Note**
> The mapping code in this example is included inline for brevity. These functions will normally be implemented and tested in separate modules.

The most interesting details are in the `toUpdateRequest` functions that implement the mapping step. We are joining the data from the different events based on the identifier (that is, `uow.event.thing.id`) of the `Thing` domain entity. Two separate rules are defined because the thing-created and thing-updated event types carry the `name` and `description` fields, and the `thing-submitted` event type carries the `status` field.

These events can arrive in any order, so we are using the DynamoDB `UpdateItem` operation as opposed to the `PutItem` operation. Both operations will create a new record if one does not exist for the specified `Key` or update the record if it does exist. But the `PutItem` operation will replace all the fields, whereas the `UpdateItem` operation only replaces the specified fields, name and description, or status. This allows us to weave together the fields from the different domain events and incrementally create the desired join records. It also allows us to do this without retrieving data first, which improves throughput. We will go into more detail later in the *Implementing idempotence and order tolerance* section.

Inbound bulkheads

Materialized views also perform the equally important job of providing the system with resilience. As depicted in *Figure 5.5*, services that have direct dependencies on other services are less resilient, because a disruption in the dependee service will impact the depender service. This results in an architecture that does not enable change, because teams become reluctant to make changes for fear of the ripple effect if they make a mistake. To counteract this impulse, we must fortify the boundaries between services by adding bulkheads that control the blast radius when we inevitably make a mistake:

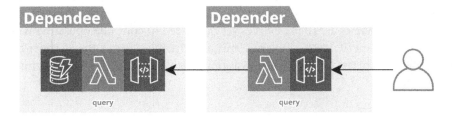

Figure 5.5 – Synchronous communication anti-pattern

The Circuit Breaker pattern attempts to solve this problem, while maintaining the synchronous communication paradigm. When the depender service detects that it is receiving too many errors from the dependee service, the depender will open a circuit and stop calling the dependee service for a period of time. This approach really only helps the dependee service, by reducing the load so that the dependee can have an opportunity to recover. Meanwhile, we force the depender service to return some form of default response to its end users.

This results in a suboptimal user experience when there is a disruption, adds overhead to every request even when there is no disruption, makes the developer experience more complicated, and increases the total cost of ownership. There are cases when the complexity of this approach is unavoidable, and we cover this in *Chapter 7, Bridging Intersystem Gaps*. But for all other scenarios, the best approach is to eliminate the dependencies by eliminating synchronous inter-service communication and leveraging materialized views.

In *Chapter 4, Trusting Facts and Eventual Consistency*, we learned how to implement asynchronous inter-service communication and use an event hub as an outbound bulkhead to protect upstream services from disruptions in downstream services. The event hub is serverless, so upstream services can rely on it to receive their events when they publish them. Downstream services will eventually consume these events and make themselves consistent.

The CQRS pattern is employed by downstream services to react to these events and create the materialized views that act as an inbound bulkhead to protect downstream services from disruptions in upstream services. Again, downstream services leverage highly available, fully managed, serverless services to implement their dedicated datastores, so we can be confident that they will respond to our queries. When an upstream service has an outage, there is no impact on downstream services, because they can continue to respond to queries with the most recent data in their materialized views, instead of a default response. This also optimizes responsiveness, because there are no additional layers involved in these requests. It also reduces the complexity of the developer experience and lowers the total cost of ownership.

Ultimately, bulkheads make services more than resilient; they make them autonomous. These materialized views are the resources services need to continue operating when other services are experiencing problems. This, in turn, gives teams the confidence to experiment and increase the pace of innovation, which is our primary architectural goal.

Live cache

Another benefit of the CQRS pattern is that materialized views act as a live cache, which solves the inherent problems of a read-through cache. As we previously discussed in the *Turning the database inside out* section, developers will ultimately turn to adding a caching layer to their technology stack to compensate for the increased latency that results from competition for scarce database resources. However, as we have seen, a read-through cache just addresses the symptoms instead of the root cause, and it introduces its own problems as well.

The first problem is cache misses. When a value is missing in the cache, we need to make an additional call back to the source database to retrieve the data, hence the name read-through. Then we add the data to the cache before we return it. As a result of this additional work, the responsiveness of the user experience is inconsistent. The extreme case is when the cache is cold (that is, empty) and all requests are cache misses.

The next problem is stale data. When there is a cache hit, we return the data from the cache instead of from the source database. This is the purpose of a cache, but it introduces the possibility that we could return stale data, if the data has changed in the source database. The workaround is to set a time to live that will expire entries from the cache to force cache misses. The trick is finding the right balance between the likelihood of returning stale data and having too many cache misses. If we set the value too low, then we will have more misses; if we set it too high, we will return stale data.

The final problem is complexity. A read-through cache adds another layer of technology to the call stack. The logic to handle a cache miss makes the developer experience more complex and increases the likelihood of introducing bugs. All in all, a read-through cache increases the total cost of ownership.

The CQRS pattern and materialized views provide a better solution because we keep the data up to date in near real time. This simplifies the developer experience because the code to materialize data is separated from the code to retrieve the data. The responsiveness of the user experience is consistent because there are no additional layers and calls. The use of a dedicated, highly available, serverless datastore, such as Amazon DynamoDB, removes the need for any additional layers because of their inherent high performance. Furthermore, we get to make this polyglot persistence decision on a query-by-query basis, which we will cover next.

Capacity per reader, per query

As we have seen, placing all data in the same database leads to competition for scarce resources and creates a single point of failure. Moving the data into separate databases and wrapping each with a service just moves these problems to another location because many services still share the data. The CQRS pattern provides a complete solution by giving each reader total control over its own derived data. We are, in essence, allocating capacity on a per-reader, per-query basis.

Each service supports a different reader (that is, actor) and creates and maintains its own materialized views and indices, instead of relying on a central, shared database. What's more, we can choose to use a different type of datastore for each query (that is, each materialized view). This gives each service complete autonomy to allocate the capacity it needs. Nothing is shared, so there is no competition for resources. If the responsiveness of a service degrades, then it is clear that the problem is self-inflicted.

This is a very powerful approach to fighting data gravity. We cannot accomplish this with a shared database, not even multiple shared databases. We are spreading the load across the cloud. In other words, we are not just turning the database inside out, we are ultimately turning the cloud into the database.

Up to this point, we have addressed the competing demands and insufficient capacity challenges that generate data gravity and impede innovation. By turning the database inside out and leveraging the CQRS pattern, we have given each service full control over its data. Now we turn to the intractable volume challenge and addressing it by keeping data lean.

Keeping data lean

Intractable volumes of data, as we have already seen, are one of the causes of data gravity. The sheer volume of data in a system can impede its evolution because the time and effort involved to reshape data is a powerful deterrent. In the *Embracing data life cycle* section, we discussed how defining boundaries between the data throughout the phases of the data's life cycle makes a big improvement as we move these groups of data into separate, leaner databases. In the *Turning the database inside out* section, we saw that a large portion of a database's size is attributable to derived data, such as indices and materialized views. Moving this derived data into the datastores of the services that use it makes the source datastores even more lean.

But we can do more. Upstream services produce events as they create data, and these events become the source of truth in the systemwide transaction log. This frees services to pick and choose the data they need to retain. Downstream services can project less data to keep their materialized views lean and all services can delete data they no longer need. Let's see how.

Projections

Duplication of data is one of the overarching concerns with the CQRS pattern. Setting aside the fact that traditional databases are full of duplicate (that is, derived) data, we can use projections to help keep downstream datastores as lean as possible. Projections are a normal feature of databases. The most common example is the SELECT clause of a SQL statement, which defines the columns to project in the response.

Similarly, when we create materialized views from upstream events, we do not need to retain all the data that is in an event. The event lake acts as the systemwide transaction log and record of truth, so that other services do not have to. This means that downstream services can project the minimum amount of data into their views that is needed to support their end users. For example, a BFF service may just need the id, name, and description from a domain entity so that it can present a drop-down list to the user.

Keeping materialized views lean obviously helps to reduce storage costs, but it also improves performance and reduces overall costs. For example, a serverless database, such as Amazon DynamoDB, is priced based on the amount of capacity that is consumed per request. The amount of capacity a query consumes is dependent on the amount of data that it retrieves. Therefore, we do not want to process any more data than is necessary. In other words, retrieving data that we will not use is a waste of money. If we keep our data lean, by excluding unneeded data from our views in the first place, we can ensure that we are not wasting capacity.

Keeping data lean also improves the performance of queries, which reduces the time that functions take to execute and thus reduces costs further. This is one of the benefits of the serverless-first approach. Doing the right thing, such as keeping data lean, provides the double benefit of reducing costs while also improving the responsiveness of the user experience. This, in and of itself, makes the cost of any duplicated data money well spent.

Projections also help reduce the impact of changes in upstream services. In *Chapter 9, Choreographing Deployment and Delivery*, we cover the Robustness principle, which states that modules should be conservative in what they send and liberal in what they receive. Following this principle, if an upstream service makes a change to a field that a downstream service does not include in its projection, then those changes can and should be safely ignored. Thus, projections have the positive effect of helping to minimize the dependencies between services.

Time to live

While projections are important for keeping individual records lean, we also need to address the total number of records. Too often do we let tables grow and grow even though we only use the most recent data on a daily basis. We typically keep the older data around just in case we happen to need it in the future, but that is a different usage scenario. In the *Embracing data life cycle* section, we covered the concept of proactive archiving. The gist is that dedicated services take responsibility for archiving data in real time, so that other services can focus on just the data they need.

In the context of a specific service, data has a useful life on a query-by-query basis. As we materialize data, we know how long we need to keep the data for each query. As we perform commands to create and modify data in a service, we also know how long we need to keep that data to support the usage scenarios of the specific service. Therefore, as we insert and update data, we should set a **time to live** (**TTL**) for each record. The following code extends the example we have been using in this chapter for populating a materialized view in a listener function:

```
toUpdateRequest: (uow) => ({
  Key: {
    pk: uow.event.thing.id,
    sk: 'Thing',
  },
  ...updateExpression({
    name: uow.event.thing.name,
    ttl: uow.event.timestamp + (60*60*24*33) // 33 days
  }),
}),
```

To support lean tables, we simply need to add a `ttl` field to each record. In this case, the value is calculated based on `uow.event.timestamp`, which indicates when the business event occurred. When performing commands to create and modify a domain entity, it is best to use data within the entity to calculate the TTL, such as the expected closing date of a mortgage application. The appropriate duration should be determined on a case-by-case basis. In this example, the useful life of the data for the hypothetical service is 33 days.

More and more databases, such as Amazon DynamoDB, are providing TTL features. This should be an important criterion when selecting a database technology for a service. We simply add the `ttl` field and the database handles, removing the data after it expires. Other services, such as Elasticsearch, support rolling indices on an hourly, daily, or weekly basis, and we can schedule functions to delete older indices. Otherwise, your scheduled function can query and delete individual records based on the `ttl` field.

Removing older data makes tables lean by keeping the number of records relatively consistent. It also helps reduce the impact of changes in upstream services. As we just covered in the *Projections* section, if an upstream change affects one of the projected fields, we need to make a change for all new records. However, we may not need to convert existing records if the TTL is short enough. The queries can continue to support the old and new format until all the old data has expired, and then it is safe to remove the legacy code. In *Chapter 9, Choreographing Deployment and Delivery*, we will see this in detail when we cover zero-downtime deployments.

Setting a TTL for records plays an important role in fighting data gravity by controlling the volume of data. This, in turn, makes it easier for systems to evolve. However, we must take care not to remove old data too aggressively as this can have an impact on the idempotence and order tolerance of the system. This is what we will cover next.

Implementing idempotence and order tolerance

In *Chapter 4, Trusting Facts and Eventual Consistency*, we learned that exactly-once delivery of messages is unrealistic. For example, a client request may time out due to network unreliability and have no choice but to resubmit the request because it cannot be certain that the service successfully processed the request. Or a stream processor may fail in the middle of a batch and retry the entire batch even though part of the batch successfully processed. Or we may replay events from the event lake to repair a service that may have dropped a subset of those events. To account for the reality of at-least-once delivery, we have to design our systems to be idempotent. In other words, no matter how many times we receive and process an event or request, it must only update the system once.

We also learned that delivering messages in order can be problematic. A stream will certainly deliver events in the order that it received them, but it may not receive them in the correct order. For example, a poorly behaving service may produce events in the wrong order. Or high traffic volumes could cause a service to delay sending events, while related services are still producing their events in real time. Or a poison event could be set aside and resubmitted later after we resolve the underlying problem. To account for this reality, we have to design our systems to be order tolerant. In other words, receiving events in order is good for throughput performance, but we have to be ready to receive events out of order and literally sort things out.

To achieve this level of resilience, first and foremost we need deterministic identifiers. From here we can employ techniques, such as inverse optimistic locking and immutable event triggers.

Deterministic identifiers

It is a very common practice to delegate the generation of identifiers to the server side, such as by using an auto-incrementing sequence number generated by the database. This is a convenient approach, but it is not idempotent. For example, if a client submits an HTTP POST request multiple times for the same logically unique domain entity payload, then the service will create duplicate records for the same entity with different identifiers. The solution to this problem is to have the client generate the identifier and submit an HTTP PUT request instead. This will ensure that the request is idempotent and will only create and update one record no matter how many times the client resubmits the request.

There are a variety of alternative techniques for generating an identifier on the client side. One seemingly simple option is to generate UUIDs. For domain entities, a V4 UUID is most appropriate because they are generated with random numbers that help avoid hot partitions. For domain events, a V1 UUID is most appropriate because they are generated based on time, which allows them to be naturally sorted.

However, there is a limitation to the UUID approach. It falls apart if the client forgets the UIDD that it just generated. For example, if a stream processor is publishing events and fails in the middle of a batch and retries, then it will publish events again with a new UUID. A similar situation happens in a SPA if the client does not remember the identifiers that it generates.

To solve this problem in a SPA client, we can leverage session consistency, as we discussed in *Chapter 3, Taming the Presentation Tier*. With this approach, the client holds everything in session storage for the duration of the user session. We can go a step further with an offline-first approach and make the data durable in local storage, which we also covered in *Chapter 3, Taming the Presentation Tier*.

Another option is to create an identifier by concatenating together a unique combination of fields from the contents of the domain entity. A major advantage to this approach is that the identifier has business meaning. This can be helpful when trying to debug a problem in the business logic. However, it is important to treat these identifiers as opaque values in the code. Otherwise, we may introduce bugs if we change the generation of the identifier.

There is a scenario when it does make sense to use an identifier that the database generates. As we will discuss shortly in the *Leveraging change data capture* section, we can create stream processors that process the stream of events that a datastore emits as we insert, update, and delete records. These events will have identifiers that the database generated. It is safe to reuse these for the identifiers of domain events because these values will not change, no matter how many times a stream processor retries. However, if you are producing more than one domain event from each database event, then you will need to add a deterministic suffix to these identifiers for each different event type to make them unique.

And finally, another approach is to generate the hash of the entire domain entity or domain event. This is a simple approach, but there is a chance that it will generate collisions. This will depend on the complexity and variability of the domain entity, so consider this option carefully.

Inverse optimistic locking

We use the traditional optimistic locking technique to prevent multiple users from updating the same record concurrently. We only allow a user to update a record if the `oplock` value has not changed since the user retrieved the data. If another user has updated the record and thus the `oplock` value, then we throw an exception when the current user attempts to update the record and force the user to retrieve the data again before proceeding with the update. This ensures that we perform updates sequentially, and it requires human interaction to resolve any potential conflicts. We can use this traditional technique in BFF services command functions when users modify data.

Conversely, we use the inverse optimistic locking technique in downstream asynchronous stream processors to provide both idempotence and order tolerance. It ensures that older or duplicate events do not overwrite the most recent data. Instead of forcing a transaction to retry when an oplock fails, they simply do the opposite; they drop the older or duplicate event.

The following DynamoDB example shows the typical structure of a mapping step for a stream processing pipeline that creates a materialized view. We are using `uow.event.timestamp` as the new `oplock` value. `ConditionExpression` compares the old `oplock` value against the new value. If the new value is greater than the old value, then we allow the update to proceed. The `attribute_not_exists` clause handles the case where the record is new and there is no old `oplock` to compare against:

```
export const toUpdateRequest = (uow) => ({
  Key: {
    pk: uow.event.thing.id,
    sk: 'thing',
  },
  ExpressionAttributeNames: {
    '#name': 'name',
    '#oplock': 'timestamp',
  },
  ExpressionAttributeValues: {
    ':name': 'Thing One',
    ':timestamp': uow.event.timestamp,
  },
  UpdateExpression: 'SET #name = :name,
                         #oplock = :timestamp',
  ConditionExpression: 'attribute_not_exists(#oplock)
     OR :timestamp > #oplock',
});
```

The first thing to notice in this example that is different with an inverse `oplock` is that the comparison is greater than instead of equals. If the value is equal to the previous value, then this indicates that we have already processed this event. If the value is less than the previous value, then this indicates that we are processing an older event out of order. When this value is greater than the previous value, we know we have a newer event, so we can proceed with the update.

The last piece of the puzzle is handling the response value returned from the call to update the database. The AWS SDK will throw an exception when `error.code` is returned. We don't want to ignore all errors, so we catch the exception and check for the `ConditionalCheckFailedException` code. We re-throw all other exceptions for fault handling, as we covered in *Chapter 4, Trusting Facts and Eventual Consistency*. When we do ignore an exception, it is good practice to log a metric so that we can track how frequently this happens and assess whether or not there is a root cause that we should address:

```
db.update(params).promise()
  .catch((err) => {
    if (err.code !== 'ConditionalCheckFailedException') {
      throw err;
    }
  });
```

When using the inverse optimistic locking technique, it is important to ensure that we are not dropping important data when we ignore older events. This could happen if we are using the same `oplock` field for different event types. For example, if the older event is of the same event type, then we know it carries the same data fields as the newer event, so we can drop it safely. However, if the older event is of a different type, then it probably has different fields that we want to capture on the same record, so we do not want to drop this older event.

This is a very typical scenario when implementing the CQRS pattern. We are essentially materializing a join record from multiple types of events. The different event types carry the same value that we are using for the identifier of the join record, plus additional fields per event type that we want to join together. If we were to use the same `oplock` field for all these event types, then we would have to receive them in the correct order.

The solution for joining multiple event types into the same join record is to use a different `oplock` field for each event type. We can refer to this as an **Inverse Oplock Join**. This allows us to incrementally build up these join records one event at a time in any order. Whichever event arrives first will create the record skeleton with the information it carries. Each additional event will flesh out the record with the additional information they carry. Within each event type, we can safely ignore the older or duplicate events.

As with most things, the inverse optimistic locking technique is not right for all scenarios. Let's take a look at immutable event triggers to see where they fit into the equation.

Immutable event triggers

One of the advantages of the inverse optimistic locking technique is that it doesn't require the stream processor to retrieve any data to perform a join. This improves the throughput of the stream processor and reduces the possibility of errors. However, it is not always possible to calculate the correct answer without performing a query to retrieve additional information. To get the best of both worlds, we can leverage event sourcing by adding a micro event store to the equation and splitting the logic into two separate stream processors.

The **first stream processor** collects events of interest from the event stream and stores them in a micro event store. This is an atomic step that optimizes the throughput, minimizes the likelihood of errors, and, most importantly, provides idempotence. Event sourcing facilitates idempotence because events are immutable. We can put the same event with the same deterministic identifier into the micro event store over and over again, yet only produce one record.

The following DynamoDB example shows the put operation for storing an event in a micro event store. This put statement is following the single table design, which we will cover shortly in the *Modeling data for operational performance* section. We use uow.event.id as the identifier (pk) for the record and we store the immutable event in the event field. We will address the data field shortly, but the ttl field deserves special attention:

```
db.put({
  TableName: options.eventTableName,
  Item: {
    pk: uow.event.id,
    sk: 'event',
    data: uow.event.thing.id,
    event: uow.event,
    ttl: uow.event.timestamp + (60*60*24*33) // 33 days
  }
});
```

In the *Keeping data lean* section, we addressed the importance of not letting our operational datastores grow unbounded. Setting a TTL for each record is the primary technique for controlling the size of a table. However, we must take care to ensure that `ttl` is not too short because this will impact the length of time that the micro event store can enforce idempotence. In this example, `ttl` is set to 33 days. If we receive an event again after this time, then we will process it again. Whether or not it is realistic that this will happen or whether it matters if it does happen is domain-specific, so consider this option carefully. And, as always, the idempotence and order tolerance of downstream logic must account for this should it happen.

The second stream processor handles the event after we insert it into the micro event store. As we will discuss shortly in the *Leveraging change data capture* section, we can create stream processors that process the stream of events a datastore emits as we insert, update, and delete records. Thanks to the immutability of events, we can be certain that the datastore will only emit the event to the stream once, when we first create the record. All additional `put` operations will not change the record and will not emit a datastore event, which provides the processing logic with idempotence.

The second stream processor also provides order tolerance by retrieving related events from the micro event store and reacting based on the events that have been received thus far. In this example, the `data` field is set to the domain entity's identifier, `uow.event.thing.id`. This allows the stream processor to retrieve all the related events for that domain entity. These events could have arrived in any order, but here the stream processor can sort the events and act accordingly. For instance, if an expected event is missing, then the processor can do nothing and reevaluate when the next event arrives. Once the necessary information is available, the processor can perform the necessary calculations and save the results to a materialized view.

In the *Calculating event sourcing snapshots* section of *Chapter 8, Reacting to Events with More Events*, you can find a detailed example that uses this technique and **ACID 2.0** properties to perform order-tolerant calculations. Now that we understand the importance of idempotence and order tolerance to the accuracy of our data, let's look at how we can model the data for optimal performance.

Modeling data for operational performance

So far, we have focused on breaking up the monolith and materializing data downstream. Now we will zero in on modeling data to support the access patterns needed during the operational phases of the data life cycle. This is where various actors (that is, users) create and use data via BFF services. These early phases of the data life cycle need particular attention because they have seen significant changes and improvements.

First, we will look at an approach to logical data modeling that is not coupled to the polyglot persistence choices we make at the individual service level. Then we will look at horizontal scalability and sharding, so that we can understand the implications that this physical model has on our operational data modeling. Then we will go through several examples of applying the single table design technique to the services in our hypothetical food delivery system.

Nodes, edges, and aggregates

For our operational datastores, we will use serverless, NoSQL databases, such as Amazon DynamoDB. How we model data for these datastores is a little different. To some extent, it is a bit of a paradigm shift. So, it is a good idea to break away from traditional modeling notations, such as relational data modeling, to help us make the shift and avoid falling back into old practices that may produce suboptimal results. We also need a notation that is reasonably neutral with regard to the type of technology that we ultimately use. But we also want a notation that is familiar.

The major distinction between the new and old approaches is that we are more focused on rows than we are on tables. More specifically, these datastores are schemaless, so we are focused on the domain entity types that we store in each row. The types stored in each row will fall into one of two categories: nodes and edges. A node represents a domain entity with a unique identifier and an edge represents an association between nodes. With this in mind, it makes sense to use a graph-style notation.

In *Chapter 2, Defining Boundaries and Letting Go*, we used the Event Storming technique to help us discover the event types that our system will emit, the relative order of those events, and the actors who produce them. During this process, we also try to identify the data that is in play when we produce the events, but at that point, we only focus on the domain aggregates.

An aggregate represents the root of a set of related domain objects. They provide perspective in the context of the larger data model. They define different starting points for navigating through the nodes and edges of the model. Ultimately, they help identify the access patterns that will be all-important to crafting high-performance, operational data models.

The aggregates also form the starting point for crafting the full logical data model. *Figure 5.6* depicts the logical model for our hypothetical food delivery system. It fleshes out the various domain entities and the associations between them. It is important to note that this is a logical model, and we will see how we can map it to the chosen datastores in a moment:

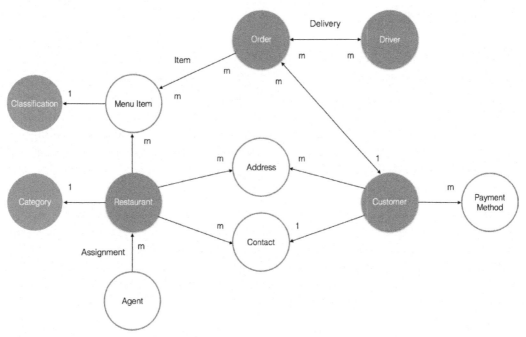

Figure 5.6 – Logical data model

The first thing to note in the logical model is that we highlight the aggregates in tan to show their importance and to indicate the various starting points for navigating through the model. We use the same colors that we use in event storming to help form the connection between the models. The aggregates will ultimately become node rows in the physical model. The other circles represent domain entities that may become node rows in the physical model, or we may embed them as immutable data in other rows depending on how we use them in a specific service.

There are several named associations in the model: **Assignment**, **Item**, and **Delivery**. These will most likely become edge rows in the physical model. The other associations will likely manifest themselves in the primary keys used in the physical model or as embedded objects. It is important to note that the cardinalities in the logical model are for the model as a whole, but in the context of a specific access scenario, they may be different. For example, a customer has many addresses, but in the context of an order, we only use one. It is often worth creating additional models per aggregate to help identify these differences without cluttering the higher-level model.

Before we look at examples of mapping the logical model to a specific datastore, let's cover sharding and partition keys. This will help explain the choices we make at the physical level.

Sharding and partition keys

The fundamental job of a database is to write data to disk. The disk drive imposes the ultimate limit on how fast we can write and read data and how many concurrent requests we can support. **Sharding** is the process of horizontally partitioning a database across many disk drives. This allows a database to support more concurrent requests. The database keeps track of which data is on which disk and evenly distributes the data across the disks to help balance the load.

On the application side, we need to properly select and use partition keys to effectively use a sharded datastore. The database uses a partition key to match a record to a partition. It stores all the records for a specific partition key on the same disk. This means we can optimize performance by modeling our operational data so that we do not need to join data across multiple disks.

We must also take care to avoid hot partition keys that are not well balanced across partitions. For example, if we use the current date as a partition key, then all writes on a given day will go to the same disk and the system would achieve no additional concurrency from sharding. A V4 UUID is a good choice for partition keys because they are generated with random numbers that result in a good distribution across partitions. We covered additional considerations for partition keys in the *Deterministic identifiers* section.

Sharding is the driving force behind the popularity of modern NoSQL databases. It also significantly increases the complexity, effort, and cost of running these databases. For example, if you need to replicate data across three cloud availability zones and you need 10 shards, then you have 30 disk drives to manage. If you have 10 services with similar configurations, then that number jumps to 300 disk drives. You should be running across two regions, so the number of disk drives doubles to 600. Just the effort alone to manage these disks makes the case for leveraging fully managed serverless datastores, such as DynamoDB.

Now let's look at some examples that use the single table design technique to fully leverage the power of sharded datastores by grouping related data within the same partition.

Single table design examples

Let's take the logical data model for our hypothetical food delivery system and see how we can apply the single table design technique to implement service-specific models that optimize performance for the specific actor's access patterns. These examples are tailored for DynamoDB, but this technique is applicable to many NoSQL databases.

First and foremost, the Single Table Design technique leverages the schemaless nature of these databases. This means that each row in the table can represent a different type of domain entity. Following from our graph-oriented logical data model, we can think of each row as either a node or an edge. A node represents a domain entity with a unique identifier and has a set of attributes. An edge represents an association between nodes and may also contain a set of attributes. We use a discriminator value to help the code determine the domain type of each row. The discriminator may be implemented as a separate field or embedded in the **sort key** (**sk**). The following examples use a separate **discriminator** field for clarity.

It is important to note that while schemaless databases do not use an *explicit* schema, there is an *implicit* schema associated with each row. We manage these implicit schemas within the code. In *Chapter 9, Choreographing Deployment and Delivery*, we will see how we do this and why it makes it easier to perform continuous, zero-downtime deployments.

The next and equally important element of the technique is the **partition key** (**pk**). As we have already seen, a partition key maps a record to a specific shard (that is, disk). We want to leverage this fact and use the pk field to pre-calculate a join between different records and ensure that we store them all on the same shard. This allows us to retrieve all the related data with a single, highly efficient query. It is helpful to think of the partition key as the unique identifier for a domain aggregate that represents a collection of related domain objects that we want to work with as a group, such as the data for a restaurant, customer, order, or driver in our logical model. Within a partition key, we use an SK to uniquely identify each of the related records.

The partition key defines our primary access pattern, which is the ability to retrieve all the data for a specific domain aggregate. However, we often need to access the same data from a different direction, across aggregates, such as implementing a basic search query. We use the **data** field for these types of queries and create an index on this field. In DynamoDB, we create a global secondary index. We can think of this as an alternate partition key that organizes the data on a different set of partitions so that we can access it with a single query as well.

Restaurant service

This example supports agents of the delivery company who manage menus on behalf of restaurants:

discriminator	pk	sk	data	fields		
Assignment	agent1	r1		Mamma Marie's		
Assignment	agent1	r2		29 Diner		
Category	cat1		meta	Italian	icon font	
Category	cat2		meta	Greek	"	
Classifier	class1		meta	Breakfast	"	
Classifier	class2		meta	Dinner	"	
Restaurant	r1		cat1	Mamma Marie's	address {...}	
Restaurant	r2		cat2	29 Diner	"	
MenuItem	r2	r2|mi1	class1	Omelet, $7.99	options {...}	image url
MenuItem	r2	r2|mi2	class2	Cheeseburger, $6.99	"	"

Table 5.1 – Restaurant service example data

Here is an explanation of the different nodes and edges:

- An **agent** is a logical node that we do not store in this table because agents already know who they are. When agents log in, they receive their employee ID as a claim in their JWT token, such as **agent1**. A different service will handle the management of assignments and that service will need to store agent nodes for the manager to choose from.

- **Category** and **Classifier** nodes contain metadata that we use for grouping restaurants and menu items. The application displays these as drop-down menus in the agent's data entry screens. The application can retrieve all this data with one simple query on the **data** field for the value **meta**.

- **Assignment** edges map agents to the restaurants they support. We materialize these records from upstream events. We use the current employee ID (that is, **agent1**) to query the table on the **pk** field to retrieve the data needed to display a list of restaurant assignments for the specific agent. In this case, **agent1** has assignments for restaurants **r1** and **r2**.

- **Restaurant** nodes contain information about each restaurant, such as its name, address, and category.

- **MenuItem** nodes contain information about the food a restaurant offers, such as its name, price, options, picture, and classifier.

- An agent can retrieve all the data for a specific restaurant, such as **r2**, with a single query on the **pk** field.

- An agent can also query for similar restaurants and menu items with a query on the **data** field for the value of a category or classifier.

In the *Leveraging change data capture* section, we will see how to produce domain events from this data to support downstream services. In *Chapter 6, A Best Friend for the Frontend*, we will see how a downstream menu service could react to these events and provide a responsive and resilient customer experience using datastores such as AWS S3 and Elasticsearch.

Customer service

This example allows customers to maintain the personal information that they need to create food delivery orders. It also supports viewing a customer's order history:

discriminator	pk	sk	data	fields		
Customer	c1			first-name	last-name	
Contact	c1	e1		contact {...}		
Address	c1	a1		address {...}		
Address	c1	a2		"		
Card	c1	p1		card {...}		
Order	o1		c1|2020	order {...}		
Order	o2		c1|2020	"		

Table 5.2 – Customer service example data

Here is an explanation of the different nodes and edges:

- When customers sign in, they receive their customer ID as a claim in their JWT token, such as **c1**. We use the customer ID to retrieve all the customer's data with a single query on the **pk** field. However, this won't include order history because we do not need that data at the same time.

- **Customer** nodes allow customers to maintain their summary information, such as first and last name. We store the customer ID in the **pk** field.

- **Contact** nodes allow customers to maintain their phone numbers and email addresses. The **sk** field contains the unique identifier and we link it to the customer via the **pk** field.

- **Address** nodes allow customers to maintain the physical locations where they want food delivered. The **sk** field contains the unique identifier and we link it to the customer via the **pk** field.

- **Card** nodes allow customers to maintain their payment information. The **sk** field contains the unique identifier and we link it to the customer via the **pk** field.

- **Order** nodes contain historical information about a customer's orders. These orders are immutable, so we embed the order details within each record. Customers can retrieve their order history by year with a query on the **data** field with the customer ID and year, such as **c1|2020**. Or we can retrieve all their orders where **data** begins with the customer ID, such as **c1|***.

Cart service

This example allows customers to prepare their current order in a cart. It does not retain the order history. We have already seen how we can retain the order history in the customer service example:

discriminator	pk	sk			
Order	c1	o1	2020-10-01	$29.99	
Restaurant	c1	o1|1	address {...}	contact {...}	
Item	c1	o1|i1	qty	price	options {...}
Item	c1	o1|i2	qty	Price	options {...}
Customer	c1	o1	address {...}	contact {...}	card {...}

Table 5.3 – Cart service example data

Here is an explanation of the different nodes and edges:

- When customers sign in, they receive their customer ID as a claim in their JWT token, such as **c1**. We use the customer ID to retrieve the contents of the customer's cart with a single query on the **pk** field.

- **Order** nodes contain summary information, such as the date of the order and the total cost. The **sk** field contains the unique order identifier and we link it to the customer via the **pk** field.

- **Restaurant** nodes contain the address and contact information of the restaurant. We retrieve this information from the menu service as the user browses and we save an immutable copy per order. The **sk** field contains the unique restaurant identifier prefixed with the order identifier and we link it to the customer via the **pk** field.

- **Item** nodes contain the items the customer wants to order from the restaurant's menu. We retrieve menu item metadata from the menu service as the customer selects an item and we store an immutable copy per item along with any customization options the customer has selected. The **sk** field contains the unique item identifier prefixed with the order identifier and we link it to the customer via the **pk** field.

- **Customer** nodes contain the address, contact, and payment information the customer has selected for the delivery. We retrieved this information from the customer service and we save an immutable copy per order. The **sk** field contains the unique customer identifier prefixed with the order identifier and we link it to the customer via the **pk** field.

Once the customer submits an order, we can flag these records for deletion with a short TTL. From here, an order tracking service will maintain a materialized view that provides the customer with order status information. I'll leave that to you as an exercise. We have already seen how the customer service retains the order history.

Delivery service

This example provides drivers with the information they need to execute a delivery. Drivers can search for unassigned orders by zone, acquire a delivery assignment, and view the order details:

discriminator	pk	sk	data		
Order	o1			order {...}	status
Delivery	zone1	o1	d1	Mamma Marie's	geo locations
Delivery	zone1	o2	unassigned	29 Diner	"

Table 5.4 – Delivery service example data

Here is an explanation of the different nodes and edges:

- **Order** nodes contain an immutable copy of the order, so that drivers can retrieve the order details. The **pk** field contains the unique order identifier.

- **Delivery** edges associate orders with delivery zones and drivers. We include the restaurant name to provide additional context information to drivers, along with the geo-locations for navigation to the restaurant and the customer. The **sk** field contains the unique order identifier and we link it to the zone via the **pk** field. We track the assigned driver in the **data** field.

- Drivers can query the table by zone to find unassigned deliveries and acquire them by setting the **data** field to their driver identifier, such as **d1**.

- Drivers, such as **d1**, can query all their current deliveries with a single query on the **data** field.

This delivery BFF service is fairly rudimentary. A **Control Service**, such as those we cover in *Chapter 8, Reacting to Events with More Events*, could match potential drivers to deliveries, and an **External Service Gateway** (**ESG**) service, such as those we cover in *Chapter 7, Bridging Intersystem Gaps*, could react by sending SMS messages to the drivers. A driver BFF service could track a driver's delivery history, similar to how the customer service tracks the order history.

From these examples, it should be clear how turning the database inside out enables the creation of responsive and resilient services that are much easier to maintain and evolve. So far, we have focused on receiving domain events from upstream services and materializing the needed data for use by a specific service. Let's switch to the upstream side and see how those services can leverage change data capture streams to produce their domain events.

Leveraging change data capture

Let's change gears a little bit. Up to this point in this chapter, we have primarily focused on the downstream query side of the systemwide CQRS pattern. Now we will look into the upstream command side of the systemwide CQRS pattern and how it intersects with the systemwide Event Sourcing pattern that we introduced in *Chapter 4, Trusting Facts and Eventual Consistency*.

In the *Turning the database inside out* section, we learned that splitting data out into multiple databases creates the need for a systemwide transaction log. We fulfill this need with the Event Sourcing pattern and the event lake. Each autonomous subsystem plays its role by providing an event hub service to collect events and an event lake service to store them. Individual autonomous services play their part by publishing events to the hub as their state changes.

Each individual database still has its own transaction log, and we leverage it as a powerful tool. **Change Data Capture** (**CDC**) is a technique that reads a database's transaction log in real time and captures these database-level events and exposes them to external consumers as a stream so that they can react as the data changes.

CDC plays an important role in turning a database inside out. We can leverage it to implement event sourcing on the upstream command side in a way that simplifies the development experience. Let's see how.

Database-first event sourcing

In the *Dissecting the CQRS pattern* section, we learned that CQRS employs separate read and write data models and that systemwide CQRS takes the approach further by splitting the models between upstream and downstream actors to optimize the experience for each user and allow them to change independently. To facilitate this approach, the upstream service must emit domain events as the data in its write model changes so that downstream services can materialize the data in their read models.

In *Chapter 4*, *Trusting Facts and Eventual Consistency*, we learned that modern databases do not support distributed transactions because they do not scale cost-effectively. Instead, we create eventually consistent systems by chaining together a series of atomic actions that each updates a single datastore. The approach we covered for initiating this chain reaction is the stream-first variation of the Event Sourcing pattern. With this variation, we first emit (that is, write) an event to the event hub, where a stream acts as a temporal datastore so that downstream services can react and materialize lean data in their own datastores. In other words, the upstream service does not immediately persist its own copy of the data it creates; it only writes to the stream.

Stream-first event sourcing is best suited for fire-and-forget scenarios where the event producer does not need to immediately interact with the outcome of the processing. In *Chapter 7*, *Bridging Intersystem Gaps*, we see that stream-first is often the right approach for *ESG* services. In *Chapter 8*, *Reacting to Events with More Events*, we see how stream-first is the best approach for Control services. However, stream-first event sourcing can be problematic for BFF services.

BFF services support end users, and end users typically need to interact with the data they create. This is where the Event Sourcing and CQRS patterns get their bad reputations. The otherwise simple process of writing the current state to the database and later reading it is now spread across two separate models and thus two different development activities. We have already seen how to materialize the read model in the *Dissecting the CQRS pattern* section, so this is not necessarily a difficult to do. But it is one more thing to do, so if we can avoid it on the upstream command side, then it is worth considering.

This is where CDC can help. CDC provides us with an opportunity to have the best of both worlds. We can have the streamlined developer experience of writing and reading the current state with a single data model, while also atomically producing domain events so that downstream services can support their own read models. This is the database-first variation of the Event Sourcing pattern:

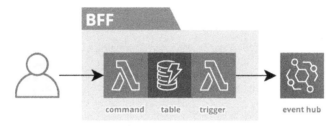

Figure 5.7 – Database-first event sourcing

Figure 5.7 depicts a **BFF** service using the database-first variant of event sourcing. The **command** function performs the single atomic action of writing the outcome of its processing to a **table** that it owns. The CDC feature of the database, such as *Amazon DynamoDB Streams*, makes the database change event visible to the **trigger** function. The **trigger** function transforms the change event and produces a domain event to the **event hub**.

It is important to recognize that with database-first event sourcing, we are relying on the at-least-once semantics of stream processing to help guarantee that we eventually publish the domain events. As with all streams, a CDC stream is a temporal datastore. In the case of an unexpected error, the **trigger** function will continue to retry until we successfully process the change event or it expires, and in the case of an expected error, the **trigger** function will produce a fault event. We covered this topic in the *Designing for failure* section of *Chapter 4, Trusting Facts and Eventual Consistency*.

Now let's look at how we implement the stream processing of a `trigger` function. The following example builds on the concept of pipeline patterns, which we covered in *Chapter 4, Trusting Facts and Eventual Consistency*:

```
import { cdc } from 'aws-lambda-stream';
const RULES = [{
  id: 'a1',
  flavor: cdc,
  eventType: /thing-(created|updated|deleted)/,
}, {
  id: 'd1',
  flavor: cdc,
  eventType: 'thing-updated',
  filters: (uow) =>
                    uow.event.raw.new.status === 'submitted',
  toEvent: (uow) => ({
    type: 'thing-submitted',
    thing: {
      id: uow.event.raw.new.pk,
      name: uow.event.raw.new.nm,
      description: uow.event.raw.new.descr,
    },
  }),
}];
```

This example emits domain events as we insert, update, and delete data. The typical steps for creating domain events from a CDC stream are as follows:

1. Filter for the desired database change events.

2. Map the data in the database change event to the desired domain event.

3. Publish the domain event to the event hub.

These steps are so typical that it makes sense to wrap them into a reusable pipeline pattern. This example uses a `cdc` pipeline pattern that works with databases such as DynamoDB that support CDC. And of course, you can create your own or implement the pattern in your favorite language and framework.

> **Note**
> The mapping code in this example is included inline for brevity. These functions will normally be implemented and tested in separate modules.

The most interesting details are in the `toEvent` functions, which implement the mapping step. The first rule, `a1`, uses a regular expression to filter for created, updated, and deleted events for the thing domain entity. This rule does not define a mapping function, so it will publish the database change events as is. Publishing the raw database change events serves two purposes. First, these events act as an audit log of exactly how the data has changed, when it changed, and who changed it. The `uow.event.raw` element includes the new and old images of the data just as they were recorded by the database's transaction log. In *Chapter 6, A Best Friend for the Frontend*, we will see how a command can pass the current user from a JWT along to the database layer to track which users are modifying which data.

As we covered in *Chapter 4, Trusting Facts and Eventual Consistency*, this raw element is for internal use only and the contents are not guaranteed to be backward-compatible. That said, the second benefit of publishing the raw database change events is to jumpstart the development process. Within a new and evolving autonomous subsystem, we can use these database change events to collaborate between services and help discover the true domain events that we should publish.

The second rule, `d1`, in this example publishes an explicit domain event. It specifically filters for the thing-updated change event and then includes an additional filter for when the `uow.event.raw.new.status` field is set to `submitted`. A `status` field is a typical approach used to track the state of a domain entity as it progresses through a workflow. It allows users to search for their work based on the status and it allows other users to determine the current status of work. We can also leverage the `status` field in our CDC pipelines, as is the case here, to determine which domain event to publish.

The `toEvent` mapping function sets the event type value to `thing-submitted` and maps the internal database fields to the contents of the thing element. These fields form the contract with downstream services, and we must ensure that any changes are backward-compatible. We will cover the versioning of domain events in *Chapter 9, Choreographing Deployment and Delivery*.

We have already seen how CDC plays a part in implementing idempotence and order tolerance. CDC is also an invaluable approach for integrating with legacy systems, as we will see in *Chapter 7, Bridging Intersystem Gaps*. We will also see how we can leverage CDC to integrate multiple datastores within a single service, in *Chapter 6, A Best Friend for the Frontend*. And in *Chapter 8, Reacting to Events with More Events*, we will see how CDC plays a role in orchestration and complex event processing.

Now let's look at the additional details of implementing soft deletes and latching.

Soft deletes

On the surface, deletion seems like a simple command, but it has some very interesting implications. Certainly, deleting data can have security ramifications, so we want to keep an audit trail per usual. And a user could delete a record by mistake, so we should be able to undo this destructive action. But there are also some additional nuances with the `delete` command that arise in eventually consistent systems.

Idempotence and order tolerance can be difficult to achieve when we perform a hard delete. For example, if an updated event arrives after a deletion event, then we would recreate the record and leave the datastore in an inconsistent state. A similar situation can happen when replaying events. We could temporarily add a deleted record back and then remove it again. The end result here is eventually consistent, but a query in the meantime could return confusing results.

Another nuance arises when we have slow data that we want to resynchronize downstream. In this case, an upstream service maintains data, such as reference data or master data, which changes very infrequently. Downstream services will cache this data and it may become stale, such as when they have defects. For example, they may drop a deletion event and continue to present the deleted data. For reasons like this, the upstream services that own slow data will produce `resync` events periodically or on demand. These `resync` events need to include information about data that was recently deleted. But how can we do this if the data is deleted? We can certainly replay these events from the event lake. But they will be spread out through the lake and time-consuming to process because the data is slow, and the events could have happened a long time ago.

The solution to these problems is to perform soft deletes instead of hard deletes. A hard delete physically removes the data, whereas a soft delete just flags the data as deleted. The following DynamoDB example shows how a `delete` command would simply set a `deleted` flag on the existing record. Any corresponding queries would filter out all records that we flagged as deleted:

```
db.update({
  Key: {
    pk: thing.id,
    sk: 'Thing',
  },
  ExpressionAttributeNames: {
    '#deleted': 'deleted',
```

```
  },
  ExpressionAttributeValues: {
    ':deleted': true,
  },
  UpdateExpression: 'SET #deleted = :deleted',
});
```

On the CDC stream, the change event will appear as an update. However, the `trigger` function will see that the `deleted` flag is set to true and publish a `thing-deleted` event instead. This trigger logic is implemented as a feature in the CDC pipeline pattern.

It is important to keep data lean, so we also need to decide how long to keep records that we flag as deleted. For slow data with limited records, it may make sense to keep these records indefinitely. Otherwise, we can set a TTL as we discussed in the *Keeping data lean* section. When the TTL expires, a hard delete will be performed. This time, the CDC stream will emit a deleted event. The trigger function can ignore it or publish another `thing-deleted` event for good measure. Publishing it again would give downstream services another opportunity to delete their record or idempotently ignore the duplicate event.

When a service emits resync events, it can include events for all records that we flagged as deleted. We will revisit slow data in *Chapter 7, Bridging Intersystem Gaps*. Now, let's look at latching.

Latching

To enable continuous change, an evolutionary architecture must support running multiple versions of functionality concurrently. We will see this need in *Chapter 7, Bridging Intersystem Gaps*, when we are incrementally modernizing a legacy system. But even the new system will evolve as new requirements emerge and as teams find better ways to satisfy existing requirements. In many cases, a service can simply evolve in place, and we will cover this in *Chapter 9, Choreographing Deployment and Delivery*.

However, much like a legacy migration, there are times when an evolution is more of a revolution. In these cases, to mitigate risks, it is best to create a new version of a service that runs concurrently with the old version. This gives beta testers an opportunity to weigh in on the new version of the feature and provide valuable feedback.

To accomplish this, we need to synchronize the data between the two versions of the service. This will allow several scenarios to potentially unfold.

1. If beta users think the new version has missed the mark, then they can switch back to the old version and pick up where they left off.

2. If the functionality needs to be migrated incrementally, then users can seamlessly perform some work in the new version and some in the old version.

3. And finally, when we release the new version to all users, the data will already be converted, and we can remove the old version.

When implementing a bi-directional synchronization like this, we must take care not to create an infinite loop. For example, the trigger function of Service A produces an event and it is consumed by the listener function of Service B. The trigger function of Service B then produces the same logical event and it is consumed by the listener function of Service A. The trigger function of Service A produces the event again and the loop continues infinitely.

Latching, much like locking a door, is the solution to this problem. The `trigger` function will not emit an event when the latch is closed. The `listener` function will close the latch when it materializes data, and a `command` function will open the latch when a user of the service performs an action. This prevents synchronization updates for looping but allows user-initiated state changes to be emitted.

The following code extends the example we have been using in this chapter for populating a materialized view in a `listener` function:

```
toUpdateRequest: (uow) => ({
  Key: {
    pk: uow.event.thing.id,
    sk: 'Thing',
  },
  ...updateExpression({
    ...uow.event.thing,
    latched: true,
  }),
}),
```

The `listener` function closes the latch by setting the `latched` field to `true`. This field tells the `trigger` function whether or not to emit a domain event. Since the value is set to `true`, the trigger function will not emit a domain event and we avoid an infinite loop. This trigger logic is implemented as a feature in the CDC pipeline pattern.

When the user of this BFF service performs a command that updates the data, the command opens the latch by setting the `latched` field to `false` or removing the field. Since the value is `false` or the field is absent, the `trigger` function will emit the domain event.

Back on the `listener` function side, a service can safely ignore the events that its trigger function just emitted. To accomplish this, we filter on the `source` tag value. Every event should contain a `source` tag that we set to the name of the service that emitted it. The `listener` function simply ignores any events with the `source` value set to its own service name.

This last point brings up an interesting difference between traditional and serverless systems. In a traditional system, we might not be concerned about the `listener` function updating the record again with the same values. We might say there's no harm, so there's no foul. But there is a cost, because the additional update consumes capacity. In a traditional system, this cost is paid for by the end users in the form of decreased performance. In a serverless system, the cost increases the monthly invoice and gives us a stronger incentive to do the right thing by avoiding the unnecessary update.

Leveraging CDC to implement database-first event sourcing is a very powerful tool that greatly simplifies the developer experience by separating the different concerns, while also producing a more responsive and resilient user experience. Now let's see how we can further improve responsiveness and resilience by replicating data across regions.

Replicating across regions

It is inevitable that a given cloud provider will experience a news-worthy regional disruption. It is not a matter of *if* but of *when*. In my experience, this happens about every 2 to 3 years or so. When such an event does occur, many systems have no recourse and become unavailable during the disruption, because they are only designed to work across multiple availability zones within a single region. Meanwhile, other systems barely experience a blip in availability because they have been designed to run across multiple regions.

In *Chapter 3, Taming the Presentation Tier*, we saw how session consistency and offline-first mechanisms help the presentation layer ensure a seamless transition during a regional disruption. In *Chapter 6, A Best Friend for the Frontend*, we will cover the regional health check and regional failover mechanisms that are leveraged by BFF services. In *Chapter 4, Trusting Facts and Eventual Consistency*, we covered the implications of multi-regional deployments on stream processing and why we rely on replication at the datastore level, instead of replicating streams.

In this section, we cover how regional data replication works at the datastore level and the role it plays in creating systems that are responsive and resilient. Specifically, we look into multi-master and round-robin replication.

Multi-master replication

Regional replication is a critical feature of modern cloud-native databases because it plays an important role in a system's responsiveness and resilences. Replicating a datastore across multiple availability zones is essential, but it is not sufficient. A system must be prepared for a regional disruption, which requires not only replicating across regions but also using all the regions on an ongoing basis to ensure they are all operational.

Running a database across availability zones is already hard enough, so running across regions may seem like a non-starter. Fortunately, fully managed, cloud-native datastores, such as DynamoDB and S3, implicitly run across availability zones and provide turnkey support for multi-master replication across regions. This empowers teams to focus effort on creating an active-active, multi-regional system that provides end users with lower latency and improves team confidence.

Figure 5.8 depicts the multi-regional deployment of a BFF service. The **East** region contains an event hub with a **stream** and a **bus**, and a BFF service with `command`, `listener`, and `trigger` functions and a **datastore**. The **West** region contains an exact copy of all these resources, and we enable bi-directional replication between the datastores in both regions:

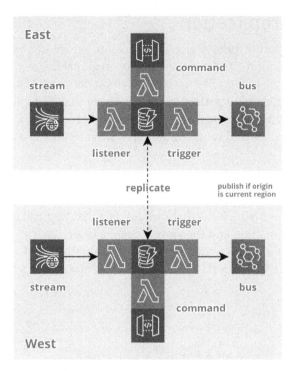

Figure 5.8 – Multi-master replication

Under normal circumstances, with no regional disruption, an end user will access a system through the closest region, and the chain reaction of events caused by the user's actions are all performed in the same region. For example, when the **command** function executes in the **East** region, it writes data to the datastore in the **East** region. The **trigger** function then executes in the same region and it emits a domain event to the **bus** in the same region. All subscribers to the domain event, such as a **listener** function, will execute in the **East** region and materialize their view data in the **East** region. Meanwhile, all the data replicates to the **West** region to support the users in that region.

In the **West** region, after the data replicates, we do not want the **trigger** function to be invoked and emit a duplicate domain event in the **West** region because this will result in a duplicate downstream chain reaction that is already being performed in the **East** region. Instead, we rely on the downstream services to replicate their own data.

This post-replication behavior will depend on the service being used. Some datastores do not emit change events to their CDC stream after replication, but some do. If the trigger function is invoked, then we can short-circuit it before it emits a duplicate event by comparing the current region to a region field in the record. If the region field is not automatically added, then we can add it and set it to the current region when writing the data.

Round-robin replication

Not all databases support turnkey regional replication, yet we still need to replicate their data across regions to improve latency and support regional failover. These will typically be read-only data stores, such as Elasticsearch, that do not provide a CDC stream. We also want to follow a consistent pattern of relying on services to replicate their own data, as opposed to replicating streams and performing duplicate work in multiple regions. To accomplish this, we can add round-robin replication to the inbound flow of these downstream services.

Figure 5.9 depicts the multi-regional deployment of a BFF service that uses Elasticsearch. The **East** region contains an event hub with a **stream**, and the BFF service has a **listener** function to consume domain events that contain data that we need to index in the **view**. Between the **listener** function and the **view**, we add a **topic**, such as Amazon SNS, a **replicator** function to implement the round-robin replication, and a **save** function to populate the **view**. The **West** region contains an exact copy of all these resources:

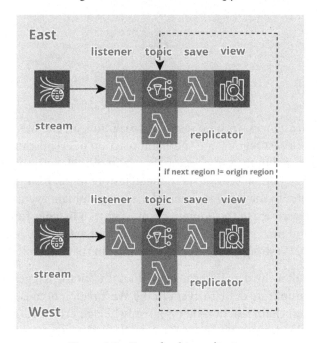

Figure 5.9 – Round-robin replication

The **listener** function in the **East** region consumes domain events from the **stream** in the **East** region. It transforms the data to the desired format and sends a message to the **topic** in the same region, along with a message attribute that indicates the originating region. Performing the semantic transformation in the **listener** function ensures that we only performed this logic once, instead of per region.

The **save** function in the **East** region reacts to the **topic** in the **East** region and updates the **view** in the same region. Meanwhile, the **replicator** function in the **East** region also reacts to the same **topic**. The **replicator** forwards the message to the **topic** in the next region, as specified by an environment variable. In this example, we configure **East** to forward to **West** and vice versa.

The **save** function in the **West** region reacts to the **topic** in the **West** region and updates the **view** in the same region. The **replicator** function in the **West** region also reacts to the same **topic** and looks to forward the message to the next region. This flow will round-robin for as many regions as necessary, until the next region is equal to the originating region.

In this example, we have two regions—East and West. The data originates in the East region, so the East **replicator** forwards the data to the West **topic**. The West **replicator** does not forward the data to the East **topic** because East is the origin. If the data originates in West, then it will forward it to East, but not back to West.

This round-robin replication technique is easy to implement and maintain. For brevity, I did not include queues, such as Amazon SQS, between the topic and the functions, but this is a best practice to add more resilience. With SQS in place, we could have all the queues subscribe to all the topics, but this would result in N x N subscriptions, with N being the number of regions. This quickly becomes difficult to manage and requires multiple deployment passes to wire everything together, so it is not the preferred approach.

Regional failover, protracted eventual consistency, and order tolerance

Timely replication of data across regions is important to facilitate a seamless user experience when a regional failover occurs. During normal execution, regional replication will occur in near real time. During a regional failover, in the best-case scenario, a user's data will already have replicated and the failover process will be completely seamless. The user's next commands will execute in the new region, the chain reaction of events will process in the new region, and the results will eventually replicate back to the failed region.

However, when there is a regional failure during a user transaction, we should expect that the results will replicate more slowly. We can think of this as protracted eventual consistency. Fortunately, we design our modern user interfaces for eventual consistency. This means they cache more data locally and are tolerant of stale data, regardless of how long it takes to become consistent. As we covered in *Chapter 3, Taming the Presentation Tier*, *session consistency* helps make the failover process appear seamless, offline-first approaches handle more significant disruptions, and the user experience provides situational awareness.

Our modern systems are also order tolerant, which comes into play when there is increased replication latency. For example, a user may perform an action and then fail over before the data replicates. The user can still perform actions on the data cached in the user's session, and we will store this updated data in the failover region. When the older data replicates it, it will be ignored because the typical replication policy lets the newest data win.

Downstream, things can be more nuanced. During a regional failover, it is likely that some subscribers in the failing region will fall behind on processing the remaining events in the regional stream. This means that the failover region can process events out of order as it processes new events without the replicated results of older event processing. The processing in the different regions can weave together in unpredictable ways, depending on the reason for the regional failure. This is one more reason why we cannot guarantee ordered processing and why we should leverage the approaches outlined in the *Implementing idempotence and order tolerance* section.

During a regional failover, it is crucial for teams to pay extra attention to how the system is performing. Now let's look into some of the most important database resource metrics to observe and alert on.

Observing resource metrics

In *Chapter 2, Defining Boundaries and Letting Go*, we covered the importance of observability and the distinction between work and resource metrics. Work metrics identify the behavior of the system from the perspective of the end user, whereas resource metrics provide the low-level supporting details. For each resource, following the USE method, we are interested in its utilization, whether it is saturated, and its error rate. Our datastores are arguable the most important resources. Let's dig into their capacity, throttling, error, and performance metrics.

Capacity

One of the most important decisions we make when we provision a datastore is how much capacity to allocate. For a serverless database, such as Amazon DynamoDB, storage is allocated automatically and we just specify the number of reads and writes needed per second. Other services follow a more traditional approach, such as Elasticsearch, where we need to specify the cluster size and proactively allocate storage. And other services, such as S3, dictate the capacity limits and we have to work within those limits.

We need to monitor capacity utilization so that we can make timely, proactive adjustments. For example, when storage reaches 60% utilization, we may want an email alert, so that we can plan to allocate more storage. We may find that we have over-allocated capacity and we can reduce it to save money. Or usage patterns may emerge that we can leverage to proactively schedule autoscaling at certain points in the day.

Threshold alerts should be set up for each utilization metric to provide an early warning sign about potential problems. These are resource metrics, so we do not want to page on these alerts, but we do want a record of each time we reached the threshold. These additional data points can be helpful later to identify trends and to perform root cause analysis.

Capacity utilization is less critical for serverless databases, but it is still important. For example, DynamoDB's on-demand mode will automatically scale capacity as needed. This is a great feature, and it results in the best total cost of ownership for most services. It certainly mitigates the risk of under-allocating capacity. However, there will be cases where it is more cost-effective to explicitly allocate capacity. To identify these cases, we can use the historical capacity metrics to determine whether or not it is worth switching to explicit allocation.

Throttling and errors

Throttling errors are an indicator that we are saturating a resource with requests. In other words, it has exceeded 100% utilization of the allocated capacity. Throttling may or may not be a problem. If it is a transient occurrence, then it may be more cost-effective to use an exponential backoff and retry to ensure that requests go through. However, if it is a persistent problem, then we will need to add additional capacity or add rate limiting to the code. We covered rate limiting in *Chapter 4, Trusting Facts and Eventual Consistency*.

Threshold alerts should be set up for throttling that exceeds an undesirable rate. These are resource metrics, so we do not want to page on these alerts, but we do want a record of each time the threshold is reached. These additional data points can be helpful later to identify trends and to perform root cause analysis. For datastores that do not support throttling, you will want to monitor the queue depth for disk reads and writes.

Throttling is a special kind of 4xx error. All other 4xx errors are an indication of a potential bug in a service's code. For example, in the *Inverse optimistic locking* section, `ConditionalCheckFailedException` is a 4xx error. Again, if these are transient, then they might not be a problem, but if they are persistent, then they most likely are a symptom of a root problem that we need to address. Thus, 4xx metrics will be useful in root cause analysis when there is an anomaly in a work metric that is impacting end users.

5xx errors are more serious. In *Chapter 4, A Best Friend for the Backend*, we will see the role that 5xx errors play in regional health checks and regional failover. A 5xx error from a fully managed, serverless datastore, such as DynamoDB, is an indication of a disruption in a region and will likely warrant a regional failover. For a datastore such as Elasticsearch, it is likely an indicator that an instance in a cluster is failing. If this leaves too few instances across too few availability zones, then these may warrant regional failover as well. Regardless, 5xx errors will most likely impact work metrics and require immediate attention.

Performance

Continuous performance tuning is a natural benefit of high observability. As we learn how a system actually performs, we can make informed decisions about optimizing its throughput.

For example, in *Chapter 4, Trusting Facts and Eventual Consistency*, we cover techniques for optimizing the throughput of stream processors. These optimizations are driven in large part by the performance of the datastore, such as latency, throttling, and the amount of data returned from queries. We can make educated optimization guesses upfront, based on expected volumes. We can perform load testing to validate these hypotheses. But it is ultimately real observability metrics that dictate proper tuning.

As always, work metrics are the place to start. If the user experience is sufficient, then it may not be worth spending the time and effort to tune the performance of a specific service.

However, for serverless systems, tuning can have a significant positive impact on cost. For a high-cost service, the historic resource metrics provide valuable insights into incremental optimizations, such as increasing capacity to reduce throttling or trimming down unneeded data fields to reduce consumed capacity and latency. We can experiment with these optimizations until the cost benefits are no longer worth the effort.

Now let's turn to the ever-important topic of securing data at rest.

Redacting sensitive data

Security is a primary requirement of all systems. We must design our systems from the ground up to be secure. Defense in depth means that every layer of a system must do its part to prevent an attack. Least-privilege access to resources is a critical part of keeping data secure. We cover authentication and authorization in *Chapter 3, Taming the Presentation Tier*, and *Chapter 6, A Best Friend for the Frontend*. However, this is not enough; we must secure data at rest.

Fortunately, serverless computing draws the line of the cloud security shared responsibility model significantly high in the technology stack, such that it allows teams to focus more of their efforts on identifying the sensitive data and securing their domain models. Most of the mundane security requirements are quickly handled through configuration and easily validated with continuous auditing. But securing data at rest is the last line of defense, and yet it is where the most shortcuts are taken, as evidenced by all the high-profile data breaches.

To truly secure data at rest, we cannot stop at simply turning on a datastore's encryption feature. Disk-level encryption only secures the data when the disk is removed from the system. While a disk is attached to the system, the data is automatically decrypted when accessed with sufficient privilege. Unfortunately, this is what happens in most data breaches. A hacker gains privileged access through an alternate channel and the data is automatically decrypted when it is read from the datastore.

To prevent this, we must redact sensitive data at the application level. This will ensure that sensitive data is unusable in the inevitable event of honest human error that inadvertently opens a hole that results in a data breach. Let's look at how teams can use envelope encryption to secure their domain models by redacting sensitive data.

Envelope encryption

Envelope encryption is the practice of using multiple layers of keys and encrypting one key with another key. We encrypt sensitive data with a data key and then we encrypt the data key with a master key. Then we store the encrypted data and the encrypted data key together to associate the data key with the data.

When we need to decrypt the data first, we decrypt the data key with the master key. Then, and only then, can we decrypt the data with the decrypted data key. Without privileged access to the master key, the sensitive data remains redacted.

Let's take an example where the thing domain entity contains **Personally Identifiable Information (PII)** in the name field. Therefore, we must encrypt this field in all events and whenever we save the field in a datastore. The following data block shows a domain event with an encrypted name field and an eem field that contains the envelope encryption metadata that we need to decrypt the object. The eem field includes the list of encrypted fields, masterKeyAlias, and the encrypted dataKeys:

```
{
  ...
  type: 'thing-updated',
  thing: {
```

```
  ...
    name: 'zzzzzzzzzzzz=',
  },
  eem: {
    fields: ['name'],
    masterKeyAlias: 'alias/my-master-key',
    dataKeys: {
      'us-east-1': 'xxxxxxxxxxxxx=',
      'us-west-2': 'yyyyyyyyyyyy=',
    },
  },
}
```

Note that we encrypted the data key twice, once per region. This example is using AWS **Key Management Service (KMS)**, which is a regional service. This means that we must declare a master key in each region. In the case of a regional failover, we need to have the data key encrypted for multiple regions to ensure that we can still decrypt if KMS is unavailable in a region. The `aws-lambda-stream` library relies on the `aws-kms-ee` library (`https://www.npmjs.com/package/aws-kms-ee`) to handle all these details.

The following code extends the example we have been using in this chapter for populating a materialized view in a listener function:

```
import { materialize } from 'aws-lambda-stream';
const RULES = [{
  id: 'm1',
  pattern: materialize,
  eventType: /thing-(created|updated)/,
  toUpdateRequest: ...,
  eem: { // envelop encryption metadata
    fields: ['name'],
    masterKeyAlias: process.env.KMS_MASTER_KEY_ALIAS,
    regions: process.env.KMS_REGIONS,
  },
}];
```

First, the `listener` function uses the `eem` data contained in an event to decrypt the data before we pass it to the pipelines. Then we must re-encrypt the data before we save it to the datastore. To do this, a rule declares an `eem` field with the metadata needed to encrypt the object, including the list of fields to encrypt, `masterKeyAlias`, and the list of regions for which we will encrypt the new data key.

The encryption process returns an `eem` structure, just like the one contained in the `thing-updated` domain event example, that contains the new encrypted data key. We save this metadata in an `eem` field alongside the domain object in the same database record so that we can decrypt the object later.

This process works in a similar manner when we process sensitive data in a `trigger` function. The `trigger` function decrypts the data it receives from the CDC stream using the data key stored in the `eem` field. Then the pipeline uses the metadata provided in the rule's `eem` field to re-encrypt the data in the domain event before publishing. Likewise, a `command` function must encrypt sensitive data before saving and a `query` function must decrypt the data before returning it to the client.

It is important to rotate the various keys. A key management service, such as AWS KMS, will rotate the master key on a yearly basis. These services retain all the previous versions of a master key so that we can decrypt existing data keys, but we encrypt all new data keys with the latest version of the master key. We should generate a new data key each time we save a domain object with sensitive data to a datastore or publish it in a domain event. This restricts the blast radius of a compromised data key to a single domain object.

General Data Protection Regulation (GDPR)

The **General Data Protection Regulation** (**GDPR**) is an EU law on data protection and privacy. One particular article of the law states that a subject can request the erasure of their personal data. At first glance, this requirement would seem to be difficult to achieve in an event-first system that leverages the systemwide Event Sourcing and CQRS patterns and maintains an event lake per autonomous subsystem. However, data life cycle architecture and envelope encryption provide a simplified solution.

First, as data moves through its life cycle, it should remain as lean as possible. If a service does not need PII data, then it should not hold a copy. If a service does need to handle PII data, then it should hold as little as possible, keep the TTL as short as possible, and use envelope encryption. And analytics services should de-identify all data.

Next, we need a solution for long-term data, such as archived data and the events in the event lakes. We want this data to continue to be useful, but we need a way to essentially de-identify the PII elements they contain. Crypto trashing provides a solution that renders data useless without deleting the data. We simply need to delete the data key that we used to perform the envelope encryption.

To support this approach, we add another layer of keys to the envelope encryption process. We still have a master key and we still create a new data key every time we encrypt data, but we encrypt the data key with a subject-specific key. We can think of this additional key as a subject-specific master key. When a subject asks for their data to be erased, we just need to delete the subject-specific key.

Finally, we leverage the inversion of responsibility principle to initiate the erasure process. When a subject requests erasure, we produce a stream-first event to record the fact the subject made the request. From here, downstream services take responsibility for performing the necessary steps, such as deleting the subject-specific key that they own.

Summary

In this chapter, you learned why data gravity impedes innovation and how to decompose monolithic databases throughout the phases of the data life cycle. You learned how the CQRS pattern turns the database inside out and ultimately turns the cloud into the database by creating a systemwide transaction log and moving derived data downstream to where it is used. And you learned how to increase team confidence by using materialized views to create inbound bulkheads.

We dug into the details and you learned how to create stream processors that are idempotent and order tolerant, and you saw how to keep data lean. You learned about using the Single Table Design modeling technique to optimize data for performance and how to create stream processors that leverage change data capture to implement the database-first variant of the event sourcing pattern. You also learned about regional data replication, important resource metrics, and redacting sensitive data with envelope encryption.

In the next chapter, we will cover the BFF pattern and see how it unencumbers teams by removing competing demands so they can focus on the end user's needs. We will look at variations of the BFF pattern throughout the data life cycle and cover OIDC security, multi-regional deployments, and more.

6
A Best Friend for the Frontend

In *Chapter 4*, *Trusting Facts and Eventual Consistency*, we covered the **event sourcing** pattern and learned how it creates an outbound bulkhead that protects upstream services from downstream outages. In *Chapter 5*, *Turning the Cloud into the Database*, we covered the **command query responsibility segregation** (**CQRS**) pattern and learned how it creates an inbound bulkhead that protects downstream services from upstream outages. Together, these bulkheads fortify the boundaries of autonomous services and give teams the confidence to forge ahead with changes, knowing that these boundaries will help control the blast radius when things go wrong.

Now we'll turn our attention to the **boundary service** patterns that work at the periphery of the system. These autonomous services are responsible for catering to the kinds of changes driven by external actors, such as end users and external systems. In this chapter, we will focus on supporting end users. You will learn how to create backend for frontend services that are responsible for catering to the kinds of changes driven by the human actors who use the system. These services segregate the requirements of different actors so that they do not compete with each other and impede innovation.

In this chapter, we're going to cover the following main topics:

- Focusing on user activities
- Dissecting the **Backend for Frontend** (**BFF**) pattern
- Choosing between GraphQL and REST
- Implementing different kinds of BFF services
- Securing a BFF in depth
- Leveraging multiple regions
- Observing BFF metrics
- Optimizing BFF performance

Focusing on user activities

In *Chapter 1, Architecting for Innovation*, we saw that the role of architecture is to enable change so that teams can continuously experiment and uncover the best solutions for their users. We enable continuous change by defining fortified boundaries around things that change together so that we can control the scope and impact of any given change. The key to defining these boundaries is to understand the driving force behind change.

In *Chapter 2, Defining Boundaries and Letting Go*, we found that people (that is, actors) are the driving force behind change. We identified three autonomous service patterns that each cater to a different type of actor. In this chapter, we dig into the details of the **Backend for Frontend** (**BFF**) service pattern. The BFF service pattern works at the boundary of the system to support end users and the activities they perform.

Before going further, it is important to put the BFF service pattern in context, because it is easy to get bogged down in all the interrelated details when we build a complex system. There are many features, different users, integrations with external systems, and overarching business processes. We need to break the larger problem down into smaller problems so that we can control the complexity and manage change.

Our three autonomous service patterns control the complexity and the scope of change. We cover integrations and the External Service Gateway pattern in *Chapter 7, Bridging Intersystem Gaps*, and we cover business processes and the *Control Service* pattern in *Chapter 8, Reacting to Events with More Events*.

The purpose of the BFF service pattern is to focus on the requirements of end user activities and let all other concerns fade into the background. Concerns about integrations should not encumber a BFF service. Each user activity is a step in an overarching business process, but only the inputs and outputs of the step are of concern to a BFF service. This level of focus is important because it minimizes coupling and increases flexibility. Let's look at how the BFF service pattern facilitates change by zeroing in on user activities, self-sufficient teams, and autonomy.

A BFF service is responsible for a single user activity

The BFF service pattern facilitates change because each BFF service has a deliberate focus on a specific user activity and eliminates distractions and competing demands.

Following on from the **Single-Responsibility Principle (SRP)**, a BFF service is responsible to one and only one human actor that interacts with the system's user interface. However, a single human actor may interact with a system in multiple ways to perform different activities. In this case, having one BFF service support multiple user activities could result in competing demands unless the activities are closely related.

In *Chapter 3, Taming the Presentation Tier*, we covered multiple approaches for breaking up a monolithic presentation tier, such as dynamically assembling many micro-apps in a micro frontends architecture or creating dedicated mobile applications for specific activities. In *Chapter 5, Turning the Cloud into the Database*, we discussed how data requirements change as data moves through its life cycle and interacts with different actors.

Taking all these considerations together, it is best to create a separate BFF service for each discrete user activity. This generally equates to creating a BFF service for each micro-app or mobile application, hence the term **backend for frontend**. For our food delivery example, we might include the following BFF services:

- A service used by restaurants to create menus, which is different from the service used by customers to browse menus

- A service used by customers to create orders, which is different from the service used by drivers to deliver orders and different still from the service used by customers to track the status of an order

- A service used by customers to view order history, another used by drivers to view delivery history, and yet another used by restaurants to view order statistics

- Separate services for customers, drivers, and restaurants to manage their accounts

Many of these examples seem very similar and their implementations may even look identical at first but avoid the temptation to merge them. They represent different actors and therefore different user activities. They are different bounded contexts. Before long, they will begin to diverge as the different actors drive different changes. Fortunately, as we covered in *Chapter 2*, *Defining Boundaries and Letting Go*, the services for the different actors will likely live in different autonomous subsystems, which will help ensure that the services remain separate.

Sometimes it is necessary to deliver the same user experience with multiple frontend implementations, such as a web application, a native iPhone application, and a native Android application. In this case, we need to make a decision regarding whether to support all the implementations with a single BFF service or one per implementation. If the functionality of all the implementations is identical, then a single BFF service is probably the right choice. If there are significant variations, then multiple BFF services may be better. If separate teams own the implementations, then that alone is a reason to have different BFF services, as we will cover next.

A BFF service is owned by the frontend team

The BFF service pattern facilitates change because the same team owns and implements the frontend and the backend.

This is a critical distinction. Traditionally, we have structured teams for the layers of the architecture with frontend teams, backend teams, and database teams. But this structure requires significant inter-team communication and coordination, which results in long lead times that impede innovation. Instead, self-sufficient, full-stack, autonomous teams own and focus on the frontend and the backend for one or more related user activities.

This enables a team to follow a UI-first approach. The team rapidly prototypes the user interfaces with no backend, to elicit fast feedback from the end user. In turn, the UI drives the requirements for the BFF service. This approach easily identifies the necessary queries and commands and eliminates the waste that arises when a separate backend team implements features that it assumes a frontend will need.

When a team is ready to implement a BFF service, they will typically leverage the same language used to implement the frontend, such as JavaScript. This allows the same developers to use the same tools to work on the frontend and the backend. This increases productivity because it reduces context switching as developers move between related frontend and backend tasks. As we will see in the *Optimizing BFF performance* section, this can also have a positive impact on runtime performance. In addition, the BFF pattern can reduce the cost of fielding a frontend team by controlling the number of necessary skill sets.

Decoupled, autonomous, and resilient

The BFF service pattern facilitates change because it eliminates inter-service dependencies.

This pattern is relatively new and has taken on various shapes and sizes as it has evolved. One common approach is to implement a BFF as a facade service that wraps and aggregates the calls to other services. But this approach is too brittle. It does eliminate the design-time coupling between the frontend and the various backend services, but it does not eliminate the runtime coupling. If any one of these other services has an outage, then the frontend user will also experience degraded functionality. Furthermore, inter-service coupling increases inter-team communication and coordination. A miscommunication between teams can lead to backward-incompatible changes that cause outages.

Instead, we implement our BFFs as autonomous services that eliminate synchronous inter-service dependencies. These services do not wrap other services. They own all the resources they need to continue operating when related services are down. They leverage the CQRS pattern to cache data from upstream services, as we covered in *Chapter 5, Turning the Cloud into the Database*, and they leverage the event sourcing pattern to produce events so that downstream services can react, as we covered in *Chapter 4, Trusting Facts and Eventual Consistency*. Together, these lower-level patterns provide the bulkheads that protect BFF services, so they can focus on delivering the responsiveness and resilience demanded by frontend users.

Let's take a look at the anatomy of a BFF service before we dive into some applications of the pattern.

Dissecting the Backend for Frontend (BFF) pattern

Creating a BFF service for each user activity does result in more services, so it is important that they all have a similar feel and structure. This will allow developers to easily work on different services. To help achieve this, it is a good practice to seed a new service with a skeleton from a standard template, stand it up, and then add the specific functionality. *Figure 6.1* depicts the resources that make up the typical BFF service.

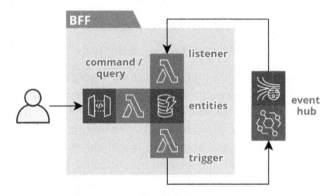

Figure 6.1 – Backend for Frontend pattern

The first thing to notice is that the typical BFF service provides a *Trilateral API*:

- It has a synchronous **command** and **query** interface that supports its frontend.

- It has an asynchronous **listener** interface that consumes domain events from upstream services via the **event hub**.

- It has an asynchronous **trigger** interface that produces domain events to the **event hub** for consumption by downstream services.

You can find a BFF service template here: `https://github.com/jgilbert01/aws-lambda-stream/tree/master/templates`. Let's dig into the different resources utilized by a BFF service.

Datastore

Each BFF service maintains its own highly available, fully managed datastore, such as AWS DynamoDB, S3, or Elasticsearch. This is how they achieve their autonomy. The datastore caches entities from upstream domain events, so the data is readily available to end users. Users make changes to the entities in the datastore, and the service produces domain events, in the background, to share the state changes.

It is important to understand that a BFF service stores data in a format that is most suitable for consumption by the frontend. This will produce a user experience that is more responsive and simplifies the frontend code by eliminating the need to continuously transform the data.

The following `serverless.yml` fragment, from the BFF service template, creates a DynamoDB table that supports the *single table design* best practice:

```
Resources:
  EntitiesTable:
    Type: AWS::DynamoDB::Table
    Properties:
      TableName: ${self:service}-${opt:stage}-entities
      AttributeDefinitions:

        . . .

      KeySchema:
        - AttributeName: pk
          KeyType: HASH
        - AttributeName: sk
          KeyType: RANGE
      GlobalSecondaryIndexes:
        - IndexName: DataIndex

        . . .

      BillingMode: PAY_PER_REQUEST
      StreamSpecification:
        StreamViewType: NEW_AND_OLD_IMAGES
      TimeToLiveSpecification:
        AttributeName: ttl
        Enabled: true
```

This standard table definition consists of generic `KeySchema`, which supports all entity types, and one or more global secondary indices. The CDC streaming and TTL features are enabled, along with on-demand billing.

We cover these database topics in detail in *Chapter 5*, *Turning the Cloud into the Database*.

API Gateway

The frontend must have access to the BFF service to perform queries and execute commands. The API Gateway provides this capability. It creates a secure and highly available perimeter around the functionality to support the frontend. We will cover this in detail in the *Securing a BFF in depth*, *Leveraging multiple regions*, and *Optimizing BFF performance* sections.

It is important to recognize that this interface supports a specific frontend and only that frontend. Other systems should not call this interface, as they are different actors. The External Service Gateway pattern fills this purpose, and we cover it in *Chapter 7, Bridging Intersystem Gaps*.

The following `serverless.yml` fragment, from the BFF service template, creates an API gateway and routes it to the functions that implement the queries and commands:

```
functions:
  rest:
    handler: src/rest/index.handle
    events:
      - http:
          path: {proxy+}
          method: any
          cors: true
```

This example routes all HTTP methods and paths to a single function and enables **Cross-Origin Resource Sharing** (**CORS**) support. We cover this function next.

Query and command functions

The all-important job of a BFF service is to provide a human actor with the ability to execute a specific set of queries and/or commands. They retrieve requested data from the datastore, and they record the results of the user's activities, in the datastore. We implement this functionality in one or more functions, using the cloud provider's **Function-as-a-Service** (**FaaS**) feature, such as AWS Lambda.

A common question regarding FaaS is whether to use many fine-grained functions or fewer coarse-grained functions. Our user activity-focused BFF services are already fairly fine-grained, so I prefer to start with a single function that executes all the BFF's queries and commands. For a GraphQL-based service, this is a natural fit. For a REST-based service, I may eventually split out a separate function for queries and one for commands if the traffic volumes are different enough. But again, these variations may represent different user activities and warrant separate BFF services instead. As the number of queries and commands grows, this may also indicate that the scope of the BFF service has grown too broad.

We will dig deeper into these functions in the *Models and connectors* section and the *Choosing between GraphQL and REST* section.

Listener function

The `listener` function plays the crucial role in an autonomous service of implementing the CQRS pattern. It is a stream processor that consumes domain events from `event-hub` and materializes entities in the datastore for consumption by end users. BFF services store data in a format that is most suitable for consumption by the frontend, so it is the job of the `listener` function to transform the entities into the desired format.

This is a single function with the single purpose of materializing entities, but there are many different domain event types to process. The function leverages the *pipeline* feature of the stream processing framework to preserve the maintainability of the logic for the individual event types.

Listener functions are optional. If a BFF service does not need to react to domain events, then it does not need a listener function. However, most BFF services will have a listener function. It is only the BFF services at the very beginning of the data life cycle that may not need a listener function.

The following `serverless.yml` fragment, from the BFF service template, creates the listener function and configures it to consume from a stream in the event hub:

```
functions:
  ...
  listener:
    handler: src/listener/index.handle
    events:
      - stream:
          type: kinesis
          arn: ${cf:event-hub-${opt:stage}.streamArn}
          ...
```

We covered stream processing in general in *Chapter 4, Trusting Facts and Eventual Consistency*, and we covered the details of creating materialized views in *Chapter 5, Turning the Cloud into the Database*.

Trigger function

The `trigger` function fills the fundamental role in an autonomous service of implementing the *database-first* variation of the event sourcing pattern. It is a stream processor that consumes change events from the datastore's **Change Data Capture (CDC)** stream and publishes domain events to the event-hub for consumption by downstream services.

This is a single function with the single purpose of publishing domain events after a user executes a command, but there are many different change event types to process. The function leverages the *pipeline* feature of the stream processing framework to preserve the maintainability of the logic for the individual event types.

Trigger functions are optional. If a BFF service is read-only (that is, it has no commands), then it does not need a trigger function. BFF services that work towards the end of the data life cycle tend to be read-only. The datastore must also support CDC streams, otherwise, we need to use the *stream-first* variant of the event sourcing pattern to produce domain events.

The following `serverless.yml` fragment, from the BFF service template, creates the `trigger` function and configures it to consume from the datastore's CDC stream:

```
functions:
  ...
  trigger:
    handler: src/trigger/index.handle
    events:
      - stream:
          type: dynamodb
          arn:
            Fn::GetAtt: [ EntitiesTable, StreamArn ]
        ...
```

We covered stream processing in general in *Chapter 4, Trusting Facts and Eventual Consistency*, and we covered the details of leveraging a datastore's CDC stream in *Chapter 5, Turning the Cloud into the Database*.

Models and connectors

In our effort to create architecture that enables change, we divide systems into autonomous subsystems, and we decompose those into autonomous services. The BFF service pattern provides a business logic tier to the presentation tier and these autonomous services own their own data tier. We can think of these building blocks as the *macro-architecture* that enables teams to work together across well-defined and fortified boundaries.

Now we need to turn our attention to the structure within each autonomous service and how it enables a single team to easily change an individual service. We have just seen how to decompose a BFF service into functions with well-defined responsibilities, such as queries, commands, listeners, and triggers. The software we write to run in these functions is not immense, but it can still become unwieldy if it is not well organized. We need to leverage some lightweight frameworks and put some simple layering in place. We can think of this as the *micro-architecture* within a service.

Akin to Alistair Cockburn's *Hexagonal Architecture* and Robert Martin's *Clean Architecture*, we want to isolate the business logic from the concerns of interacting with the technical resources, such as the datastore and event hub and the function execution environment. Therefore, we implement the business logic in `Model` classes and wrap all resource calls in `Connector` classes. Then we inject the connectors into the models using simple constructor-based injection. This does make the code more *portable*, but most importantly, it makes it more *testable*.

The following example shows the structure of a typical `Model` class:

```
export default class Model {
  constructor( connector ) {
    this.connector = connector;
  }
  save(id, input) { ... };
  getBy(id) {
    return this.connector.get(id);
  };
  queryBy(username) { ... };
  submit(id) { ... };
  delete(id) { ... };
}

export const toUpdateRequest = (uow) => ({ ... });
export const toDomainEvent = (uow) => ({ ... });
```

A BFF service works with a small slice of the system's overarching logical domain model. Each model class represents a separate domain aggregate used in the BFF service. Each method in a model, such as `save`, `submit`, and `getBy`, corresponds to a command or query provided by the service to the frontend.

A BFF service stores the domain entities in a format best suited for the frontend. The models provide mapper functions, such as `toUpdateRequest` and `toDomainEvent`, that transform the data between the internal and external data formats. These mapper functions support the `listener` and `trigger` functions, respectively.

A model class has a constructor for injecting connectors. The following example shows the structure of a typical `Connector` class:

```
class Connector {
  constructor( tableName ) {
    this.tableName = tableName;
    this.db = new DynamoDB.DocumentClient({ ... });
  }
  get(id) {
    const params = {
      TableName: this.tableName,
      KeyConditionExpression: '#pk = :id',
      ...
    };
    return this.db.query(params).promise()
      .then((data) => data.Items);
  }
  update(Key, inputParams) { ... }
}
```

In this specific example, we see a connector that is wrapping the calls to AWS DynamoDB. The `Model` class dictates the signatures of the `Connector` intance's methods and the connector encapsulates all the details of interacting with the resource. This will allow the model to work with different connector implementations. For example, during the early stages of development, it may be helpful to implement a connector that holds data in memory, so that we can quickly experiment with the functionality. Then we plug in the real connector when we are more confident with the requirements.

The connectors also make it easier to write unit tests that execute in isolation, because it is easier to write mocks for connectors than it is to write mocks for resources. Developers only need to write a small set of connector unit tests that have the complexity of mocking the resources. Then, for the model unit tests, which account for the majority of test cases, it is only necessary to mock the connectors.

Each connector defines a constructor with configuration options. This provides a clean separation between the connector and the execution environment. For example, at runtime, a function will receive connection information in environment variables, whereas unit tests will simply assign test values.

Models and connectors are also agnostic to the execution environment. For example, we should be able to implement a BFF service using REST or GraphQL without having to change the model and connector classes. Now, let's take a look at using GraphQL versus REST and how these interact with the models and connectors.

Choosing between GraphQL and REST

GraphQL has become very popular in recent years, which raises the question of whether it is better to use REST or GraphQL. The short answer is that it depends on the user activity.

Does a user activity involve many users interacting with the same data or a few users interacting with different data? Taking our food delivery system as an example, a few employees from each restaurant will interact with just the menu of their restaurant, whereas many customers will interact with the menus of many restaurants. Furthermore, the customers are only reading the menus and the restaurant employees are editing the menus.

This means that we can use the `cache-control` header to improve the responsiveness of the system for customers and reduce the cost of the system. This is where *REST* excels. **Representational State Transfer (REST)** was designed to take full advantage of the infrastructure that makes up the internet, such as routers and content delivery networks. So, it makes sense to use REST for a customer-facing menu service.

GraphQL, on the other hand, uses the `POST` operation, so it is not well suited for read-only scenarios. But it is very well suited for more ad hoc activities where the user is navigating through and editing data, such as restaurant employees maintaining menus or customers maintaining their account information and user preferences.

In *Chapter 7, Bridging Intersystem Gaps*, we will cover the topic of *webhooks*, which usually require RESTful endpoints. We will also cover the topic of external interfaces, which traditionally expose a RESTful endpoint. These are akin to a BFF service, but they support an unbounded number of external systems. This means that versioning and backward compatibility are of utmost importance. Versioning is another area where GraphQL excels because clients declare the exact fields they need. This makes it easier to track how clients use the interface and craft backward-compatible changes.

The major advantage of GraphQL is that its client-driven query approach is less chatty than REST. A typical RESTful interface will require an application to make several calls to retrieve a full domain aggregate. This kind of lazy retrieval may be preferred if the user does not need the full object. GraphQL, on the other hand, lets the client specify the fields to return and the associations to traverse, which allows the client to retrieve more data all at once. This level of flexibility is less important for a highly focused BFF service, but it is very helpful for an external interface.

My general guideline is to use REST for customer-facing read-only services and GraphQL for everything else. Sometimes, it may be necessary to support both. Let's see how models and connectors help us do this.

REST

REST is the traditional choice for implementing services. As we have discussed, it is better for read-only services, webhooks, and external interfaces. The following code fragments implement the **handler** for the **rest** function we declared in the *Dissecting the Backend for Frontend (BFF) pattern* section:

```
const api = require('lambda-api')();
import Connector from '../connectors/dynamodb';
import Thing from '../models/thing';
const connector = new
  Connector(process.env.ENTITY_TABLE_NAME);
api.app({
  models: {
    thing: new Thing(connector),
  }
});
...
export const handle = async (req, ctx) =>
  api.run(req, ctx);
```

The handler uses the `lambda-api` framework, which is very similar to Express, but with a significantly smaller footprint. It works with both AWS API Gateway and AWS Application Load Balancer and hides the differences. The handler function simply needs to wire the pieces together. First, we register the `models` with the framework and inject the connectors on startup, so that this logic does not need to be repeated for each request.

Next, we implement the `route` that will handle requests to retrieve `Thing` entities by their identifier:

```
api.get('/things/:id', (request, response) =>
  request.namespace.models.thing.get(request.params.id)
  .then((data) => response.status(200).json(data)));
```

The `route` function has access to the `models` through the `request` object. The model handles the business logic, and the connector interacts with the datastore. This means the `route` function only needs to implement the glue code to map the inputs from the `request` object to the `model` and map the output from the `model` to the `response` object.

Now let's take a look at how we can use the same model and connector in a GraphQL function.

GraphQL

GraphQL is becoming the preferred choice for implementing services. As we have discussed, it is better for more ad hoc user activities that include editing data. It also has benefits for versioning and backward compatibility, it can be more efficient, and it is self-documenting. Furthermore, it has great framework support for both the client side and the server side.

Here is an example of hooking up GraphQL in a Lambda function. The following `serverless.yml` fragment creates an API gateway for the service:

```
functions:
  graphql:
    handler: src/graphql/index.handle
    events:
      - http:
          path: graphql
          method: post
```

There is one route that directs POST requests for the `graphql` path to the function that implements a GraphQL schema. Next, we have a fragment of a GraphQL schema that defines the `Thing` domain entity and a query to retrieve `Thing` by ID:

```
type Thing {
  id: String!
  name: String
  description: String
}

extend type Query {
  thing(id: String!): Thing
}
```

This schema corresponds to the `model` class we defined in the *Models and connectors* section. There will typically be a one-to-one relationship between schema fragments like this one and `model` classes. We will see how resolvers bring the two together in a moment. Next, we implement the **handler** for the `graphql` function:

```
import { ApolloServer, gql } from 'apollo-server-lambda';
import schema from './schema';
import Connector from '../connectors/dynamodb';
import Thing from '../models/thing';
const connector = new
  Connector(process.env.ENTITY_TABLE_NAME);
const handler = new ApolloServer({
  ...schema,
  context: () => ({
    models: {
      thing: new Thing(connector),
    },
  }),
}).createHandler();

export const handle = (req, ctx, callback) =>
  handler(req, ctx, callback);
```

The handler uses the **Apollo** framework to do the heavy lifting of processing GraphQL requests. The handler function simply needs to wire the pieces together. Once again, we register the `models` and inject the connectors on startup, so that this logic does not need to be repeated for each request. We also register the GraphQL `schema`. Finally, we implement the `resolvers` that map the schema to the `models`:

```
export default const resolvers = {
  Query: {
    thing(_, { id }, context) {
      return context.models.thing.get(id);
    },
    ...
  },
  Mutation: { ... },
};
```

In this case, we see the resolver that handles queries for `Thing` entities by their identifier. The resolver has access to the `models` through the `context` object. The model handles the business logic, and the connector interacts with the datastore. This means the resolver only needs to implement the glue code to map the inputs from the query to the model and return the output from the model.

These examples demonstrate how we can decouple the business logic from the execution environment. The business logic lives in the model classes and the connector classes encapsulate the external dependencies. Then we glue everything together in the execution environment with the appropriate framework. Now that we have seen some of the lower-level details, let's see how we can put all this to work in applications with some different kinds of BFF services.

Implementing different kinds of BFF services

Up to this point, we have learned how to control the scope of a BFF service and we have seen its major building blocks. In *Chapter 5, Turning the Cloud into the Database*, we discussed how different actors interact with data in different ways as it moves through its life cycle. Let's look at some different kinds of BFF services that cater to the different phases of the data life cycle. These include **Task**, **Search**, **Action**, **Dashboard**, **Reporting**, and **Archive** BFF services.

Task BFF services

A **Task BFF service** is a variation of the BFF service pattern that supports a step (that is, a task) in a larger business process.

Tasks are the workhorses of BFF services, as they constitute the majority of BFF services. A Task BFF provides a well-defined query to access the data the user needs to perform the specific task. It also provides the set of commands the user needs to accomplish the task, including a command to signal when the task is complete.

For example, from our food delivery system, the **Delivery BFF** allows drivers to acquire a delivery assignment, access the delivery information, and indicate when the delivery is complete. The **Restaurant BFF** provides agents with access to their assigned restaurants, so they can manage menus on behalf of restaurants. And the Account BFF allows customers to manage their locations and payment methods.

Figure 6.1 in the *Dissecting the Backend for Frontend pattern* section depicts the resources involved in a Task BFF service.

In its most basic form, a Task BFF may just provide **Create, Read, Update and Delete (CRUD)** capabilities. These tasks typically manage master data that support all the business processes. Or the task may sit at the beginning of the data life cycle where the user creates the domain data and then invokes a `submit` command to publish the domain event that initiates a business process.

A Task BFF may implement a step in a business process. In this case, the `listener` function of the Task BFF consumes domain events that initiate the tasks. It materializes the data so users can query their work. These domain events may come from control services that orchestrate the business processes or the individual services may choreograph the business processes themselves. We cover orchestration and choreography in *Chapter 8, Reacting to Events with More Events*.

The `trigger` function produces domain events to record the outcome of any intermediate commands. And it ultimately produces the domain event that signals the completion of a task and moves the larger business process forward.

Search BFF services

A **Search BFF** service is a variation of the BFF service pattern that provides read-only access to the data produced by one or more upstream services.

Whereas a Task BFF service provides its own well-defined queries, a Search BFF service helps users narrow in on what they are looking for. The users may not know exactly what they are looking for or even if the information exists. They may only have a general idea of what they want and be looking to see what is available.

For example, the Menu BFF service in our food delivery system provides the ability to search for restaurants and menu items by name, category, location, and more. The Restaurant BFF service allows restaurants to maintain their menus, but the Menu BFF search service provides the high performance and scalability needed to support millions of customers. In the back office, a search service would provide a central location for employees to search for all the business's domain information, such as customers and cases in a customer support system.

The following figure depicts the resources involved in a Search BFF service.

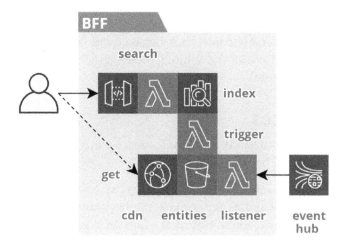

Figure 6.2 – Search BFF service

At the heart of a search service is an **index**, such as *Elasticsearch*. The **search** interface provides access to the index through an API gateway and a search function. Each search result contains summary information and the URL to access the detailed entity information.

The domain **entities** data is the perfect candidate for object storage, such as an AWS S3 bucket, because the volume of data is unbounded and it is read-only, reasonably static, and only accessed by the identifier. We store the data in the JSON format that we will return to the client, along with any images. The object keys should follow a good RESTful structure, such as `/restaurants/123/menuitems/987`.

For public information, like the Menu service, we serve the domain entities from the edge of the cloud using a **Content Delivery Network (CDN)**, such as AWS CloudFront. We accomplish this by setting the `cache-control` property on the objects in storage so that we can cache the requests on the browser and the CDN. This provides the low latency and massive scale needed to support an unbounded number of customers. We discussed the origins of this approach in the *Turning the database inside out* section of *Chapter 5, Turning the Cloud into the Database*. For private data, such as a back-office search service, the client will access the data through a signed URL with a short time to live.

The **listener** function is responsible for materializing the entities and images in the S3 bucket. Then, the **trigger** function indexes the data, only after it is available in the bucket. Chaining these steps is important because each step is atomic, as we discussed in *Chapter 4, Trusting Facts and Eventual Consistency*. Splitting these steps ensures that the index will not return a result with a broken link.

Action BFF services

An **Action BFF** service is a variation of the BFF service pattern that performs a specific action in the context of another BFF service.

For example, the Menu BFF service in our food delivery system is a search BFF that supports browsing and navigating restaurants and menu items, but it does not support adding items to a cart. This is the job of an action BFF, such as a Cart service. This action BFF supports adding items to a cart, and stores the menu item's identifier, the quantity, and any configured options. Once the customer submits the order, the Cart service no longer needs to retain the cart information, because it is not editable, and the `order-submitted` domain event is a record of the state.

The following figure depicts the resources involved in an action BFF service.

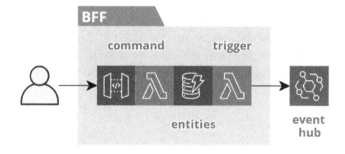

Figure 6.3 – Action BFF service

An action service is responsible for performing a set of commands. We can think of these services as *headless* because they need other services to provide context for the inputs to a **command**. In other words, we pass all the necessary information into a **command**. They have no **listener** to create materialized views that the service can **query** to provide its own context. An action service may have a query to return the results of its own actions, but the service does not retain this information for any longer than necessary. Finally, a **trigger** function produces domain events to record the outcome of the commands.

Dashboard BFF services

A **Dashboard BFF** service is a variation of the BFF service pattern that provides users with a read-only, running tally of important domain values.

For example, a banking application will provide users with a dashboard of all their balances. In our food delivery system, restaurants can see statistics on how many customers viewed their menus, the top viewed items, and order statistics, so that they can gauge the value of using the food delivery service.

The following figure depicts the resources involved in a Dashboard BFF service:

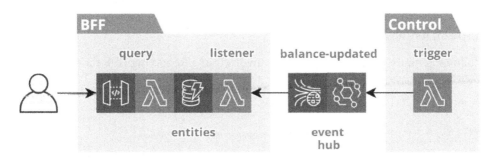

Figure 6.4 – Dashboard BFF service

These example dashboard user activities have a well-defined access pattern. For example, each record contains a specific value, with pk set to the user's identifier or group, and sk set to the value identifier. The **query** simply returns the set of pre-calculated values for the current user.

These user activities are typically externally-facing and therefore require fast response times and high availability. These requirements, combined with the fact that the user experience is not ad hoc, mean that these services do not need and should not rely on complex analytics infrastructure.

Instead, a dashboard BFF service works with a control service that leverages ACID 2.0 transactions to perform the necessary calculations, as we cover in the *Calculating event sourcing snapshots* section in *Chapter 8, Reacting to Events with More Events*. The control service consumes lower-order domain events, calculates the current value, and produces a higher-order domain event, such as **balance-updated**.

This leaves the BFF service with the simple responsibility of delivering the read-only information to the user. The **listener** function consumes the higher-order events and materializes the values for the **query** to return. As the dashboard service is autonomous, it can always return the most recently received pre-calculated values.

Reporting BFF services

A **Reporting BFF** service is a variation of the BFF service pattern that provides users with a historical view of the data in the form of periodic reports.

In *Chapter 5, Turning the Cloud into the Database*, we learned how to control the volume of data and keep data lean in the individual services. Upstream services set a time to live on each record so that data expires when they no longer need it. However, it is common to have reporting requirements on historical data. This is a different user activity, for a different actor, in a later phase of the data life cycle. So, we create reporting services downstream for these activities.

The following figure depicts the resources involved in a Reporting BFF service:

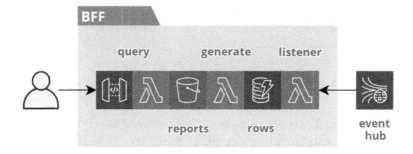

Figure 6.5 – Reporting BFF service

On a periodic basis, an actor expects to have access to reports, such as the monthly report on their area of responsibility. Traditionally, this data lives in a monolithic relational database and the users execute jobs to generate the reports and then wait for the jobs to complete. Instead, we can continuously prepare the reports so that they are ready at the desired frequency.

We organize, version, and store the generated **reports** in an S3 bucket with an appropriate key structure, such as `/division/yyyy/mm/dd/report-name.pdf`. The **query** interface allows the user to browse the reports.

The **listener** function consumes domain events and materializes the data in a table as `rows` formatted for a specific report. The `pk` field is set to the identifier of the report instance, which is equal to the S3 key and the `sk` field identifies the sorted rows in the report. The database stream triggers the **generate** function as we insert new rows. The function retrieves all the rows for the same `pk` value, produces the report, and stores it in the bucket.

At any time, the user can see the latest version of a report with the most recent data. The rows in the table have a time to live that is short enough to control the size of the table but long enough for late-arriving data to generate a new version of the report. We can retain the reports themselves indefinitely and age them into cold storage.

Archive BFF services

An Archive BFF service is a variation on the BFF service pattern that serves as the ultimate data collector at the end of the data life cycle. These services are governed by record management requirements that specify how long a company must retain various data.

In *Chapter 5*, *Turning the Cloud into the Database*, we learned about the importance of *proactive archiving* and how it enables services to keep data lean. Upstream services set a time to live on each record so that they delete data when they no longer need it. Downstream services collect the data they need and the cycle repeats. Archive BFF services allow all other services to remain lean.

The following figure depicts the resources involved in an Archive BFF service:

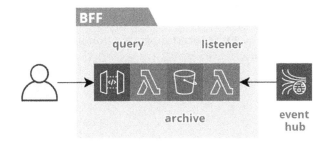

Figure 6.6 – Archiving service

Archive BFF services are proactive because they do not wait to collect data at the end of the life cycle. They continuously collect data from the moment users create it, so that upstream services can delete data freely.

The **listener** function consumes domain events and stores the data in an S3 bucket. This is akin to an event lake, but we organize the data around a specific domain entity identifier, such as customer, restaurant, or driver. A detailed history accumulates that we can use in the future for auditing and restoration. The **query** interface allows a user to browse the archive. The data ages in cold storage and we purge it after a regulated time period.

To put the archive service in context, we can use a case management system as an example. A Task BFF service is responsible for active cases. While a case is active, the index in the search BFF service points to the data in the task BFF service. When a case officer closes a case, the Task BFF service deletes the case data and we update the search index to point to the case data that has accumulated in the Archive BFF service. If we need to reopen a case, then we restore the case data from the archive to the Task BFF service and update the search index.

Each autonomous subsystem should have an archiving service for its domain aggregates so that its services remain lean. If a subsystem has many domain aggregates, then it may warrant multiple archives. As a whole, a system should have an archive subsystem at the end of the data life cycle that is responsible to the regulatory actor. This allows the other autonomous subsystems to remain lean.

Now let's turn our attention to securing our BFF services from top to bottom.

Securing a BFF in depth

BFF services are the most interesting to secure. They expose a synchronous interface to the frontend, which means they have the largest attack surface. Fortunately, securing a serverless BFF service in depth is mostly a declarative exercise. The following diagram enumerates the various resources a BFF service interacts with and the different security topics we must address, such as authentication, encryption in transit, least privilege, encryption at rest, and auditing.

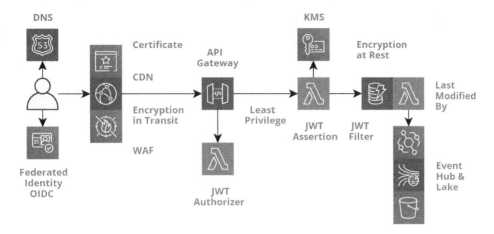

Figure 6.7 – Security in depth

Let's discuss these topics in the order that user activity will encounter them.

The perimeter

We need to take steps to secure the channel through which all requests to a BFF service will flow. Any BFF service that exposes a public interface outside of a private network, such as an AWS VPC, is vulnerable to **Distributed Denial of Service** (**DDoS**) attacks. This is a system-level concern that we addressed in *Chapter 2, Defining Boundaries and Letting Go*.

From the standpoint of an individual BFF service, the team must take advantage of these system-level capabilities. For example, each BFF service should have a CDN, such as AWS CloudFront, and associate it with the system-level **Web Application Firewall** (**WAF**) policies. The team should also be aware of and familiar with the continuous auditing and security monitoring that we perform at the system level.

Federated identity

Authentication is the first step for a private user activity. The frontend will initiate the authentication process with a federated identity provider, such as AWS Cognito, when the current user is unknown. We covered this process in detail in *Chapter 3, Taming the Presentation Tier*. The identity provider will implement the **OpenID Connect** (**OIDC**) protocol and the output of a successful login process is a **JSON Web Token** (**JWT**). The frontend retains the token and passes it as a bearer token, in the Authorization header field, on every request to a BFF service.

In transit

All calls to a BFF service must encrypt the data in transit. At a minimum, this is necessary to secure the JWT bearer token. A bearer token gives access to any bearer of the token, so we must not expose it in transit. We must encrypt all other sensitive data as well, so it is best to encrypt all calls.

Serverless services, such as AWS API Gateway, Lambda, and DynamoDB, require the use of HTTPS. Therefore, we only need to take steps to encrypt the calls to the CDN. This requires a custom SSL certificate. A cloud provider's certificate management service, such as **AWS Certificate Manager** (**ACM**), can create the certificate and automatically rotate it each year. Then we associate the certificate with the CDN and configure the CDN to require HTTPS.

JWT authorizer

Once a request reaches the BFF service, the first step is to authorize the request. This step is performed by the API gateway, so that we separate the technical concerns of handling the JWT token from the business logic. This also eliminates unnecessary calls to the query and command functions when the request is unauthorized.

The authorization process verifies the signature of the token and checks the expiration time, at a minimum. The process will usually validate the issuer and the intended audience as well.

Verifying the signature requires access to the key used to generate the token. A third-party provider will expose its public key, following the **JSON Web Key Set** (**JWKS**) standard, with a URL similar to `https://my-identity-provider/.well-known/jwks.json`. We configure the API gateway with this URL, so it can perform the verification.

Alternatively, we can implement a custom authorizer function that verifies the token. Authorizer functions provide the flexibility to verify custom and non-standard tokens, as well as standard tokens. Choosing between the alternatives depends on the needs of the token and the features of the API gateway service.

The following `serverless.yml` fragment, from the BFF service template, configures the `rest` function to use the `authorizer` function provided by AWS Cognito:

```
functions:
  rest:
    handler: src/rest/index.handle
    events:
      - http:
```

```
. . .
authorizer:
    arn: arn:aws:cognito-idp:REGION:ACCOUNT:
                userpool/ID
```

If the JWT token is valid, then the API gateway includes the claims in the request context when it forwards the request to the query and command functions. From here, we can perform JWT assertions and JWT filters as needed.

JWT assertion

So far, we have used a JWT to authorize access to a service as a whole. This may be all that is necessary for some services. For others, we may need to use the claims in the token to grant role-based authorization to the individual queries and commands in the service.

First, we need access to the claim that contains the user's assigned roles. The following code shows how to access the groups claim that AWS Cognito includes in its JWT token:

```
const getUserGroups = (request) => request
  .requestContext.authorizer.claims['cognito:groups'];
```

Next, we need the code to assert that the user has the required role. The following middleware code asserts that the user is a member of a group with the required role name, before continuing. Otherwise, it returns a 401 HTTP status code in the response:

```
export const forRole = (roleName) => (req, res, next) => {
  const groups = getUserGroups(req);
  if (groups.includes(roleName)) {
    return next();
  } else {
    res.error(401, 'Not Authorized');
  }
}
```

Then we add the middleware to the individual routes and specify the required role name, such as forRole('Admin'):

```
api.get('/things', forRole('Admin'), getThings);
```

We can implement role-based assertions in GraphQL by decorating the model with directives, such as @hasRole:

```
extend type Query {
  things(...): [Thing] @hasRole(role: 'Admin')
}
```

We can also implement fine-grained assertions in the model class, if need be. However, we should pass the claims to the model in a normalized format.

JWT filter

So far, we have used a JWT to authorize access to a service and used the claims in the token to assert role-based authorization to the queries and commands in the service. Now, we need to control access to the data at the record level. For example, customers should only have access to their own data, or employees should only have access to their team's data.

To accomplish record-level security, we need to carefully craft the queries that grant users access to the data. A request may explicitly include the data for these filters. However, we cannot trust these values, because they can be set to any arbitrary value by the caller.

Instead, we need to use the claims from the JWT to set the filter values. For example, the token will include the subject's identity and should include the roles and groups the subject is a member of. We can trust these values because we have asserted the authenticity of the token signature. In other words, the caller cannot tamper with the contents of the signed token. You should also assert the claims against the requested values to help find bugs or suspicious activity.

Last modified by

Auditing is another common security requirement. We need to track who changed what data and when. Our event-first architecture already provides auditing in the form of events and the event lake. We do not need to build another mechanism. We simply need to ensure that we produce all the right events and that they have all the necessary information.

In addition to domain events, the trigger function should produce lower-level data change events as users insert, update, and delete records in the entities datastore. We have already seen how to do this in the *Leveraging change data capture* section of *Chapter 5, Turning the Cloud into the Database*. This tells us what changed and when.

Now we need to know who invoked the command that changed the data. This information is available in the JWT. We need to pass this information down to the model class, so we can set a lastModifiedBy field on each record. The following code block provides an example of accessing the username from a JWT token in an AWS Lambda function:

```
const getUsername = event => event
  .requestContext.authorizer.claims.['cognito:username'];
```

In the rest or graphql handler function, we use getUsername to pull the username from the claims and pass it to the constructor of the model class in a normalized format:

```
export default class Model {
  constructor( connector, username ) {
    this.username = username;

    ...
  }
  save(id, input) {
    return this.connector.save(id, {
      ...input,
      lastModifiedBy: this.username,
      });
  };
  ...
}
```

The methods in the model class assign the username to the lastModifiedBy field, so all the data change events record who performed the command. The event lake can now serve as an audit of all user activity. We can also use this information in a *Reporting BFF service*, as we covered in the *Implementing different kinds of BFF services* section, to make the audit information more accessible.

Least privilege

As always, we should assign permissions to the least privileges necessary. In addition to assigning permissions to users, we also have to assign permissions between resources. For example, we have to grant the API gateway permission to access the functions in a service and we have to grant the functions permission to access the datastore and the event hub.

The following `serverless.yml` fragment, from the BFF service template, grants the `rest` function permission to query and update the datastore:

```
iamRoleStatements:
  - Effect: Allow
    Action:
      - dynamodb:Query
      - dynamodb:UpdateItem
    Resource:
      Fn::GetAtt: [ EntitiesTable, Arn ]
```

The Serverless Framework will automatically generate any permissions it can implicitly infer from the specified metadata. For example, the API gateway will need permission to access the `rest` function, whereas we have to explicitly grant the permissions for the resources accessed within the function code. Do not use wildcards when granting permissions.

At rest

Encrypting data at rest is the last line of defense. If a hacker breaches all the other layers of security, the data will still be secure if we have properly redacted the sensitive information. We covered the details of encrypting data at rest in the *Redacting sensitive data* section of *Chapter 5, Turning the Cloud into the Database.*

The majority of data in a system originates from a BFF service. Therefore, it is crucial that we identify all the sensitive information used in a BFF service and ensure we redact it in the datastore and in the domain events. This will force all downstream services to follow suit because they will need to decrypt it before using it, which should make it obvious that they should re-encrypt it before saving it.

This means that the developers of a BFF service are the first line of defense. Fortunately, the cloud's *shared responsibility model* handles many of the lower-level security details, which frees developers to focus more time and effort on identifying all the sensitive information used within a BFF service and redacting it when we save and publish the data. In other words, *security-by-design* starts with the developers of BFF services. We need to know our domain models and take responsibility for redacting sensitive information.

Now let's turn our attention to running BFF services in multiple regions.

Leveraging multiple regions

Designing a system to run across multiple regions is a multifaceted problem and a running theme throughout this book. Each layer of the system plays its role. In *Chapter 3, Taming the Presentation Tier*, we saw how session consistency and offline-first mechanisms help the presentation layer ensure a seamless transition during a regional disruption. In *Chapter 4, Trusting Facts and Eventual Consistency*, we covered the implications of multi-regional deployments on stream processing and why we rely on replication at the datastore level, instead of replicating streams. In *Chapter 5, Turning the Cloud into the Database*, we covered the different strategies for data replication. And in *Chapter 9, Choreographing Deployment and Delivery*, we examine how to leverage multiple regions for canary deployments.

In this section, we cover how BFF services leverage multiple regions to provide users with a more responsive and resilient experience. Specifically, we look into latency-based routing, regional health checks, and regional failover.

Latency-based routing

Why should you run your system in multiple regions? It will require additional effort, but not much more effort, as we will see in *Chapter 9, Choreographing Deployment and Delivery*. And the benefits of regional failover may seem remote, until that day when you really need it.

The simple answer is, for your users' benefit. BFF services are user-facing services and responsiveness is important to users. More and more, users are spread across many geographic regions, whether they are your customers or fellow employees. This means that latency will be an issue for some of your users if the services are only running in a single region.

The following diagram depicts a BFF service running in two regions, east and west.

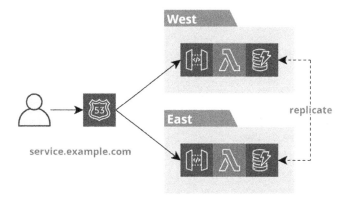

Figure 6.8 – Latency-based routing

We deploy a BFF service and all its resources twice, once in each region. This results in two separate and independent stacks. The stacks are only related with regard to data replication, as we covered in *Chapter 5, Turning the Cloud into the Database*, and because they share the same domain name.

When the frontend resolves the domain name, the cloud provider's **Domain Name System** (**DNS**) service, such as AWS Route 53, will return the IP address of one instance of the BFF service. There are many strategies for picking an instance. The latency-based strategy will pick the region that is closest to the location of the user.

The following `serverless.yml` fragment configures a BFF service for latency-based routing:

```yaml
provider:
  name: aws
  endpointType: REGIONAL
...
Resources:
  ApiRegionalDomainName:
    Type: AWS::ApiGateway::DomainName
    Properties:
      DomainName: ${opt:stage}-${self:service}.
          mysubsys.example.com
    ...
  ApiRegionalBasePathMapping:
    Type: AWS::ApiGateway::BasePathMapping
    ...
  ApiRegionalEndpointRecord:
    Type: AWS::Route53::RecordSet
    Properties:
      HostedZoneId: ${cf:global-resources-${opt.stage}
          .hostedZoneId}
      Name: ${opt:stage}-${self:service}
          .mysubsys.example.com
      Region: ${opt:region}
      SetIdentifier: ${opt:region}
      Type: A
      AliasTarget:
```

```
      HostedZoneId:
        Fn::GetAtt: [ ApiRegionalDomainName,
                      RegionalHostedZoneId ]
      DNSName:
        Fn::GetAtt: [ ApiRegionalDomainName,
                      RegionalDomainName ]
```

First, set `endpointType` for the API Gateway to `REGIONAL` to disable the creation of a default CloudFront distribution. We will see how to create a custom distribution shortly in the *Optimizing BFF performance* section. Then, configure the API gateway with a custom `DomainName` and `BasePathMapping`, in the same way as for a single region configuration.

Next, configure the DNS `RecordSet`. Point the recordset to the subsystem's Route 53 hosted zone. Each autonomous subsystem should have its own subdomain and corresponding Route 53 hosted zone. Then assign a unique domain name for the BFF service within the subsystem's subdomain and point `AliasTarget` to the BFF service instance.

Finally, set the `Region` and `SetIdentifier` properties to enable latency-based routing. Each deployment of the BFF service will register with the same domain name. The `SetIdentifier` property differentiates each instance, so each recordset is unique.

You can find a full example in `serverless-multi-regional-plugin` here: `https://www.npmjs.com/package/serverless-multi-regional-plugin`.

Regional health checks

Like so many other things, serverless is different when it comes to health checks. The cloud provider is responsible for running its serverless services across multiple availability zones within a single region and performing health checks on this infrastructure. But this does not absolve teams of the responsibility to perform health checks. Instead, we have to check the health of the cloud provider's services.

For example, what do we do when one of the cloud provider's services has a regional outage? We really have no recourse other than to fail over to another region. The only other option is to take an outage as well, which really isn't a good option. So, we need to know when a region is unhealthy.

A traditional health check asserts that a service instance has access to all the necessary resources. For example, it may ping the database to ensure it has connectivity. A regional health check does the same thing but at the autonomous subsystem level instead of the instance level. We treat the cloud provider's serverless services as resources and assert that they are all healthy.

The following diagram depicts a regional health check service:

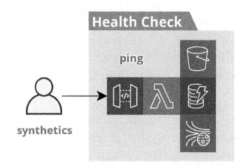

Figure 6.9 – Regional health check service

The service asserts the health of the resources used by the autonomous subsystem. In this example, the subsystem uses API Gateway, Lambda, S3, DynamoDB, and Kinesis. We deploy the service to each region and it provisions its own resources of these types. The monitoring system's `synthetics` feature pings the health check in each region at least once a minute. The service tests each resource in parallel by executing one or more calls, such as writing and reading. We implement the service with API Gateway and Lambda, so they are tested implicitly. If any call fails, then the service returns a 503 status code.

A region is unhealthy when the regional health check service produces a high rate of errors. The following `serverless.yml` fragment adds a `CloudWatch Alarm` and Route 53 `HealthCheck` to the regional health check service:

```
Resources:
  Api5xxAlarm:
    Type: AWS::CloudWatch::Alarm
    Properties:
      Namespace: AWS/ApiGateway
      MetricName: 5XXError
      Dimensions:
        - Name: ApiName
          Value: ${opt:stage}-${self:service}
```

```
        Statistic: Minimum
        ComparisonOperator: GreaterThanThreshold
        Threshold: 0
        Period: 60
        EvaluationPeriods: 1
  ApiHealthCheck:
    Type: AWS::Route53::HealthCheck
    Properties:
      HealthCheckConfig:
        Type: CLOUDWATCH_METRIC
        AlarmIdentifier:
          Name:
            Ref: Api5xxAlarm
          Region: ${opt:region}
        InsufficientDataHealthStatus: LastKnownStatus
```

The regional heath check service triggers the CloudWatch `Alarm` when the `5XXError` rate exceeds the threshold. `Tune` this threshold to your desired sensitivity. The alarm informs the Route 53 `HealthCheck` instance and the BFF services will reference it to control failover, which we cover next.

Regional failover

All the BFF services in an autonomous subsystem should fail over to another region when the regional health check service deems a region unhealthy. Some services may be more affected than others, but all should fail over, because it is the simplest solution. Reasoning about the behavior of the system if only a subset of services fail over can be confusing and lead to mistakes.

The following `serverless.yml` fragment extends the latency-based routing example to include the health check identifier:

```
  ApiRegionalEndpointRecord:
    Type: AWS::Route53::RecordSet
    Properties:
      ...
      HealthCheckId: ${cf:health-check-${opt:stage}
          .healthCheckId}
      ...
```

Route 53 takes the health check status into account when resolving a domain name. It will not return the address of an unhealthy resource unless all the resources are unhealthy.

After a failover, all queries and commands will execute against in the next closest, healthy region. In *Chapter 3, Taming the Presentation Tier*, we saw how session consistency ensures a seamless transition, and in *Chapter 5, Turning the Cloud into the Database*, we covered the implications of the protracted eventual consistency that can arise during a regional failover.

Now let's turn our attention to observing the health of our BFF services so that we can jump into action when there are runtime problems.

Observing BFF metrics

Observability is instrumental in reducing lead time. The metrics of BFF services are critical because the health of these services directly impacts the end user. Having visibility into the inner workings of a service gives a team the confidence to experiment with changes. Let's look at how work metrics and resource metrics apply to BFF services.

Work metrics

In *Chapter 2, Defining Boundaries and Letting Go*, we discussed the importance of work metrics. These metrics represent the user-visible output of the system. BFF services support end users so they are the predominant producer of work metrics. The execution rate of queries and commands, their durations, and their error rates are all key performance indicators of the health of a system.

Any anomalies in these metrics are an indicator that the team may need to take action. We can set up anomaly detection algorithms, such as those provided by AWS CloudWatch or the Datadog monitoring service, to alert us to variations in these metrics. The metrics produced by the API gateway are the leading candidates for anomaly detection. The metrics for the domain events produced by commands are additional candidates.

Over time, teams will identify which work metrics of which BFF services are the best indicators of the system's health.

Throttling and concurrency limits

Once we detect an anomaly in a work metric, we will leverage the resource metrics to help us identify the root cause of the problem. The datastore is a BFF service's most significant resource, but the API gateway and the functions themselves are also resources. These serverless resources have implicit autoscaling, but they do have soft limits. These soft limits protect against runaway bugs that can drive up costs.

We can request an increase of these soft limits, but we need to know when the current limits are insufficient. Therefore, it is important to set up an alert on the utilization of concurrent functions against the limit. This alert is an early warning sign that you may need to request an increase in the concurrency limit to avoid throttling.

Throttling errors indicate that we have breached a limit. Prolonged throttling will trigger the work metric alerts so that we can jump into action. However, requesting an increase to a soft limit takes time, hence the importance of the early warning.

Now let's turn our attention to optimizing the performance of our BFF services.

Optimizing BFF performance

Performance is an important consideration in the design of all services. But, of all the autonomous service patterns, performance is of utmost importance for BFF services, because they are user-facing, and users have high expectations.

We have optimized the BFF service pattern for high performance by employing the CQRS pattern, which we covered in *Chapter 5, Turning the Cloud into the Database*. This eliminates competition for resources and allows each service to take full control of its resources.

Latency-based routing helps to ensure that all users experience similar performance, as we covered in the *Leveraging multiple regions* section. But there is still more we can do to improve performance. We can tune function memory allocation, minimize cold starts, avoid timeouts and retries, and leverage cache control.

Function memory allocation

The cost of running a function is typically calculated in Gigabyte-seconds. The price of a Gigabyte-second is based on the amount of memory allocated. The more memory allocated, the higher the price per Gigabyte-second. However, the correlation between price and cost is counter-intuitive, because memory allocation also corresponds with CPU power and network I/O throughput. This means that paying more per Gigabyte-second may result in a lower overall cost and better performance.

For example, on AWS Lambda's pricing scale, when you double the memory allocation but consequently cut the execution time in half, the cost is the same. The corollary is, when you cut memory allocation in half and consequently double the execution time, you are spending the same amount of money for less performance.

Start with a moderate allocation of memory as the default for all functions, such as 1,024 MB. Then focus on tuning the most expensive functions based on the production runtime metrics.

Cold starts

Cold start performance is a common concern regarding the performance of **Function-as-a-Service (FaaS)**. A cold start occurs when the FaaS service receives a request to execute a function and it needs to initialize a new function instance first. This happens when there is a long period between invocations or when there are many concurrent invocations.

The first thing a new function instance must do is download the function bundle. The size of the bundle has an impact on the cold start time. Increasing the memory allocation of the function and thus the network I/O performance is the simplest way to increase the download speed. We also strive to minimize the size of the bundle. For Node.js functions, we can leverage the Webpack module bundler, which performs tree shaking to remove unused code from the bundle.

Once the download completes, the function instance can start the runtime environment. The choice of language runtime has an impact on the cold start time. Scripting languages, such as JavaScript, are the best option because they do very little at startup. It is also important to avoid heavy-weight frameworks, such as dependency injection and object-relational mapping, which perform introspection on startup. The lightweight alternative covered in the *Models and connectors* section is more than sufficient for autonomous services.

Timeouts and retries

Networks are unreliable. For example, a call from a query function to the datastore can hang for no particular reason and the next call will go straight through. This scenario is common enough that libraries, such as the aws-sdk, have retry logic built in and turned on by default. However, we need to take control of the timeout period so that the end user does not need to wait long for the retry.

The following example sets the timeout for calls to DynamoDB:

```
class Connector {
  constructor() {
    this.db = new DynamoDB.DocumentClient({
      httpOptions: { timeout: 1000 },
    });
  }

  ...

}
```

The default timeout period in Node.js is 2 minutes. This is obviously much longer than a user is willing to wait. So, we need to set the `timeout` to a more reasonable value. The value needs to be long enough to support the required queries and commands, but short enough to retry quickly.

Next, we need to set the timeout for the query and command function itself, so that it is long enough to support multiple retries. For example, the default timeout for an AWS Lambda function is 3 seconds. This provides the connector with enough time to perform at least one retry but may not be long enough for two retries.

Finally, the network performance of a function is associated with memory allocation. Lower network I/O capacity will increase the likelihood of failures and the need for retries. If a function is performing a lot of retries, then this is an indication that it needs more resources.

cache-control

The response times of BFF service queries are highly optimized. A BFF service uses a high-performance cloud-native database, which it does not share, and we specifically design the materialized views to support the needed access patterns. This provides great performance for most usage scenarios.

However, for high-volume usage scenarios, we can further improve performance and control cost, by adding `cache-control` headers and leveraging a **Content Delivery Network (CDN)**. The following example sets the `cache-control` header on a query response:

```
api.get('/things/:id', (request, response) =>
  request.namespace.models.thing.get(request.params.id)
  .then((data) => response.status(200)
    .header('cache-control', 'max-age=3')
    .json(data)));
```

This example sets the cache value to a meager 3 seconds. However, for a high-traffic resource, this has the potential to significantly reduce the cost if at least one request has a cache hit. Adding `cache-control` headers to our responses tells a browser not to repeat a request and also tells the CDN to reuse a response for other users. As a result, we reduce the load on the API gateway and the function and reduce the necessary capacity for the database, which reduces the cost for all of these resources.

The following `serverless.yml` fragment extends the latency-based routing example, from the *Leveraging multiple regions* section, to configure a BFF service with a custom CloudFront distribution:

```yaml
ApiDistribution:
  Type: AWS::CloudFront::Distribution
  Properties:
    DistributionConfig:
      Origins:
        - Id: ApiGateway
          DomainName:${opt:stage}-${self:service}.mysubsys.
example.com
            ...
      DefaultCacheBehavior:
        TargetOriginId: ApiGateway
        CachedMethods: [ HEAD, GET, OPTIONS]
        ...
ApiGlobalEndpointRecord:
  Type: AWS::Route53::RecordSet
  Properties:
    Name: ${self:service}.mysubsys.example.com.
    ...
    AliasTarget:
      DNSName:
        Fn::GetAtt: [ ApiDistribution, DomainName ]
        ...
```

First, we create a CloudFront distribution, point the origin to the multi-regional endpoint of the BFF service, and specify `CachedMethods`. Then, we configure DNS RecordSet for the distribution.

As traffic flows through it, the CloudFront distribution will use the `cache-control` header to determine which requests to cache and for how long. When there is a cache hit, then it returns the cached response. When there is a cache miss, then the latency-based routing directs the request to the closest region and the distribution caches the response. As an added benefit, CloudFront optimizes the network traffic between the edge locations and the cloud regions, which provides improved response times even when there is a cache miss.

You can find a full example in `serverless-multi-regional-plugin` here, `https://www.npmjs.com/package/serverless-multi-regional-plugin`.

Summary

In this chapter, you learned why it is important to create services that focus on user activities and how this helps teams accelerate the pace of innovation. You learned about the BFF pattern and how to combine the event sourcing and CQRS patterns to create user-facing services. And you learned how to apply the BFF pattern throughout the different phases of the data life cycle.

We dug into the details and you learned how to choose between GraphQL and REST, how to implement latency-based routing with regional health checks and failover, and you learned how to verify JWT tokens and how to secure a BFF service in depth. You also learned about important BFF resource metrics and how to optimize the cold start performance of a BFF service.

In the next chapter, we will cover the **External Service Gateway (ESG)** pattern and see how it creates an anti-corruption layer that frees teams to focus on the functionality of their system. We will look at variations of the ESG pattern and cover integration with third-party systems, legacy systems, other autonomous subsystems, and more.

7
Bridging Intersystem Gaps

In *Chapter 6, A Best Friend for the Frontend*, we covered the Backend for Frontend autonomous service pattern. These services work at the boundary of the system to support end users. They are responsible for catering to the kinds of changes driven by human actors. Now, in this chapter, we turn our attention to integrating with external systems. We will create boundary services that are responsible for catering to the kinds of changes driven by these external system actors, so that external concerns and changes do not corrupt your system.

In this chapter, we're going to cover the following main topics:

- Creating an anti-corruption layer
- Dissecting the External Service Gateway pattern
- Integrating with third-party systems
- Integrating with other subsystems
- Integrating across cloud providers

- Integrating with legacy systems
- Providing an external API and SPI
- Tackling common data challenges
- Managing shared secrets
- Addressing multi-regional differences

Creating an anti-corruption layer

In *Chapter 2, Defining Boundaries and Letting Go*, we highlighted the role that the **Single Responsibility Principle** (**SRP**) plays in helping to define a system's boundaries. Each bounded context should be responsible to one and only one actor. In other words, it is the actors who interact with a system that are the driving force behind any reason to change the system. So, we are obliged to draw boundaries around the interactions of the various actors to limit the impact of any changes they will cause.

We also identified *three autonomous service patterns* that each cater to a different type of *actor*. In this chapter, we dig into the details of the **External Service Gateway** (**ESG**) pattern. The ESG pattern works at the boundary of the system to provide an *anti-corruption layer* that encapsulates the details of interacting with other systems, such as third-party, legacy, and sister subsystems. These ESG services act as a bridge to exchange events with the external systems.

External systems are owned by a different organization. This may be another organization in your company or another company altogether. The implication is that we have little to no control over the design and architecture of these systems. Nor do we have much say over when and how they might change. This means it is in our best interest to isolate the interactions with external systems, to protect the rest of our system and allow each to change independently.

The term *anti-corruption layer* was popularized by Eric Evans in his book *Domain-Driven Design*. The Gang of Four institutionalized the *Adapter* pattern in their pivotal book *Design Patterns: Elements of Reusable Object-Oriented Software*. Robert Martin recommends an *Interface Adapter* layer in his book *Clean Architecture*, and in Alistair Cockburn's hexagonal architecture, core components expose *ports* and *adapters* glue them to the outside world. The overarching idea is to separate and decouple external concerns from internal concerns by creating an isolation layer.

The ESG pattern provides this same function, but at the macro or system level, in a system of autonomous services. As we covered in *Chapter 6, A Best Friend for the Frontend*, each autonomous service (that is, BFF, ESG, or Control) employs layers of classes within, to promote the clean, decoupled code that allows us to easily test services in isolation from external resources. But the focus here is that ESG services themselves act as an isolation or anti-corruption layer for the system as a whole, from external systems. Borrowing from the hexagonal architecture, we can think of domain events as *ports* and ESG services as *adapters*.

In *Figure 7.1*, we see a representation of a typical autonomous subsystem. The relative position of services from left to right implies the flow of events on a timeline, with upstream services to the left and downstream services to the right. Events flow in from upstream systems via ingress ESGs; the core BFF and Control services of the subsystem make their contributions and produce more events. Events flow out to downstream systems via egress ESGs. The core of the subsystem is completely decoupled from the external systems:

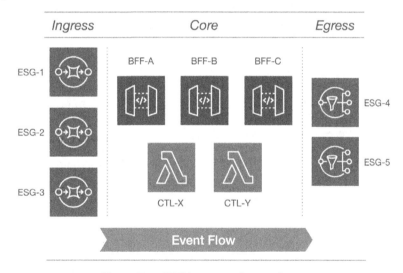

Figure 7.1 – ESG ingress and egress layers

Each ESG service is focused on adapting a single external system to the internal model of the system. Each ESG is a separately deployable autonomous service. This allows us to employ the **Liskov Substitution Principle** (**LSP**). For example, over time there may be a business reason to switch from one third-party system to another, by simply replacing one ESG with another. Or, as in the case with legacy migration and the use of the Strangler pattern, we can leverage the ESG pattern to run the old and new simultaneously and simply turn off the old when it is no longer needed, without upstream or downstream impacts.

ESG services act as a *bulkhead* as well. They protect systems from each other. For example, if an external system is experiencing an outage, then an ESG can leverage a *circuit breaker* to minimize the impact on our system. Conversely, the natural *backpressure* of event stream processing can prevent our system from overpowering a less robust external system. In either case, the volatility and/or limitations of an external system are absorbed by its corresponding ESG service, because the ESG addresses any impedance mismatch between the two systems.

Let's take a look at the anatomy of an ESG service, before we dive into various applications of the pattern.

Dissecting the External Service Gateway pattern

In *Chapter 2, Defining Boundaries and Letting Go*, we did some event storming to identify a system's domain events, human actors, and external system actors. We also divided the system into autonomous subsystems, and we treated each sister subsystem as an external system.

For each external system, we create at least one ESG service in the appropriate subsystem. We need to identify whether events will flow in from the external system, flow out to the external system, or both. We also need to determine which domain events the ESG services will consume and produce.

From here, we need to understand the options for connecting to the external system, define the semantic maps between the external and internal domain entities, establish whether we are aiming to invoke an action or elicit a reaction, implement the ingress and/or egress pipelines, and decide how to package the service.

Connectivity

How we connect to an external system is driven almost entirely by the type of external interface it provides. Does the system support a real-time interface or only a batch? Is the interface synchronous or asynchronous? What protocol does it support, REST, SOAP, JMS, AMQP, or so forth? Is the payload formatted in JSON, XML, or something else? How is the interface secured? Is it owned by a third party or is it a legacy system? Is it running on-premises or in the cloud? How can we mock the system to support isolated testing? Does the system support synthetic transactions for live testing?

All these questions, and more, are the kinds of challenges an ESG is responsible for handling and hiding from the rest of the system. Throughout this chapter, we will flesh out variations on the ESG pattern that account for many of these scenarios. We will address security topics at the end of this chapter. In *Chapter 9, Choreographing Deployment and Delivery*, we will cover techniques for testing.

Semantic transformation

After encapsulating connectivity, the primary function of an ESG is to perform the semantic transformations between the internal and external domain entity formats. All the details of connectivity may be a challenge upfront, but once they are solved, the majority of the business logic and churn in requirements will most likely be in the transformations.

As we discussed in *Chapter 2, Defining Boundaries and Letting Go*, our domain events form the system's contracts. By adapting to these contrasts, the ESG pattern enables the system to evolve as the requirements for and by the external systems change. This is the LSP at work, allowing us to substitute different ESG services as business needs change.

Sometimes the information needed to perform the semantic transformations is not readily available in the message payloads themselves. In this case, the ESG will handle enriching the data. We will cover an approach for this later in the chapter, in the *Tackling common data challenges* section.

We will also leverage the event lake to keep an audit trail of what was sent to and received from an external system. As we saw in *Chapter 4, Trusting Facts and Eventual Consistency*, the raw field in the standardized event envelope can be used to store the external payloads to ensure that there is no loss of information after any transformations.

Action versus reaction

For each ESG, it is helpful to classify whether it is intending to invoke an action or elicit a reaction. The **Inversion of Responsibility** principle is one of the key benefits of event-driven systems. It stipulates that we should defer important decisions to downstream services where they can react to upstream events. The application of this principle is clear with core BFF and Control services. However, it can be less clear in ESG services, because they provide a layer of indirection to the service that will ultimately carry out an action. A couple of examples will help make this clear.

First, an ESG for a third-party service will typically have an egress flow that invokes a specific action in the external system. Then an ingress flow receives an event from the third-party webhook that contains the results of the action. It transforms the external event into an internal domain event, so that downstream services can decide how to react to the outcome of the action. This keeps the ESG as a simple bridge.

Second, we will use the ESG pattern to connect autonomous subsystems. These services are focused on transforming between internal and external domain events and relaying them between subsystems so that the downstream subsystem can react to upstream events. This scenario includes an egress flow upstream and an ingress flow downstream. Neither flow actually invokes a business action. They simply react in order to make domain events available to the BFF or Control services that provide the business actions.

Finally, we leverage the ESG pattern to integrate different systems by synchronizing (that is, replicating) data between them. This is most evident when implementing a bi-directional integration with a legacy system. Either system can carry out a business action and the ESG layer is simply reacting to keep the two systems in sync.

This distinction becomes important when dealing with many ESG services of different flavors. Let's look at the essential elements of egress and ingress flows before covering the details of the more advanced scenarios.

Egress

An egress flow is responsible for reacting to an internal domain event and integrating it with an external system. In this basic example, the external system has the ability to receive events and we are simply forwarding the logical domain event from one system to the other. This means that we are only intending to elicit a reaction in the external system, but not necessarily a specific reaction. In this example, we will assume that the external system exposes an AWS SNS topic that it consumes from. *Figure 7.2* depicts the resources involved:

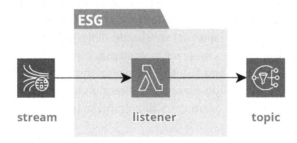

Figure 7.2 – External Service Gateway – egress

Here is sample code for the `listener` function. It implements a stream processor, such as what we covered in *Chapter 4, Trusting Facts and Eventual Consistency*:

```
export const handler = async (event) =>
  fromKinesis(event)
    .filter(onEventType)
    .map(toExternalFormat)
    .through(send())
    .through(toPromise);

const onEventType = uow => uow.event.type.match(/thing-*/);
const toExternalFormat = (uow) => ({
  ...uow,
  sendRequest: { // variable expected by the `send` util
    TopicArn: process.env.TOPIC_ARN,
    Message: JSON.stringify({
      f1: uow.event.thing.field1,
      f2: uow.event.thing.field2,
      f3: uow.event.thing.field3,
    }),
  },
});
```

The domain events of interest are available on a stream in the event hub. The `listener` function consumes from the stream and filters for the event types of interest, such as all events for the `thing` domain entity. The `toExternalFormat` step *transforms* the internal format to the external message format. The `send` step *connects* to the external system and sends the message.

All the stream processing optimizations we discussed in *Chapter 4, Trusting Facts and Eventual Consistency*, such as pipelines, backpressure, fault handling, and so forth, are excluded here for brevity.

Ingress

An ingress flow is responsible for integrating with an external system to receive external domain events and transform them into internal domain events so that our system can react as needed. In this basic example, the external system has the ability to emit events and we are simply forwarding the logical domain event from one system to the other. This means that we are only intending to elicit a reaction to the external system, but not necessarily a specific reaction. In this example, we will assume that the external system exposes an AWS SNS topic where it emits events. *Figure 7.3* depicts the resources involved:

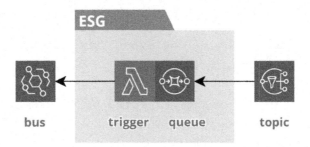

Figure 7.3 – External Service Gateway – ingress

Here is sample code for the `trigger` function. It implements a stream processor, such as what we covered in *Chapter 4, Trusting Facts and Eventual Consistency*:

```
export const handler = async (event) =>
  fromSqs(event)
    .map(toInternalFormat)
    .through(publish())
    .through(toPromise);

const toInternalFormat = (uow) => ({
  ...uow,
  event: { // variable expected by the `publish` util
    id: uow.record.messageId,
    type: `thing-${uow.record.body.action}`,
    timestamp: uow.record.SentTimestamp,
    thing: {
      field1: uow.record.body.f1,
      field2: uow.record.body.f2,
```

```
      field3: uow.record.body.f3,
    },
  },
});
```

The external system emits events on an AWS SNS topic. The ESG creates an AWS SQS queue to *connect* to the external system and receive events from the topic. The `trigger` function consumes messages from the queue. The `toInternalFormat` step *transforms* the external format to the internal event format. The `publish` step puts the internal domain event on the event hub, so that core services can react to the event.

All the stream processing optimizations we discussed in *Chapter 4, Trusting Facts and Eventual Consistency*, such as pipelines, backpressure, fault handling, and so forth, are excluded here for brevity.

Packaging

Each ESG lives in its own source code repository and cloud stack, like all autonomous services, as we covered in *Chapter 2, Defining Boundaries and Letting Go*. As a default starting point, there should be one ESG per external system that contains all the ingress and egress pipelines.

Alternatively, we can create a separate ESG for ingress and egress pipelines per external system. This is useful when the way the ESG connects to the external system is significantly different for ingress and egress.

For large and complex external systems, it can be advantageous to create multiple ESG services that group related pipelines and that change together, such as per external system capability. This approach can also be combined with the packaging by flow direction approach.

Use a service naming convention that makes it easy to recognize the purpose of the specific ESG. A good convention will alphabetically group related services in the source code tool and cloud console, such as `<external-service-name>-ingress|egress-<capability-name>-gateway`.

Separate cloud accounts

Most ESGs, such as third-party integrations, fit nicely into the functional flows of a particular autonomous subsystem. Other ESGs are specifically intended to integrate the various autonomous subsystems. Still others are best isolated in their own autonomous subsystems with their own cloud accounts.

Legacy system integrations are candidates for their own subsystems. This is particularly important when the legacy system is running on-premises. This allows all access to the on-premises network to be isolated to a controlled number of cloud accounts. It also makes it possible to simply shut down a cloud account once a legacy system is retired.

Your external interface is another candidate to isolate and treat as an autonomous subsystem in its own cloud account. This subsystem will integrate with the core subsystems, like any other subsystem, but it will expose your external domain model to the outside world, which you will have little to no control over. It will also be responsible to a single generic external actor, which you define, that represents the prototypical external system the external interface is designed to support. Therefore, it is best to create this outer layer as a bulkhead to isolate security concerns and provide for the strongest backward compatibility guarantee.

Integrating with third-party systems

One easy way to accelerate the pace of innovation is to avoid building software that you don't need to build. If a piece of functionality is not part of your core competency's value proposition, then you should not build it. More than likely it is already offered as a service by a third party.

This is akin to the serverless-first approach. We leverage a fully managed, third-party capability and defer commitment so that we can focus on building our value proposition and create knowledge about what works and what does not work. Then, once we know what capabilities are actually required, we can make an informed decision to stay with the third party, switch to another provider, or implement the functionality ourselves.

To facilitate this process, we employ the ESG pattern to decouple this decision from the core of the system. We wrap the third-party system with an ESG service that adapts the external system to the core model. Then we can simply substitute a different ESG service when we change directions. We can even run multiple implementations simultaneously for different scenarios.

Let's look at the egress flow for performing an action and the ingress flow for receiving updates about the progress of the action.

Egress – API call

Software as a Service (SaaS) products typically provide a well-documented REST API for invoking their functionality. From our Food Delivery example, this includes the likes of authorizing a payment or sending email messages and push notifications to customers.

These egress flows are responsible for reacting to an internal domain event and invoking an action on a third-party system to perform a specific business function. *Figure 7.4* depicts the resources involved:

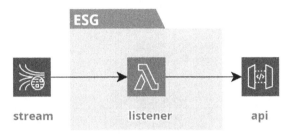

Figure 7.4 – Egress – API call

The domain events of interest are available on a **stream** in the event hub. Once again, the `listener` function is a stream processor that consumes from the stream and filters for the right event type, such as `OrderSubmitted`. It transforms the data to create the external request and invokes the action via a `REST POST`:

```
. . .
    .map(toPostRequest)
    .ratelimit(opts.number, opts.ms)
    .through(post())
. . .
```

One thing of note is that third-party APIs are typically throttled, and pricing may be based on the rate at which they are invoked. Therefore, it is recommended to add explicit backpressure with a rate-limiting feature. We covered this and other stream processing optimization techniques in *Chapter 4*, *Trusting Facts and Eventual Consistency*.

In *Chapter 4*, *Trusting Facts and Eventual Consistency*, we also covered the important role that atomic actions play in resilient systems. In this context, it means that we should not attempt to invoke an external action and then produce an internal event about the success of the action in the same unit of work. Instead, we will rely on the third-party system's webhook feature to notify us about the success of the action.

Ingress – webhook

SaaS products provide webhooks as a generic way to integrate with other systems. These allow other systems to register a callback, so that they can be notified about internal changes and progress updates. Some examples include a payment service emitting an event when a payment is completed or an email service emitting an event when a message is flagged as junk.

These ingress flows are responsible for integrating with a webhook to receive external domain events and transform them into internal domain events so that the system can react as needed. *Figure 7.5* depicts the resources involved:

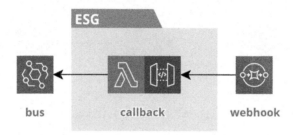

Figure 7.5 – Ingress – webhook

The third-party system emits events via its webhook feature. The ESG uses an *API gateway* to implement a **callback** endpoint that will receive external events from the **webhook**. The **callback** function transforms the external format to the internal event format and forwards the domain event to the event hub, so that core services can react to the event.

Asynchronous request response

The interactions with external systems are typically the least resilient part of a system, because they require a synchronous call to another system that you do not control. This is why it is preferable to have ESG services that are completely asynchronous and react to events from other services. This supports the majority of scenarios where a fire-and-forget flow is appropriate, such as when one user performs a step and another user performs the next step after any automated steps have successfully completed in between.

However, there are scenarios where a single user performs a step and needs a response from an external system before continuing to the next step. It is important that the user proceeds to the next step as quickly as possible, but the user shouldn't have to wait for a flaky and/or slow response. In these scenarios, we can employ an asynchronous request-response flow to make the user experience more resilient and responsive. *Figure 7.6* depicts the resources involved:

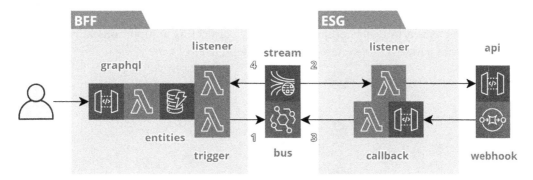

Figure 7.6 – Async request response

The BFF's `graphql` function provides a mutation to initiate the request. It stores a request object in the `entities` datastore. The `trigger` function publishes a request event, such as `<entity>-<action>-requested`.

The ESG's `listener` function consumes the `request` event and makes the external API call. The external system's **webhook** feature invokes the `callback` with the results of the action. The `callback` function publishes a response event, such as `<entity>-<action>-completed`.

The BFF's `listener` function consumes the response event and updates the `request` object in the `entities` store. Meanwhile, the frontend polls the BFF's `graphql` function to query for the status of the request. The polling implements an exponential backoff and results in an error after several attempts. If the response arrives later, then a fresh query will return the results, which provides for more resilience. Alternatively, a live update approach can be used, such as was presented in *Chapter 3, Taming the Presentation Tier*.

Third-party systems are the most obvious kind of external system. However, as a system grows larger, it will need to be divided into multiple related systems. Next, we will look at how to integrate these related pieces into a unified whole.

Integrating with other subsystems

For any large system, it is necessary to divide the system into a set of manageable subsystems. In *Chapter 2, Defining Boundaries and Letting Go*, we discussed the concept of autonomous subsystems. Like autonomous services, these subsystems employ bulkheads to protect themselves from each other. Each autonomous subsystem is fortified in its own cloud account, has its own event hub, and only exposes a set of *external domain events* for inter-subsystem communication.

We can then create arbitrarily complex systems by connecting autonomous subsystems in a simple fractal pattern. This system topology is depicted in *Figure 7.7*:

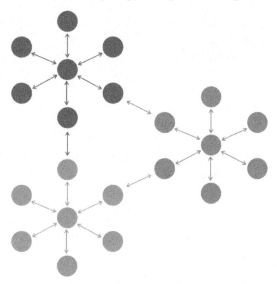

Figure 7.7 – Autonomous subsystem topology

The nodes in the diagram that are connected across the subsystems represent the *egress* and *ingress* ESG services. In this section, we will cover the tactical aspects of transforming between internal and external domain events and connecting the subsystems across accounts.

Egress – upstream subsystem

Upstream subsystems make a set of external domain events available and route them to downstream subsystems. *Figure 7.8* depicts the inter-subsystem egress flow and the resources involved:

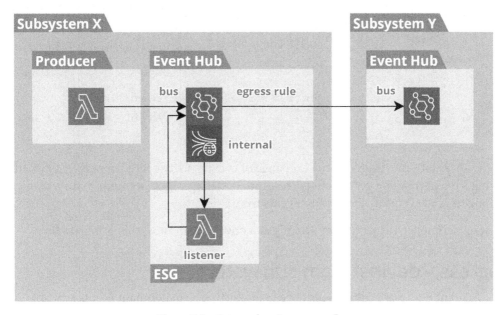

Figure 7.8 – Inter-subsystem egress flow

The autonomous services within a subsystem exchange internal domain events. The backward compatibility of these event types is only guaranteed within the subsystem. The `Producer` services publish internal domain events to the **bus** as usual and remain completely decoupled from downstream subsystems.

Each subsystem produces a set of external domain events that contain the information they are willing to share and support. This hides the internal dirty laundry of a subsystem and provides stronger backward compatibility guarantees to downstream subsystems. One or more `ESG` services consume the internal domain events and *transform* them into external domain events. Then these events are published to the **bus** as well.

From here, the fully managed event bus service, such as AWS EventBridge, is responsible for forwarding events from the **bus** in one account to the **bus** in another account. One or more **egress rules** are defined to relay the external domain events to downstream event hubs.

Here is an example of an egress rule for AWS EventBridge that routes all external domain events to one or more downstream subsystems. The ESG services set the `source` field to `external` to simplify the routing rules. We add a target for each downstream **bus** that will receive the upstream subsystem's events:

```
EgressEventRule:
  Type: AWS::Events::Rule
  Properties:
```

```
EventPattern:
  source: ['external' ]
Targets:
  - Id: SubsystemY
    Arn: arn:aws:events:*:123456789012:event-bus/
                                      event-hub-bus

...
```

Both subsystems must agree to the exchange of events. A trust agreement is established by configuring permission policies in both accounts stating which accounts a subsystem is willing to send events to and receive events from.

Now let's complete the picture by looking at a downstream subsystem's ingress flow.

Ingress – downstream subsystem

At this point, upstream subsystems have made their external domain events available and routed them to downstream subsystems. Next, each downstream subsystem makes the events of interest available to its own services. *Figure 7.9* depicts the inter-subsystem ingress flow and the resources involved:

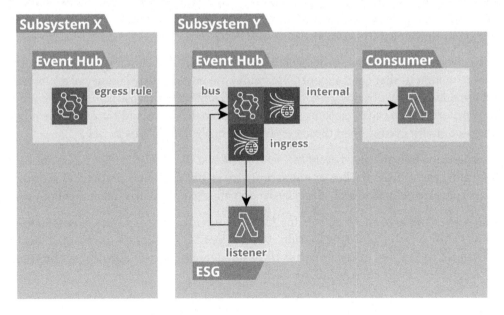

Figure 7.9 – Inter-subsystem ingress flow

The **bus** of a downstream event hub receives external domain events from an upstream subsystem and routes the events to an **ingress** stream to isolate them from internal domain event flows. One or more **ESG** services consume the external domain events and transform them into internal domain events. Then the internal domain events are published to the **bus** and routed to the **internal** streams for further processing, as usual, by **Consumer** services.

Note that the **ingress** stream is optional. If the volume is low, then it may not be necessary. You can start without it and add it as needed. It can also be excluded in lower environments to control cost.

This variation of the ESG pattern allows subsystems to evolve independently. Only the ESG logic needs to be modified when the definition of an internal or external domain event changes. The Robustness principle is followed when a change is necessary, so that both sides do not have to change at the exact same time. This anti-corruption layer is the primary benefit of this ESG pattern scenario. We will cover the details of applying the Robustness principle in *Chapter 9, Choreographing Deployment and Delivery*.

Implementing subsystems on the same cloud provider allows leveraging the features of common services. Next, we will look at integrating subsystems that are deployed on different cloud providers.

Integrating across cloud providers

Polycloud is the notion that we should use the right cloud provider for the job on a service-by-service basis. This is similar to the concepts of *polyglot programming* and *polyglot persistence*. We will discuss the business value supporting this approach in *Chapter 10, Don't Delay, Start Experimenting*. In this section, we will cover the tactical aspect of connecting a system that operates across cloud providers.

Fundamentally, polycloud is employed at the service level, but from a practical standpoint, it operates at the subsystem level. For example, if you only have a single service that you want to run on a different cloud provider, then we can think of it as a subsystem consisting of a single service. However, in reality there would most likely be several related services that all benefit from running on the alternate cloud provider and others that are just better off running as closely as possible to related services.

This subsystem point of view actually makes integrating across cloud providers much easier, because it builds on the inter-subsystem integration approach that is used between all autonomous subsystems. The subsystem ingress flow we just covered remains completely unchanged, while the subsystem egress flow just needs a small tweak. An example will make this clear.

In this example, subsystem **X** runs on cloud provider **X** and subsystem **Y** runs on cloud provider **Y**. By definition, each of these subsystems benefits from the bulkheads of not only separate cloud accounts but also separate cloud providers. We will also follow the same bulkhead approach of exchanging external domain events between these subsystems:

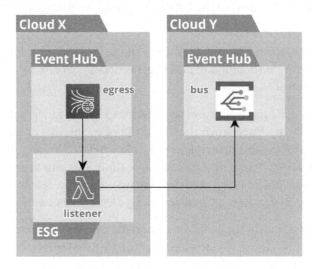

Figure 7.10 – Polycloud egress

As we previously covered, subsystem **X** will have egress ESGs that are responsible for transforming internal domain events into external domain events. From here, we cannot rely on out-of-the-box cloud service features to route events between cloud providers. For example, if subsystem **X** is using AWS EventBridge as its event bus and subsystem **Y** is using Azure Event Grid or GCP Pub/Sub, then we need to implement a forwarding mechanism.

To accomplish this, we simply add an additional ESG to bridge the gap. The `listener` function of this ESG consumes external domain events from an `egress` stream and sends them to subsystem **Y**. It batches up events and invokes the API provided by the bus of the downstream cloud provider. The *ingress flow* in the target subsystem remains the same with ESGs dedicated to transforming the external domain events into internal domain events.

Integrating subsystems and third-party systems is challenging because the systems have different owners. Legacy systems present additional challenges, because they are often not designed to support integration. Next, we will look at techniques to overcome these hurdles.

Integrating with legacy systems

Delivering new business value at a faster pace is the major goal of digital transformation. Achieving this goal usually involves migrating off of existing (that is, legacy) systems. This migration process does not happen overnight. Therefore, it is crucial that we do not put the existing systems at risk. They need to continue delivering business value until they are retired.

To provide this continuity of business, we follow an event-first migration approach that iteratively adds new business value and incrementally upgrades existing features, until the legacy systems are no longer needed. This is often called the Strangler pattern. We will discuss the business value supporting this approach in *Chapter 10, Don't Delay, Start Experimenting*. In this section, we will cover the tactical aspects of integrating with a legacy system.

There are two main objectives of this approach:

- We do not want to modify the existing systems, if at all possible. This is consistent with the **Open-Closed principle**. Any change puts an existing system at risk, so we will employ the least invasive alternatives.

- We want to simply turn the existing systems off when they are no longer needed, with zero downtime and zero modifications to the new system. This is consistent with the **LSP**. In essence, we want to choreograph a smooth evolution from the old to the new.

We effectively need to turn legacy systems into autonomous services by wrapping them with the ability to produce and consume domain events. A legacy system will exchange events with the new system so that both can react to each other, maintain their own state (that is, data), and stay synchronized. This enables users to use the old and the new concurrently. We can incrementally transition features from old to new and easily fall back to the old when we miss the mark.

At its core, this is the time-honored approach of **Enterprise Application Integration (EAI)** that we discussed in *Chapter 1, Architecting for Innovation*. This approach is the heart of our evolutionary architecture, but it is most evident when integrating with legacy systems.

In this section, we will enumerate a set of common legacy integration scenarios. The number of potential scenarios may seem limitless, bounded only by the number of legacy systems. But in all cases, we are integrating the legacy system into the event hub, so that it can act as another spoke in the overall system.

Ingress – Change Data Capture

Many legacy systems do not have a mechanism that emits events to notify the outside world when its state has changed. Systems that do have such a mechanism may not emit the right level of detail. Fortunately, there is a non-invasive way to add this capability to many systems.

Change Data Capture (CDC) is an approach that leverages a database's *transaction log* to identify when data has changed, so that the changes can be captured and shared with other systems. CDC tools are non-invasive, because they only need the ability to read the transaction log. Every insert, update, and delete is recorded in the transaction log. A database can use a transaction log to completely replicate its state. This means that CDC can provide all the detail needed to synchronize the legacy system to the new system. *Figure 7.11* depicts the resources involved:

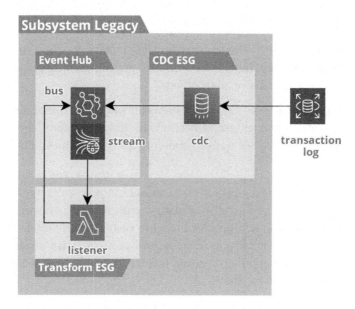

Figure 7.11 – Ingress – CDC

First, we are isolating access to the legacy database within its own autonomous subsystem and cloud account. Next, a CDC tool, such as AWS's fully managed **Database Migration Service** (DMS), is granted access to the legacy database's transaction log. The CDC tool publishes an event to the event hub for every insert, update, and delete performed on all tables of interest. These internal events contain the raw details about the individual statements that changed the data.

One or more ESG services are responsible for transforming the database events into the external domain events that will be consumed by the new systems. To create the external domain events, an ESG will likely need to aggregate the contents of several low-level database events. We will cover this enrichment process in the *Tackling common data challenges* section later in this chapter. From here, the external domain events are routed to downstream subsystems following the approach discussed previously for integrating autonomous subsystems.

Egress – Direct SQL

Many legacy systems do not have an external interface for invoking business logic. In these systems, the logic to update the database is usually coupled with the presentation logic. They often rely on **Extract, Transform, and Load** (**ETL**) processes for periodically ingesting external data. In this scenario, we can use Direct SQL to create a real-time integration. *Figure 7.12* depicts the resources involved:

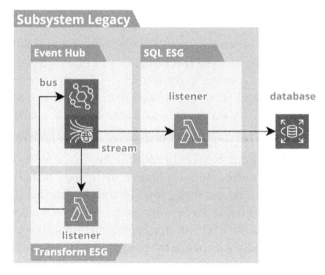

Figure 7.12 – Egress – Direct SQL

Again, we are isolating access to the legacy database within its own autonomous subsystem and cloud account. This egress flow would be part of the same subsystem that contains the CDC ingress flow and would share the same access to the legacy database. External domain events from upstream subsystems are routed to this subsystem following the approach discussed previously for integrating autonomous subsystems.

One or more ESG services are responsible for transforming the external domain events into internal domain events that contain one or more SQL statements. These events form an audit trail in the event lake of the changes made to the legacy database. The SQL ESG is responsible for executing the SQL statements in a transaction against the legacy database.

Egress – circuit breaker

Autonomous services are designed to avoid the need for the Circuit Breaker pattern. This is accomplished by eliminating all inter-service synchronous communication, leveraging fully managed, highly available, serverless resources, and creating inbound and outbound bulkheads. We have covered this in detail in *Chapter 4, Trusting Facts and Eventual Consistency*, and *Chapter 5, Turning the Cloud into the Database*.

Unfortunately, the Circuit Breaker pattern may not be avoidable when integrating with external systems. Egress flows typically require synchronous calls to the external system and a circuit breaker may be necessary if the external system is not reliable. In this case, the ESG encapsulates these details and accommodates for the impedance mismatch.

A third-party SaaS system is hopefully reliable enough and you may only need backpressure and rate-limiting to avoid throttling. On the other hand, legacy systems are frequently less reliable and take longer to recover when they experience a failure. In this case, we need to ensure that an ESG does not exacerbate the problem by continuing to overload the external system. We also want to avoid the increase in cost that results from the stream processor function repeatedly waiting for the calls to timeout and retry.

The solution is to include a circuit breaker in the ESG connector logic. The state machine diagram in *Figure 7.13* depicts the approach. The circuit breaker is in the `closed` state when the external system is operating properly, and the external calls are mostly successful. When the calls reach `failure-threshold`, then the circuit breaker transitions to the `open` state. The ESG will stop calling the external system for a period of time to give the external system a chance to recover. After the `timeout` period, the circuit breaker transitions to the `half-open` state. In this state, the ESG will try the next call to test whether the external system has recovered. If the call is successful, then the circuit breaker transitions to the `closed` state, and if it is a failure, then it transitions back to the `open` state and waits again before attempting another test:

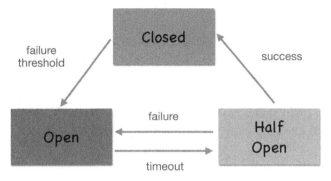

Figure 7.13 – Circuit breaker state machine

Next, we need to determine whether to maintain the state of the circuit breaker in memory, a datastore, or both. *Figure 7.14* depicts the resources involved:

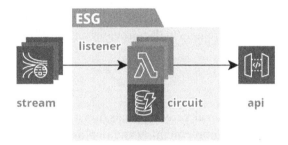

Figure 7.14 – Egress – circuit breaker

The ESG's stream processor is implemented as a `listener` function, so there is no guarantee that the next batch of events pulled from the stream will invoke the same function instance and memory space. In practice, these function instances may live upward of a few hours, so memory may be sufficient. However, if the stream has multiple shards, then there will be multiple function instances, each maintaining its own circuit breaker state. Thus, the most accurate approach is to store the circuit state in a database, such as AWS DynamoDB, and leverage memory as an optimization.

Finally, we need to decide how the ESG will handle events when the circuit breaker is in the `open` state. The simplest approach is to just ignore these events, but this is usually not functionally accurate. We can produce `fault` events, as we discussed in *Chapter 4, Trusting Facts and Eventual Consistency*, but this will require us to manually resubmit these faults after the target recovers. Or, preferably, we can retry the batch from the first failure until the target recovers. A fourth approach is applicable when another service is expecting a timely response event. The ESG would produce an informative response event and delegate the decision to the other service.

Ingress – relay

The security of the connections between your cloud accounts and your on-premises network is a natural concern. The attack surface may seem limitless due to the wide variety of legacy architectures. One consideration is whether to open connections from the cloud to on-premises or from on-premises to the cloud. This **ingress relay** approach gives resources on-premises access to cloud resources, but not the other way around. This eliminates the need for complexities, such as on-premises domain name resolution.

Relay services are implemented and deployed on-premises. These services should comply with the guidelines that are already established for your on-premises services. However, lead times for on-premises resources can be protracted. Therefore, we want to limit the functionality that these relays perform and let them focus on the technical requirements for connecting between on-premises resources and cloud resources. Therefore, relays should do as little transformation as possible. This minimizes the possibility of failure on the legacy side. It allows the transformation rules to be changed more readily on the cloud side as the requirements change. It also provides an audit trail of the raw external messages in the event lake.

Messages

In this scenario, the legacy system already supports messaging, such as JMS, and has a well-understood approach for implementing and deploying message processors on-premises. One or more new processors are created to consume from the on-premises topics of interest. A native queue is allocated on-premises for each topic and the processors relay the messages to cloud-native queues, such as SQS:

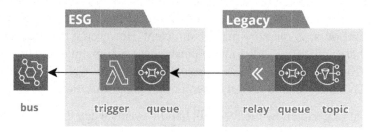

Figure 7.15 – Ingress – messaging relay

On the cloud side, an ESG is responsible for handling the external messages. A `trigger` function consumes from the serverless queue, transforms the external messages into internal domain events, and publishes them to the event hub's bus.

Files

This scenario is a variation on the ingress message flow that supports moving files from on-premises to the cloud. A message processor on the legacy side listens to a queue for notifications about new files. The processor pulls the file from the filesystem on-premises and pushes the file to object storage in the cloud, such as an S3 bucket:

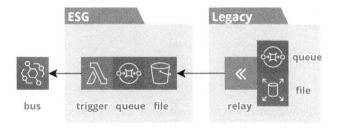

Figure 7.16 – Ingress – file relay

On the cloud side, an ESG is responsible for mediating access to files downstream. A `trigger` function consumes from the serverless queue that contains notifications of new files in the object store. For example, an S3 bucket can be configured to forward triggers to SQS for durable messaging. The `trigger` function publishes an internal domain event with important metadata about the contents of the file and a URL to the file. Downstream services use the URL to pull the file and store it according to their needs, freeing the ESG to purge files as it sees fit. For example, task-oriented services can consume the file for specific activities and a records management service can handle archiving regulations.

Egress – relay

The egress relay approach addresses the same concerns as the ingress relay, just in the opposite direction. Again, cloud resources have no knowledge of the on-premises network and resources. Relay services running on-premises access cloud resources, pull available data, and forward it on to the legacy systems.

Messages

In this scenario, the legacy system already supports messaging, such as JMS. The ESG `listener` function consumes internal domain events of interest, transforms them into the external format, and sends them to a serverless queue, such as SQS. Legacy systems usually assume that messages are arriving in order, in which case the serverless queue should support FIFO:

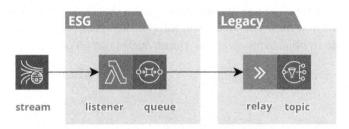

Figure 7.17 – Egress – messaging relay

One or more message processors are implemented and deployed on-premises to consume from the serverless queues and relay the messages to the internal topics. We will cover multi-regional consideration in the final section of the chapter, *Addressing multi-regional differences.*

Files

This scenario is a variation on the egress message flow that supports moving files from the cloud to on-premises. The ESG `listener` function consumes internal domain events of interest that contain a URL to files that were produced upstream. The function retrieves the file and puts it in its own object storage, such as an S3 bucket. This minimizes race conditions if the upstream service archives the file. The bucket triggers a message to a serverless queue, such as S3 to SQS:

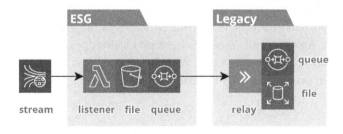

Figure 7.18 – Egress – file relay

A message processor on the legacy side listens to the serverless queue for notifications about new files. The processor pulls the file from the cloud object storage and pushes it to the filesystem on-premises. Finally, the processor notifies the legacy system of the new file by sending a message to an internal queue. We will cover multi-regional consideration at the end in the *Addressing multi-regional differences* section.

We have just covered a variety of scenarios for integrating with legacy systems, but it is far from an exhaustive list. Another approach that can be used to integrate with legacy systems, sister systems, and external systems in particular is the creation of an external interface. We will cover these scenarios next.

Providing an external API and SPI

Non-invasive integration is one of the goals of the ESG pattern. This is important when you do not have control of the other systems. But it means that you are taking on the responsibility of implementing the integrations that adapt the other systems to your system. This is only manageable for a limited number of systems.

If you are implementing your own SaaS product, then the number of external systems that want to integrate with your system can be limitless. In this case, the only manageable solution is to provide your own *external interface* and make the external systems responsible for integrating with your system.

External interfaces expose your external domain model to the outside world. They act as a façade to hide the inner workings and provide strong backward compatibility guarantees. They simplify the process of integrating with your system and enable external systems to take on the responsibility for *connecting* to your system and *transforming* between their external model and your external model.

An external interface includes an **Application Programming Interface** (**API**), so that other systems can call your system, and a **Service Provider Interface** (**SPI**), so that your system can notify other systems about important events. They support asynchronous ingress and egress flows to receive and emit events and synchronous flows to perform actions and queries. A developer portal may also be provided so that organizations can register to use the external interface.

There are two types of ingress APIs that we will cover in this section. Most SaaS systems only provide a more traditional synchronous ingress API, but we will also cover an asynchronous ingress API that supports an event-first approach. We will then look at two types of egress interfaces: a webhook's push events to external systems and queries allowing external systems to pull desired data.

Ingress – event

This ingress interface is essentially the inverse of a webhook. It allows external systems to notify your system about their state changes. In other words, they have already performed an action and they want to give your system an opportunity to react. Following our Food Delivery example, when a restaurant updates its menu, then it will need to notify all its food delivery partners. *Figure 7.19* depicts the resources involved:

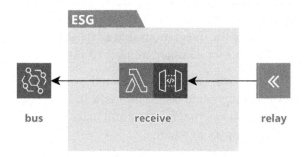

Figure 7.19 – External API – ingress – event

The ESG provides a RESTful endpoint to **receive** events from external systems. The interface defines an explicit set of external domain events that it accepts. To improve throughput, the interface may support receiving events in batches. Each external system implements its own egress ESG service that will transform its external domain events to your external domain events and **relay** them to your endpoint.

The **receive** function validates the incoming events and forwards them to the event hub's **bus**. From here the ESG variation for integrating with other subsystems will forward the events downstream to elicit reactions from other subsystems.

Ingress – command

This ingress interface is the flip side of the third-party egress integration. It allows external systems to submit a request for your system to perform an action on its behalf. Following our Food Delivery example, this interface may allow another system to request a driver. *Figure 7.20* depicts the resources involved:

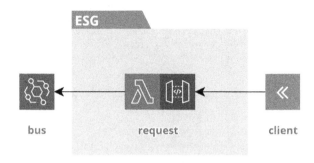

Figure 7.20 – External API – ingress – command

The ESG provides a RESTful endpoint so that an external system can submit a **request** for a specific command to perform an action. Each external system implements its own egress ESG service that will transform its internal domain entities to your external domain entities and act as a **client** to call your endpoint.

The actual details regarding how to perform the requested command are not the responsibility of this ingress ESG. The request function validates the incoming request and publishes an event that the request was submitted. From here, the ESG variation for integrating with other subsystems will forward the event to a downstream subsystem, so that a downstream service can perform the actual work.

The act of receiving the request and producing the event is an atomic transaction with a low likelihood of failure and the event is an audit trail of receiving the request. The external system can trust that the request will be fulfilled and it can receive status events through the webhook ESG, which we will cover next.

Egress – webhook

This egress interface allows external systems to register for notifications about state changes in your system. In other words, your system has already performed an action and the external system wants the opportunity to react. Following our Food Delivery example, when an order has been submitted, the restaurant needs to be notified so that it can start preparing the food. *Figure 7.21* depicts the resources involved:

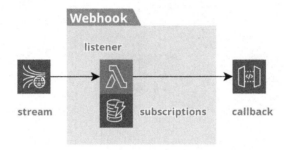

Figure 7.21 – External API – egress – webhook

The external system provides a RESTful endpoint that implements a **callback** to receive your external domain events, such as what we covered in the *Integrating with third-party systems* section. A developer will register a **callback** endpoint using your developer's portal, which would be implemented using the BFF pattern as we covered in *Chapter 6, A Best Friend for the Frontend*. The BFF will emit events for these registrations. The ESG's `listener` function will consume these registration events and cache the **subscriptions** in a datastore.

The `listener` function will also consume external domain events and look up registered subscriptions. For each subscription, the `listener` will invoke the registered **callback** endpoint with the external domain event. For example, restaurants would subscribe to `OrderSubmitted` events. When an `OrderSubmitted` event is received the `listener` looks up **subscriptions** for the restaurant specified in the order and passes the event to the callback URL registered for the `OrderSubmitted` event.

Egress – query

This egress interface allows external systems to pull data from your system on demand. Following our Food Delivery example, third-party systems might want read access to the restaurants and their menus. *Figure 7.22* depicts the resources involved:

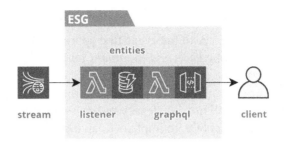

Figure 7.22 – External API – egress – query

The listener function consumes external domain events and caches the data in the entities table. A graphql or RESTful interface is provided to allow external clients to query for data. In this case, graphql is preferred because its client-driven nature will make it easier to provide backward compatibility to a large set of external systems, as we discussed in *Chapter 6, A Best Friend for the Frontend*.

One thing you may have noticed is that this API looks very much like a BFF service. In essence, it is a generic BFF that is designed to support many external frontends. It employs the CQRS pattern to cache data, specifically allocates capacity for external systems, and creates a bulkhead to the rest of the system. If the interface was to support mutations, then it would look like a full BFF with a trigger function as well.

But a distinction is made here, because it breaks the BFF pattern of the frontend and backend being owned by the same team. This distinction is important because of the impact it has on the pace of innovation. This external interface is intended to change slowly and provide a strong guarantee of backward compatibility. It is included here for completeness, but the event-first approach of using webhooks is recommended.

Up to this point, we have covered a variety of scenarios for integrating with external systems. Next, we change gears a little and cover some cross-cutting concerns related to common data challenges and securing secrets and address multi-regional differences.

Tackling common data challenges

Let's look at some common considerations that are applicable across many of the ESG scenarios we covered throughout this chapter, such as idempotence, data enrichment, latching, and resynchronizing slow data.

Idempotence

Idempotence is an important piece of the event-first approach. We cover different approaches in *Chapter 4, Trusting Facts and Eventual Consistency*, and *Chapter 5, Turning the Cloud into the Database*. The external systems that ESGs integrate with may or may not support idempotence. For example, a third-party SaaS product most likely will support it, but a legacy system probably will not. The legacy system's API will dictate which approach can be used, such as using Direct SQL to implement an inverse OpLock.

If the external system does not provide idempotence, then it can be implemented in the ESG with a micro event store. *Figure 7.23* depicts the resources involved:

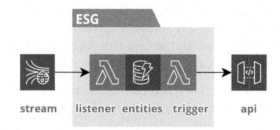

Figure 7.23 – Egress – idempotence

For an egress flow, the `listener` function inserts an event in the `events` store. The first time an event is stored, the `trigger` function will be invoked and perform the logic needed to integrate with the external system. If the `listener` receives an event again, then the `trigger` will not be invoked.

It may be necessary to provide idempotence on the ingress flow of your external interface as well. *Figure 7.24* depicts the resources involved:

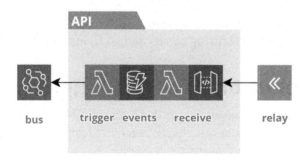

Figure 7.24 – Ingress – idempotence

For an ingress flow, the `receive` function stores the incoming events in the `events` store and the `trigger` function is invoked for each unique event. To support idempotence, the external system must provide a deterministic event ID; otherwise, an event that is logically a duplicate will be treated as unique when the ID changes.

Enriching data

An individual event may not contain all the information needed to produce an external domain event or make a call to an external system. For example, the ingress CDC flow produces internal events at the granularity of individual tables that may only contain foreign keys to related entities. In this case, the ESG needs to enrich the data before proceeding. The ESG can accumulate the related data by consuming more events and caching the needed information. *Figure 7.25* depicts the resources involved:

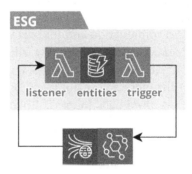

Figure 7.25 – Data enrichment

In this example, a specific ESG is responsible for producing external domain events for one or more aggregate domains. The `listener` function consumes events from all the tables that make up the aggregate domain and accumulates the data in an `entities` table following the single table pattern that we covered in *Chapter 5, Turning the Cloud into the Database*. The `trigger` function is invoked when data is added. It retrieves all the related data and will produce an external domain event once all the needed data is present.

For example, in a typical relational model, for something such as a purchase order, there will be reference data for products and the customer, a master record for the order that references the customer, and then a record for each line item that references the master order record and a product record. The reference data will usually arrive first (possibly long before), next the master record arrives, followed by each line item. An `OrderItemAdded` external domain event can be produced for each line item as it arrives, so long as the master record and reference data are available. If the events arrive out of order, such as if the master record arrives after some line items, then the events for those line items can be produced once the master record arrives.

Latching and cross-referencing

Latching is an approach for controlling infinite loops in a situation where we have bi-directional integration. This situation is very normal in an evolutionary architecture, because we may have multiple versions of functionally running concurrently from time to time as we upgrade a capability. We first covered this concept in *Chapter 5, Turning the Cloud into the Database*, where we discussed building it into our systems as a first-class capability so that we are ready to evolve.

When we are migrating from a legacy system, we will certainly have bi-directional integration. But it is unlikely that the legacy system will have a latching feature, so we will need to add it non-invasively. We can accomplish this by storing *cross-reference* and *latching* information in an `entities` table following the single table pattern.

In this table, we store a cross-reference between the internal and external identifiers of the entity. For example, the partition key of a DynamoDB table would contain the internal `namespace|type|id` combination and the sort key would contain the external `namespace|type|id` combination. The row will also contain a `latched` field. The egress flow will set `latched` to `closed` when it sends updates to the legacy system. The update will trigger the ingress flow, but it will see that `latched` is `closed`, so it will short-circuit and set `latched` back to `open`. Then, when a user performs an update in the legacy system, the ingress flow will not short-circuit and will publish an external domain event.

Slow data resync

We touched on the concept of fast versus slow data before, in *Chapter 5, Turning the Cloud into the Database*. Fast data is transactional data that produces events continuously; whereas slow data is reference data that is essentially static and produces data infrequently. This means that the events for slow data are spread out through the event lake, which makes it more tedious to replay those events.

As discussed previously, we can solve this problem by periodically publishing resynchronization events about the current state of the slow entities. This allows downstream services to ensure they are up to data and also records these events in the event lake, so they are easily included during a replay. We can also think of this as similar to creating a *snapshot* in *event sourcing*.

During a migration, the slow data will typically live in the legacy systems. After a migration, much of this data will typically live in an upstream subsystem, following the data life cycle approach for dividing up subsystems, as we discussed in *Chapter 2, Defining Boundaries and Letting Go*. In either of these cases, it may be beneficial to build a resynchronization capability into an ingress ESG, so that your team does not have to rely on coordinating with an upstream team to initiate a resynchronization in an emergency situation. *Figure 7.26* depicts the resources involved:

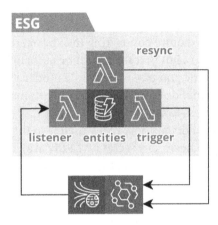

Figure 7.26 – Ingress slow data resync

The `listener` function of the ingress ESG consumes external domain events, transforms them into the internal format, and stores them in the entities table following the *single table pattern*. The `trigger` function produces internal domain events when an entity changes. Note that this provides a layer of idempotence, in the case that an upstream system publishes the same event multiple times or if it performs a resynchronization itself.

The `resync` function scans the `entities` tables and produces internal domain events, such as `thing-resync`, for all the entities. This includes deleted entities as well, with a `deleted` flag, following the *soft delete* approach covered in *Chapter 5, Turning the Cloud into the Database*. This allows downstream services to bring themselves up to date if they have become out of sync.

One of the major challenges of integrating with external systems is handling the differences in security protocols. Many legacy systems have proprietary security systems, while modern SaaS systems follow modern protocols and others use legacy standards. These are precisely the kinds of details that the ESG pattern is designed to encapsulate and hide from the rest of the system. Let's cover how to efficiently manage this next.

Managing shared secrets

We have already touched on security topics, such as isolating legacy systems and external interfaces in their own cloud accounts and having on-premises components pull data from the cloud instead of granting the cloud access to on-premises. These techniques help control the attack surface that exists at the interactions between disparate systems. In this section, we will address shared secrets such as passwords, access keys, and API keys.

Securing secrets

The various egress scenarios require connecting to external resources. These interactions are secured in transit with SSL, but first they must be authenticated. Legacy systems will most likely require a username and password, while modern systems typically require some sort of long-lived token. For example, a SaaS system may use API keys and a cloud provider may require an access token. In reality, these are all semantically the same; they are all secrets. The syntactical details only really matter to the external system. What matters to an ESG is that the necessary secret is readily available and that it remains a secret.

It is important to note that we are not authenticating users in these scenarios; we are authenticating systems. We discussed end user authentication in *Chapter 3, Taming the Presentation Tier*, and *Chapter 6, A Best Friend for the Frontend*. In the BFF pattern, an end user is authenticated at the beginning of a session and the token they receive is short-lived. In the ESG pattern, the token is long-lived and periodically rotated. Of course, a legacy system username and password blurs this line, but we can think of these as system users.

The ESG pattern encapsulates the details of interacting with secrets. A secret must be encrypted at rest and the ESG service should have least privilege access to the secret. To accomplish these requirements, a secret should be stored using a fully managed cloud service, such as AWS Secrets Manager. The ESG function will retrieve the secret, cache it in memory, and use it when connecting to the external system. The actual value of the secret must never be logged.

Secrets are long-lived, but they should not be perpetual. It is best to rotate them periodically. A cloud service, such as AWS Secrets Manager, will provide a rotation feature with scheduling and the ability to implement custom code that calls the external system to create a new secret. A typical rotation algorithm might add a new secret every 90 days, disable the previous secret several days later, and delete it several days after that. This allows in-flight transactions to continue to work and supports rolling back to the previous secret if need be.

Using API keys

The external interface and third-party webhook scenarios involve exposing endpoints on the public internet. In *Chapter 6, A Best Friend for the Frontend*, we covered the details of how this is accomplished using cloud services, such as AWS API Gateway and AWS CloudFront. In the BFF pattern, these endpoints are secured with an *OIDC JWT* that represents an end user's authenticated session. For these ESG scenarios, we use an API key to identify the specific external system making the call, not the end user.

An API key grants an external system access to a specific interface. Therefore, it is best to limit the features exposed by each interface to ensure that an external system has the least privileges necessary. The developer's portal of a SaaS product should provide the ability to request and revoke a key for each API. An API Gateway service should provide the capability to define usage policies that protect interfaces by throttling access with rate limits and upper limits per API key. Tiered usage policies may also be applicable, such that freemium accounts have lower thresholds and so forth.

It is important to keep in mind that API keys are long-lived bearer tokens. If they are stolen, they can be used to access resources until they are revoked. Therefore, these secrets must be secured as we discussed previously. They should also be rotated, so your external interface should provide this capability.

We have covered a lot of ground in this chapter. Let's turn our attention to one last topic on the implications of different multi-regional scenarios.

Addressing multi-regional differences

ESG services are deployed to multiple active-active regions just like other autonomous services, but with one major difference. ESGs interact with external systems that may have very different architectures with different regional approaches. Addressing the differences is a multi-dimensional problem that can make your head spin as you consider the challenges from all angles:

- There is the perspective from your system and from the external system's.
- Whether the flow is egress or ingress.
- Are you using a push or pull technique?
- Is the external system in the cloud or on-premises?
- Is it active-active or active-passive?
- Does it perform regional routing or will you have to perform routing on the client side?

Following the happy path, a logical transaction starts with a user of your system being routed to the closest healthy region. From that point on, the chain of events and reactions happens in that region and data replicates to the other regions. When we reach an ESG, it should invoke the closest healthy instance of the external system and ideally, this is transparent to the ESG. In the opposite direction, logical transactions from the external systems flowing into your system should behave similarly.

In the ideal failure scenario, new logical transactions are no longer routed to the unhealthy region and all those that are already in flight are drained from the streams and processed with minimal delay. In a system that is designed for eventual consistency, this is just a case of protracted eventual consistency. Sooner or later the system will become consistent. In the meantime, the end user has enough visual clues to understand the situation, as we covered in *Chapter 3*, *Taming the Presentation Tier*.

These ideal scenarios become less so when an external system does not transparently route requests to the closest healthy instance. Once again, the purpose of the ESG pattern is to encapsulate and hide these details. The best way to look at these differences is to understand what happens during a regional failure by flow direction, across the various scenario categories.

Egress routing and failover

In *Chapter 6*, *A Best Friend for the Frontend*, we covered the concepts of regional health checks, latency-based routing, and failover, and we leveraged services such as AWS Route 53 to perform most of the heavy lifting for us. In the best case, an external system will have similar support and free an ESG from these responsibilities.

Third-party SaaS systems will typically handle routing and failover for you. However, you should still understand the details of their approaches. For example, if an external system is active-passive, then that means that some of your regional users will experience more latency than others. If the external system uses the same cloud provider as you, then it may be susceptible to the same regional disruptions.

Most legacy systems, particularly those running on-premises, only support active-passive deployments. Worse yet, the failover process may be extremely protracted. In this case, the Circuit Breaker pattern we discussed earlier may be your only recourse. During the failover period, the circuit would stay open until the passive site is brought online and the DNS routing is switched over.

A legacy system may have multiple active sites, but it delegates routing and failover to the client. In this case, the Circuit Breaker pattern can be extended by adding an ordered list of endpoints. The client would try each endpoint before opening the circuit. Alternatively, the client may give each endpoint its own circuit and only move down the list once the preceding circuits have been opened. Another variation assumes clients will invoke the endpoints in a *round-robin fashion* to balance the load and allow failover. Finally, if the external system provides a health check, then the circuits can be opened and closed proactively.

The legacy egress relay scenario turns the routing equation on its head, because components running on-premises are pulling from queues in multiple cloud regions. In the case of a cloud region disruption, it is important that the relays continue to drain the queues in the unhealthy region and resume polling those queues once the region is healthy again. In the case of an on-premises data center failure, the passive center can resume pulling messages when it comes online. If the data centers are active-active, then each center can pull from a specific cloud region. In the case of an outage, the relays can coordinate, so that one center can handle the additional regions during an outage.

Ingress routing and failover

The external interface and third-party webhook scenarios expose endpoints that are implemented using an API gateway and follow the same latency-based routing and failover approach outlined in *Chapter 6, A Best Friend for the Frontend*. Therefore, it is preferable to use these interfaces whenever possible.

Once again, legacy integrations pose the biggest challenge. For example, an ingress relay pushes data from on-premises to the cloud. If the on-premises data centers are active-passive, then it must be decided whether the active center should route all messages to one region and let the data replicate to the regions, or can it perform intelligent content-based routing to reduce latency? Regardless, the relay should proactively test the regional health checks and redirect all messages when a cloud region is unhealthy.

In the case of a data center failure, the implications for an ingress relay are dependent on the capabilities of the on-premises messaging system. In general, we must make sure that all messages are drained from the failing center. If the on-premises messaging system supports global queues, then an active-active approach can account for both regional and data center failures. Each center can pull from the global queues and push messages to a specific region. If a region is down, then that center will stop pulling from the global queue and the other center will pull all messages. The same behavior will happen if a center is down.

The legacy CDC scenario presents challenges because on-premises databases are typically deployed as active-passive. If the active data center has an outage, then the CDC service would need to switch to the passive data center once it comes online. A similar situation occurs when a cloud region becomes unhealthy and another region must be switched on to pull from the active data center. However, the database in the passive center must be hot, so that replication can take place. Therefore, one region can pull from the active data center and the other pulls from the passive data center. Due to replication latency, the secondary region pulling from the passive data center will typically lag and publish duplicate internal domain events. Leveraging idempotence, these events will ultimately be ignored. However, if the primary region or the active data center experiences an outage, then this secondary region and the passive data center will seamlessly take over as primary.

Summary

In this chapter, you learned why it is important to create an anti-corruption layer between your system and external systems, so that changes in external systems have minimal impact on the internals of your system. You learned about the ESG pattern and how to use it to integrate with other systems.

We dug into the many variations on the ESG pattern and you learned how to handle ingress and egress flows with third-party and legacy systems, how to create a system topology of autonomous subsystems, and how to integrate across cloud providers. You also learned how to tackle common data challenges and various security and multi-regional considerations.

In the next chapter, we will cover the Control Service pattern and see how it facilitates collaboration between BFF and ESG services. We will look at variations for orchestration, complex event processing, event sourcing, compensation, and more.

8
Reacting to Events with More Events

In *Chapter 6, A Best Friend for the Frontend*, and *Chapter 7, Bridging Intersystem Gaps*, we covered boundary service patterns. These services work at the boundary of the system, to support end users and external systems, and are responsible for catering to the kinds of changes driven by these actors.

Now, we turn our attention to the inter-service collaborations that represent the business policies and control logic of a system. We will learn how to create control services that are responsible for catering to the kinds of changes driven by the actors who own these business policies.

In this chapter, we're going to cover the following main topics:

- Promoting inter-service collaboration
- Dissecting the Control Service pattern
- Orchestrating business processes
- Employing the Saga pattern
- Calculating event-sourcing snapshots

- Implementing **complex event processing (CEP)** logic
- Leveraging **machine learning (ML)** for control flow
- Implementing multi-regional cron jobs

Promoting inter-service collaboration

In *Chapter 1, Architecting for Innovation*, we saw that the role of architecture is to enable change so that teams can continuously experiment and uncover the best solutions for their users. We enable continuous change by defining fortified boundaries around things that change together so that we can control the scope and impact of any given change. The key to defining these boundaries is to understand the driving force behind change.

In *Chapter 2, Defining Boundaries and Letting Go*, we found that people (that is, actors) are the driving force behind change. We identified a set of *autonomous service patterns* that support the different kinds of actors so that each service is responsible to a single actor. In this chapter, we dig into the details of the **Control Service** pattern.

Control services work between the boundary (that is, **Backend for Frontend (BFF)** and **External Service Gateway (ESG)** services) as mediators, to promote collaboration between the different actors. They embody the rules and business processes that constitute the policies of the organization. These policies are apt to change frequently as the business adapts to its dynamic environment. Thus, control services are responsible to the stakeholders who own these policies.

One way to understand the value of control services is to look at the pros and cons of the alternative. In an event-driven system, services collaborate by exchanging events. **Choreography** is by and large the most common form of inter-service collaboration. It is characterized by the lack of a central coordinator. Upstream services emit events, and downstream services react and produce more events. We design and assemble a sequence of these interactions, and the individual services control the flow.

The following diagram depicts a choreography that promotes the *flow of data* through a system so that we can materialize data in downstream services. Following our food delivery example, when a restaurant updates its menu, then other services react to keep their cache synchronized:

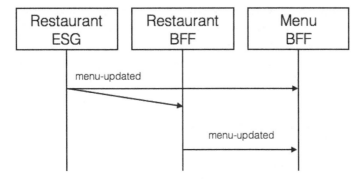

Figure 8.1 – Data-flow choreography

The restaurant's system invokes the external interface provided by **Restaurant ESG** to produce a **menu-updated** event. The **ESG** does not explicitly know what downstream services will consume the event. We design the **Menu BFF** to react to this event so that customers can order off the most up-to-date menu.

Restaurant BFF supports restaurants that do not have their own system and enables system administrators to make menu corrections. As such, this BFF will both consume and produce the **menu-updated** event.

This data-flow example highlights some of the benefits of the choreography approach. Upstream and downstream services are not explicitly coupled to each other. Upstream services can publish an event and do not expect a response. We can added or removed downstream services over time, and multiple services can play similar roles. Any number of services can participate in the collaboration, so long as they uphold the event contract. *Choreography is the best approach for implementing these data-synchronization flows.*

The following diagram depicts a choreography that promotes the *flow of control* through a system so that multiple services can collaborate to perform the steps of a business process. Following our food delivery example, when a customer submits an order, then the restaurant needs to receive the order and communicate that the meal is being prepared:

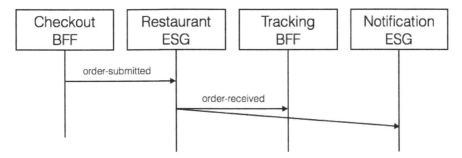

Figure 8.2 – Control-flow choreography

Checkout BFF produces an **order-submitted** event. The **Restaurant ESG** egress flow reacts by invoking the callback endpoint provided by the specific restaurant. The restaurant's order system receives the order, and then the **Restaurant ESG** ingress flow is invoked by the external system's webhook to receive confirmation and produces an **order-received** event. **Tracking BFF** and **Notification ESG** each consume the **order-received** event and make the information available to the customer.

In this control-flow example, the choreography approach works perfectly well up to this point. But the business process is far from over, and things get much more complicated from here. For example, the **order-submitted** event also needs to trigger the selection of a driver, and we need to track the driver's status. It might be straightforward to use choreography for this happy path, but the driver functionality becomes much more complicated as we include all the alternate paths and error paths

It wouldn't be reasonable to put all this logic in **Driver BFF**. **Driver BFF** will change with the needs of the drivers, and the functionality for selecting drivers will change with the needs of the business. Furthermore, **Tracking BFF** and **Notification ESG** should just be *observers* of the driver functionality and consume a generic status event that shields them from the details of how the status is determined. Thus, a service that sits in the middle and acts as a mediator between the boundary services may be a better approach when the business logic is more intricate.

Choreography has the advantage of being straightforward and easy to implement. It is perfect for *data synchronization and observation flows*. It works well for basic control-flow scenarios, but may not scale well for more complex scenarios. As the highly inter-related control-flow logic spreads across the system, choreography becomes harder to understand, trace, debug, test, and maintain. Real duplication of logic, as opposed to false duplication, can also become a problem.

Instead, we can move control-flow logic upstream and consolidate it in dedicated control services. These services consume lower-order events, evaluate rules, and produce higher-order events. They come in many variations, such as business process orchestration, Sagas, CEP, ACID 2.0 calculations, and more. It is reasonable to start with choreography and evolve to control services as the optimal solution becomes clear. Ultimately, a solution may warrant a mixture of both approaches.

Let's take a look at the anatomy of a control service, before we dive into some applications of the pattern.

Dissecting the Control Service pattern

Up to this point, we have learned how to identify the actors of a system and create boundary services for the end users and external system actors. BFF services produce events as the users perform actions. ESG services bridge events between systems and invoke external actions. We use choreography to synchronize data across the services to create the inbound bulkheads that protect the services from upstream failures.

In the early days of a system, it is typical to use choreography to implement the control flows of the system's business processes, but as the system evolves and matures, it becomes beneficial to refactor these control flows into control services. The following diagram depicts the resources that make up a typical control service:

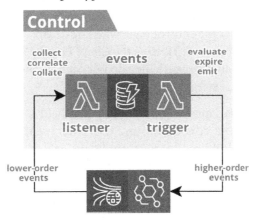

Figure 8.3 – Control Service pattern

Control services act as *mediators* between collaborating boundary services. They only consume and produce events; they do not expose a synchronous interface. The job of a **listener** function is to **collect**, **correlate**, and **collate lower-order** events in a micro **events** store. The job of a **trigger** function is to **evaluate** rules against the collected and correlated events and emit **higher-order** events that constitute the appropriate reaction to the identified conditions. They also implement time-based logic and produce expired events.

In essence, control services react to events by producing more events. We can think of these services as implementing a continuous **action-event-reaction loop**. The flow of arrows in *Figure 8.3* implies this loop. Boundary services produce events and control services consume them and produce more events, then boundary services react to these events, and the cycle continues. Control services may even consume and react to their own events. The events that control services emit simply represent higher-order *facts* that they infer from lower-order facts. They record these facts with a *stream-first atomic action* of publishing an event so that downstream services can take responsibility to react.

It's a recursive implementation of the **inversion of responsibility principle (IRP)**, with boundary services delegating decision logic to control services and control services delegating action logic to boundary services. Each control service embodies a cohesive set of rules. You can find a control service template project here: (`https://github.com/jgilbert01/aws-lambda-stream/tree/master/templates/control-service`). Let's dig into the different kinds of rules.

collect

The job of a control service's `listener` function is to collect events of interest and store them in a micro events store. The purpose of this is twofold: *idempotence* and *correlation*.

Storing events in a serverless database, such as **Amazon Web Services (AWS)** DynamoDB, helps to protect the control logic when upstream services produce duplicate events. As we covered in *Chapter 5, Turning the Cloud into the Database*, these databases implicitly provide idempotence because they do not send duplicate records to their **change data capture (CDC)** stream.

Following the single table design, the **primary key (pk)** field is set to `event.id`, the **sort key (sk)** field is set to the `EVENT` constant, and the actual event is stored in the body. The logic to collect events is reusable and a great candidate for declarative rules.

The following example builds on the concept of *pipeline patterns*, which we covered in *Chapter 4, Trusting Facts and Eventual Consistency*:

```
import { collect } from 'aws-lambda-stream';
const RULES = [{
  id: 'r1',
  pattern: collect,
  eventType: [
    'order-submitted', 'order-received', 'driver-assigned', . .
.
  ],
}];
```

Collection rules are very straightforward, as only a list of event types is required. Events of these types will be inserted into the micro events store, and all other events will be ignored. From here, things start to get more interesting as we address *correlation*.

correlate

Some rules are *simple*, in that they only need to evaluate the state of a single event. Other rules are considered *complex*, because they need to evaluate the state of multiple related events. Storing events in a micro events store gives us the opportunity to correlate related events so that we can easily retrieve them when a complex rule needs to be evaluated.

By default, the `collect` pipeline uses `event.partitionKey` as the correlation value. This is based on the good assumption that we are using the partition key to route related events to the same stream shard. Following the single table design, covered in *Chapter 5, Turning the Cloud into the Database*, the `data` field is set to the correlation key. Later, when an event triggers an evaluation rule, we use the correlation key stored in the `data` field to retrieve all the related events with a single query. This query leverages a global secondary index that we configure with the `data` field as the *primary key*.

Sometimes, there is more than one way to correlate events. In this case, we can declare additional `correlate` rules in the `trigger` function. The `collect` rule still handles idempotence, and once an event is inserted, the `trigger` function will create the additional correlations.

In the following example, a set of `order` events are correlated by `customerId` instead of `order.id`. This will allow the evaluation of conditions across multiple orders instead of a single order:

```
import { correlate } from 'aws-lambda-stream';
const RULES = [{
  id: 'r2',
  pattern: correlate,
  eventType: ['order-submitted', . . .],
  correlationKey: 'order.customer.id',
}];
```

To support multiple correlations, we use the main index of the table with the **primary key** (**pk**) field set to `correlationKey`. When these records trigger an evaluation rule, we use the correlation key stored in the **pk** field to retrieve all the related events with a single query.

collate

Order tolerance is another important benefit of *collecting* and *correlating* events in a micro events store. As we covered in *Chapter 4, Trusting Facts and Eventual Consistency,* when everything is running smoothly, the throughput of the system benefits from events arriving in the correct order; however, our services must have the resilience to accommodate situations where events arrive in the wrong order.

To support order tolerance, a service needs to take into consideration all the work that has already been performed and recognize when it has not performed certain work—for example, if a `cancellation` event arrives before an `initialization` event, then the logic will need to decide whether to defer reacting to the `cancellation` event or proceed and ignore the `initialization` event when it arrives later. Collecting events in a micro events store allows a service to remember which events it has already seen. A service can even consume its own events to record which actions it has already taken.

Collating the events in the micro events store allows the correlated events to be retrieved in chronological order. This increases the efficiency of the rules as it minimizes the programmatic sorting that each must perform. To accomplish this, a service needs to choose the best field to use as the *sort key* for any *indexes*. The typical choices include `event.timestamp`, stream `sequenceNumber`, and `event.id`.

The `event.timestamp` is frequently the best option, so long as it does not result in duplicates, because it represents the time that a domain event occurred. The `sequenceNumber` is certain to avoid duplicates, but it represents the order in which events were added to the stream and not necessarily the order in which they happened. The `event.id` will also avoid duplicates and may be a good candidate if it contains **Version 1 (V1) universally unique identifiers (UUIDs)**, as they are timestamp-based.

To fully support order tolerance, it is necessary to enumerate all the potential scenarios and declare rules that account for all the combinations. Let's move on and look at the elements of evaluation rules.

evaluate

Every time a new event is inserted into the micro events store, the `trigger` function has another opportunity to assess the state of the system, based on the current state in its micro events store, and determine how to react. This is accomplished by consuming from the CDC stream of the database, such as an AWS DynamoDB stream, and *evaluating* rules against the incoming and correlated domain events.

The overall flow of evaluating events and reacting is a great candidate for declarative rules.

The following example builds on the concept of *pipeline patterns*, which we covered in *Chapter 4*, *Trusting Facts and Eventual Consistency*:

```
import { evaluate } from 'aws-lambda-stream';
const RULES = [{
  id: 'r3',
  pattern: evaluate,
  eventType: ['order-submitted'],
  filters: [(uow) => uow.event.order.category === 'xyz'],
  emit: . . .
}];
```

The first step in the `evaluate` flow is to match rules to the incoming domain events based on their `eventType` value. In many cases, this may be all that is necessary to proceed to the outcome of a rule. It may also be necessary to filter based on the content of an event. In this first example, the rule tests the content of the `order.category` field. These are considered *simple* rules because they only evaluate conditions against an incoming domain event.

This next example is considered a *complex* rule because it needs to evaluate conditions against multiple correlated domain events. This rule applies to two event types, `order-received` and `driver-assigned`, and the condition is that both events must be present before the rule reacts. This condition is declared as an expression that contains a block of code. The presence of the expression directs the rule to retrieve the `correlated` events before invoking the `expression` function:

```
import { evaluate } from 'aws-lambda-stream';
const RULES = [{
  id: 'r4',
  pattern: evaluate,
  eventType: ['order-received', driver-assigned'],
  expression: (uow) => {
    const found = uow.correlated.find((e) =>
      ['order-received', 'driver-assigned']
        .contains(e.type));
    if (found.length === 2) {
      return found;
```

```
    } else {
      return false;
    }
  emit: . . .
}];
```

In this particular example, the order of the events does not matter. If the `driver-assigned` domain event arrives first, then the condition will not be met. When the `order-received` event does arrive, then the condition is met and the rule reacts. The same will hold true if the domain events arrive in the opposite order. In many cases, such as this one, it is straightforward to account for *order tolerance* within a single rule. In other cases, it is better to define multiple rules with different guard conditions to account for the various scenarios.

Note that in these examples, the conditional logic is implemented inline for brevity. In practice, it is better to implement and test the conditions as separately declared functions. As a control service grows, these functions will begin to form a **domain-specific language (DSL)** with reusable code fragments that we can combine in different ways to account for the many scenarios.

These two examples represent just one possible way to implement the *evaluate* phase of the Control Service pattern. We will look at some other variations later in the chapter, but before we move on, we need to look at the intended outcome of a control service, which is to produce more events.

emit

The purpose of a control service is to react to lower-order events by producing higher-order events. These lower-order events provide a layer of indirection that helps to decouple downstream services from upstream services. The logic that controls when we emit these higher-order events also tends to change independently of the upstream and downstream services, which reinforces the value and purpose of the Control Service pattern.

A *higher-order* event represents the *fact* that a specific condition was met, therefore it is only necessary for the control service to record these facts. In *Chapter 4, Trusting Facts and Eventual Consistency*, we covered the importance of *atomic actions* in eventually consistent systems. In control services, we leverage *stream-first* atomic actions to persist the facts. Once a fact has been persisted to the stream, the control service is free to continue its *action-event-reaction loop*, and it defers to downstream services to take responsibility and react accordingly.

The following code fragment completes the preceding example by adding the `emit` logic. Again, the code is included inline for brevity:

```
const RULES = [{
  id: 'r4',
  . . .
  emit: (uow, rule, template) => ({
    ...template,
    type: 'delivery-initiated',
    order: uow.event.order,
  }),
}];
```

The `template` argument contains default values, including a unique and deterministic event ID, plus a timestamp, partition key, tags, and references to the events that triggered this new event. We can override any and all of this template and adorned it with additional data, such as the domain object and the event type to emit.

expire

Following from the data life cycle architecture philosophy covered in *Chapter 5*, *Turning the Cloud into the Database*, the control service's micro events store should remain lean and retain events for only as long as necessary. The **time to live** (**TTL**) feature of the database, such as AWS DynamoDB, is leveraged to remove events after they are no longer needed. For example, a default TTL of 33 days is likely sufficient for most business scenarios, while also ensuring idempotence in the case of event replays.

It is important to note here that control services are very time-sensitive, which has implications on replaying events to them. We should take caution when replaying events that are older than the TTL. In this case, it is often more appropriate to replay the events of the control service to downstream boundary services.

We can also use the TTL feature to implement *dynamic expiry* logic. The following example contains rules that will trigger an escalation when a step in a business process is taking too long:

```
const RULES = [{
  id: 'r5',
  pattern: timer,
  eventType: ['order-submitted'],
  ttl: (uow) => uow.event.timestamp + 600, // 10 minutes
```

```
},{
  id: 'r6',
  pattern: expired,
  eventType: ['order-submitted'],
  expression: (uow) => uow.correlated.find((e) =>
    ['order-received'].contains(e.type)).length > 0),
  emit: 'order-submission-expired',
}];
```

Following our food delivery example, once the order-submitted event is produced, we expect the restaurant to respond with an order-received event within 10 minutes. After the time period expires, we want to produce an order-submission-expired event to trigger a downstream escalation process. The escalation logic will likely be part of the same control service, but this rule is focused on recording the fact that the time has expired.

Note that the **service-level agreement (SLA)** for a database's TTL feature may be low, which means that this approach is most applicable for *event-time*-based logic instead of *processing-time*-based logic. For example, a slight delay in emitting an order-submission-expired event is probably tolerable, or using expiration to calculate end-of-month totals could tolerate a much longer delay, so long as it eventually happens.

We must also pay attention to order tolerance when implementing time-sensitive logic—for example, an order-received event could be delayed by an error condition, but the restaurant is working on the order. So, when the order-received event is ultimately received, there may be a need to compensate for an escalation that was already triggered by an order-submission-expired event. We will be covering compensation transactions in the *Employing the Saga pattern* section.

This kind of order tolerance logic is tedious, but it is where many systems fall short and get into trouble. It is also where the Control Service pattern and the rule-driven approach comes in very handy.

As I mentioned previously, declarative rules are just one way to apply the Control Service pattern. In some cases, it may be best to have a completely bespoke implementation, but the collect, correlate, collate, evaluate, emit, and expire concepts will still be applicable. Now that we are familiar with these concepts, let's take a look at some different ways to apply the pattern.

Orchestrating business processes

A *business process* is a long-lived flow of activities, executed in a specific sequence, to achieve the desired outcome. These activities consist of human tasks and atomic actions. The duration of a business process can range from minutes to days, or longer, depending on the nature of the human tasks that must be performed. For example, the Food Delivery process, which involves preparing and delivering food, should be measured in terms of minutes, whereas a typical business process that requires a management approval step may involve waiting hours or days for a manager to approve a task.

There are two approaches to implementing business processes: *choreography* and *orchestration*. These terms are borrowed from the arts and are used as metaphors for software techniques—for example, a team of dancers work together to perform a choreographed set of movements but the choreographer is not in control of the actual performance, whereas an orchestra is led by a conductor as it performs a musical composition.

As we have seen, there are limits to the *choreography* approach and it is only recommended for the most basic of business processes. *Orchestration* is the preferred approach. Orchestration is distinct from choreography as the flow of control is managed centrally by a conductor or mediator. This is the role that a *control service* plays. We can model the logic of a control service (that is, business process) as a state machine using an activity diagram, such as the one shown here:

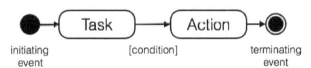

Figure 8.4 – Activity diagram

A process is initiated by a specific event, and the end of the process is signaled by another event. Each step in the process represents a different state, indicating when a specific activity—such as a human task or an atomic action—should be performed. The directed lines between the states represent the state transitions and their guard conditions.

A *control service* is responsible for orchestrating (that is, mediating) state transitions, but not for implementing the individual activities, which are instead implemented by collaborating services—for example, a BFF service will implement a human task, and an ESG service might invoke an atomic action on an external system. Let's take a deeper look at how we implement state transitions with entry and exit events.

Entry and exit events

If you are familiar with traditional **business process management** (**BPM**) tools such as AWS Step Functions, then you will notice a difference in how control services orchestrate business processes. For example, to perform an atomic action step, a traditional BPM tool will directly invoke other services and wait for a response. It may also support publishing an *entry event* when the step starts and an *exit event* when a response is received so that others can observe the flow of control, but these events are completely optional.

Of course, having one service directly invoke another service violates the goal of creating autonomous services with fortified boundaries. *Control services*, on the other hand, implement orchestration using just *entry and exit events*. This approach eliminates synchronous invocation dependency and builds on the **dependency inversion principle** (**DIP**), *IRP*, and the *substitution* principle to create a completely decoupled solution. It is also implicitly supporting observers, such as an event lake, without additional effort.

Following this approach, the control service acts as a policy-setting module that establishes the contracts that other services must implement to participate in the business process. These contracts are the pairs of entry and exit events. The following sequence diagram provides an example of these events for a process that is similar to the one depicted in *Figure 8.4*. In this example, a user wants to perform an action but approval is required first:

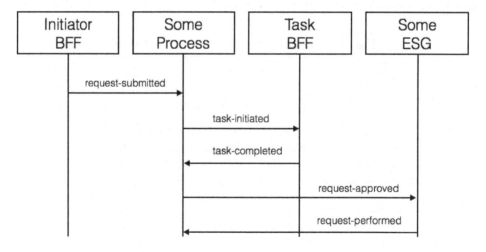

Figure 8.5 – Orchestration sequence diagram

The **Initiator BFF** service signals its intention to start a business process by publishing a **request-submitted** event. The **Some Process** control service transitions to the **Task** state when it receives the **request-submitted** event and emits a **task-initiated** event to indicate that it has *entered* that state. To *exit* this state, the process expects to receive a **task-completed** event.

The **Task BFF** service implements the human activity. It consumes **task-initiated** events and presents tasks to users in a work list. When a user completes a task, it produces a **task-completed** event with the user's disposition.

The **Some Process** control service receives the **task-completed** event, evaluates the conditions, and determines whether to transition to the next state. If the user completed the task with an approval, then the business process transitions to the **Action** state and emits a **request-approved** event to indicate that it has *entered* that state. To *exit* this state, the process expects to receive a **request-performed** event.

The **Some ESG** service consumes the **request-approved** event, performs the atomic action, and produces a **request-performed** event when it has confirmation that the action is complete. At this point, the process is complete. The **Some Process** control service collects the **request-performed** event, but has no further reaction.

The following code block shows how a control service can implement the business process using a set of rules. The first rule emits the **task-initiated** event in reaction to the **request-submitted** event. The second rule emits the **request-approved** event in reaction to the **task-completed** event. These rules are where we wire the outputs of one activity to the inputs of another activity as well—for example, in the first rule, uow.event.request is mapped to task.artifact, and in the second rule, uow.event.artifact is mapped to request:

```
import { evaluate } from 'aws-lambda-stream';
const RULES = [{
  id: 'o1',
  pattern: evaluate,
  eventType: ['request-submitted'],
  emit: (uow, rule, template) => ({
    ...template,
    type: 'task-initiated',
    task: {
      subject: `Review request: ${uow.event.request.id}`,
      role: 'Reviewer',
```

```
        artifact: uow.event.request,
    }}),
  },
  {
    id: 'o2,
    pattern: evaluate,
    eventType: ['task-completed'],
    filter: (uow) => uow.event.task.outcome === 'approved',
    emit: (uow, rule, template) => ({
      ...template,
      type: request-approved',
      request: uow.event.artifact,
    }),
  }];
```

Leveraging entry and exit events allows us to completely decouple the various collaborators—for example, the **Initiator BFF** service does not know or care which business process handles the request, and the **Some Process** control service can be initiated by any service. The control service, in turn, does not know or care which service reacts to an entry event, so long as it emits the expected exit event. These are examples of the flexibility provided by the IRP, as upstream services defer to downstream services that take responsibility for reacting to the upstream events.

Following the DIP, the high-level control service is only concerned with when to emit an entry event and not with how to react. It establishes the contract of each *entry/exit* event pair and delegates the details to the low-level boundary services, and—as just mentioned—the control service has no dependency on which services implement the activities.

Following the **Liskov substitution principle** (**LSP**), we can substitute different collaborators—for example, a legacy system may implement an activity until the capability has been re-architected. Multiple collaborators can also participate simultaneously, with each filtering for and reacting to a subset of the events. This can be useful for beta-testing different potential implementations or for supporting different needs under different scenarios. In any case, the important aspect is that these details can change independently of the control service that defines the business process.

The low-level boundary services are also not coupled to the actual business process and can potentially participate in multiple business processes. For example, a boundary service such as the **Task BFF** service can define a generic pair of *entry/exit* events that it supports, and thus can participate in any business process that uses those events.

An activity in a business process can also be implemented by another control service that is essentially implementing a sub-process. In this case, the *entry* event would *initiate* the sub-process, and the *terminating* event of the sub-process would be the *exit* event expected by the parent process.

Ultimately, the most important characteristic of orchestrating business processes with control services is that we are implementing all the control-flow logic for the business process in one place. This has three key benefits, as follows:

- It makes learning and understanding the policies easier because they are not spread across the system.

- When the policies change, the impact has a higher likelihood of being limited to a single control service.

- The policies can be tested in isolation from the details of the boundary services.

Now, let's look at how to implement more complicated business processes with parallel execution paths.

Parallel execution

The previous business process example is considered to be a simple process because the steps in the process are executed sequentially. More complex business processes include parallel execution. Parallel execution can take the form of *fan-outs* or *forks and joins*.

A *fan-out* is applicable when multiple activities can execute in parallel but there is no need for all the activities to complete before continuing on to the next activity. For example, at a certain point in the flow, it may be necessary to send the customer a status update, but there is no need to hold up the rest of the process while this happens.

The following diagram depicts how this might look, with **Step 1** fanning out to **Step 2** and **Step 3**. **Step 2** transitions to **Step 4** when it is complete, whereas **Step 3** has no follow-on steps. Implementing a fan-out is straightforward. We only need to emit an entry event, and there may not be a need to react to an exit event:

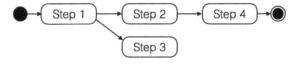

Figure 8.6 – Fan-out

This is also an opportunity for multiple services to react in parallel to the same entry event, such as one ESG service sending a status update by email and another ESG service sending it by **Short Message Service (SMS)**.

Forks and joins are applicable when multiple activities can execute in parallel but they must all complete before continuing on to the next activity. For example, in our Food Delivery system, sending an order to the restaurant and selecting a driver can happen in parallel, but we may not want to dispatch the driver to the restaurant until we have confirmation that the order was received.

The following diagram depicts how this might look. The first black bar represents the *fork*, with **Step 2** and **Step 3** executing in parallel. The second black bar represents the *join*, which must occur before transitioning to **Step 4**. To implement a join, we leverage the correlated events that the control service keeps in its micro events store. The join rule asserts the presence of all required exit events before emitting the next entry event:

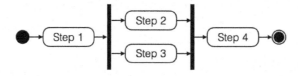

Figure 8.7 – Fork and join

The following code block shows how a control service can implement a join using rules. We have already seen a similar example of CEP in the *Dissecting the Control Service pattern* section. The join utility function asserts whether or not all the listed events have been correlated in the micro events store. When each step completes, the rule has an opportunity to evaluate if the other step has completed. The entry event for **Step 4** is emitted once the expression evaluates to true:

```
import { evaluate } from 'aws-lambda-stream';
import { join } from './utils';
const RULES = [{
  id: 'o3',
  pattern: evaluate,
  eventType: ['step2-completed', 'step3-completed'],
  expression: join(['step2-completed', 'step3-completed']),
  emit: 'step4-initiated',
}];
```

Parallel execution is just one example of how a business process can become complex. First-order alternate paths, such as a rejection flow in an approval process, are straightforward to model with activity diagrams. However, second-, third-, and *Nth*-order alternate paths are much easier to reason about as straight rules, with help from tools such as decision tables. One pattern for handling alternate paths is called the Saga pattern. Let's look at this next, and we will cover rules for CEP later.

Employing the Saga pattern

In *Chapter 4*, *Trusting Facts and Eventual Consistency*, we addressed the reality that modern distributed systems no longer rely on distributed transactions because they do not scale well and because of the heterogeneity of the many technologies involved. Instead, we create resilient, eventually consistent systems by breaking long-lived transactions down into a sequence of atomic actions. The outcome of each action is emitted as an event that is recorded as a fact. Downstream services react and the cycle repeats until the system reaches a consistent state in near-real time.

However, we do need to account for scenarios when something goes wrong downstream and the long-lived transaction is not able to move forward to a consistent state. In these cases, we need to undo the sequence of actions performed up to the point of failure so that the system is returned to a consistent state. This pattern is referred to as a Saga pattern and was first discussed by Hector Garcia-Molina and Kenneth Salem in their 1987 Princeton University paper entitled *SAGAS* (`http://www.cs.cornell.edu/andru/cs711/2002fa/reading/sagas.pdf`).

Let's dig into how we implement Sagas using compensating transactions and abort events.

Compensating transactions

Boundary services that participate in long-lived transactions may need to implement compensating transactions. These are atomic actions that undo the effects of a previous action, and they may be as simple as flipping a status field or canceling an outstanding task for a human activity. Alternatively, they might need to redo a complicated calculation or create a new task for a human to perform a manual activity. The scope of a compensating transaction is only limited by the scope of the transaction it is intending to reverse.

It is important to note that a compensating transaction is not akin to a rollback. The objective is not to erase the evidence of the previous transaction. The previous transaction is a historical fact and the compensating transaction will become a fact as well, with a clear audit trail in the event lake. An analogy is available in the field of public accounting, where nothing is ever erased and mistakes are corrected by adding adjustment-journal entries to the standard general ledger.

Compensating transactions may be further complicated by the fact that multiple transactions may have interlaced and updated the same data since the previous transaction was executed. In this case, the effects of the subsequent transactions should not be undone. This may be as simple as subtracting the incremental value instead of setting a discrete value, or it may require keeping a micro events store so that the state can be recalculated.

It will also be necessary to account for the cascading effect of the events that will be produced by the compensating transaction. These events will provide the audit trail, but they may also cause downstream services to react. This will usually be the intended behavior, but it is still necessary to reason about these impacts when designing the compensation algorithm.

Abort events

A boundary service emits an *abort event* when it is unable to complete its work. Abort events are distinct from the concept of *fault events*, which we covered in *Chapter 4, Trusting Facts and Eventual Consistency*. Fault events signal that an unexpected error condition occurred, whereas an abort event signals that an expected condition occurred. A fault event can be resubmitted once the condition is corrected so that the system can move forward to reach a consistent state. Abort events, on the other hand, indicate that there is no way forward and signal upstream services to perform their compensating transactions so that the system can be returned to a consistent state.

As with any other collaboration, we can implement a Saga using choreography or orchestration. The following sequence diagram provides an example of implementing the Saga pattern with *choreography*:

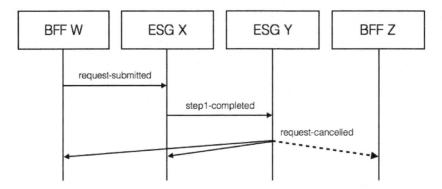

Figure 8.8 – Choreography Saga

The **BFF W** service initiates a long-lived transaction with the **request-submitted** event. The **ESG X** service reacts and emits a **step1-completed** event. The **ESG Y** service reacts but is unable to complete its step and *aborts* by broadcasting a **request-cancelled** event. The **BFF W** and **ESG X** services react by performing their compensation transactions.

Broadcasting the **request-cancelled** event makes the **ESG Y** service's job easier because it doesn't worry about which services will react. However, this means that services that would have performed subsequent steps, such as the **BFF Z** service, will need to determine if they can ignore the abort event or not.

And as always, the choreography approach is reasonable for the happy path, but it begins to lose its appeal as the alternate paths begin to emerge. In this case, all the services are coupled to the **request-cancelled** event for signaling an abort scenario. To alleviate this coupling, we can use an orchestration approach. The following sequence diagram provides an example of implementing the Saga pattern with *orchestration*:

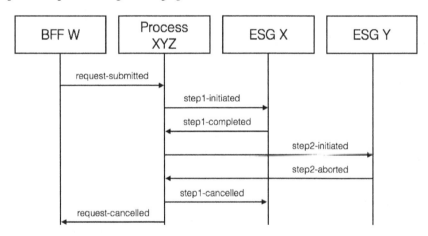

Figure 8.9 – Orchestration Saga

Once again, the **BFF W** service initiates a long-lived transaction with the **request-submitted** event. The **Process XYZ** control service reacts by initiating *Step 1* and then *Step 2*. The **ESG Y** service is unable to complete its step and *aborts* by emitting a **step2-aborted** event. At this point, the **Process XYZ** control service knows exactly which compensating transaction needs to be performed and emits **step1-cancelled** and **request-cancelled** events.

Here, we have expanded on the *entry and exit events* contract that we covered in the *Orchestrating business processes* section, by adding *abort and compensate events* to the contract. Each collaborator has its own events, which gives the control service precise control over which steps need to compensate. It also makes it possible for boundary services to participate in multiple business processes.

The following code block shows how a control service can implement a Saga using rules. The first rule signals to the **BFF W** service to compensate when *Step 1* or *Step 2* abort. The second rule signals to the **ESG X** service to compensate when *Step 2* aborts:

```
import { evaluate } from 'aws-lambda-stream';
const RULES = [{
  id: 's1',
  pattern: evaluate,
  eventType: ['step1-aborted', 'step2-aborted'],
  emit: 'request-cancelled',
},
{
  id: 's2,
  pattern: evaluate,
  eventType: 'step2-aborted',
  emit: 'step1-cancelled',
}];
```

The details for implementing a compensation transaction may be complicated for a specific service but they are encapsulated by the service, which makes it easier to reason about the solution as a whole. Coordinating all the compensations that are necessary in a long-lived transaction is best managed with orchestration because these policies are managed in one place. All this improves our confidence in eventually consistent systems, and—more importantly—it improves our confidence with regard to making changes to the system.

Now, let's turn our attention to another transactional approach known as ACID 2.0, and look at how we can use it to improve the event-sourcing pattern.

Calculating event-sourcing snapshots

Event sourcing is arguably the most important pattern in our architecture because it turns events into facts. Instead of treating events as ephemeral messages, they become first-class citizens and live on in the event lake. They serve as an audit trail of activity within the system and enable replaying of events to seed new services, repair ailing services, or help validate hypotheses for system improvements.

Unfortunately, event sourcing has a bad reputation for being overly complex for most use cases. This complexity revolves around the need to recalculate the current state from events over and over again to perform basic user scenarios, but instead of abandoning event sourcing and all its benefits, it is better to employ approaches that eliminate the need to recalculate the current state.

Database-first event sourcing is a variation of the pattern we covered in *Chapter 5, Turning the Cloud into the Database*, and it gives us the best of both worlds. With this approach, we implement a BFF service in the traditional manner, whereby it only stores and interacts with the current state of domain entities in its database. On the other side of the database, the CDC stream emits change events, and a *trigger* function produces domain events to the event hub. This simplifies the development experience of the BFF service and improves performance for the user, while maintaining the benefits of event sourcing for downstream services.

We can also improve on the event-sourcing pattern by moving the calculation of current state to *control services* in the middle of the system. As depicted in the following diagram, these control services collect the detailed events, calculate the current state, and emit *higher-order snapshot* events. They also collect their own snapshot events and leverage them to optimize their calculations. Downstream BFF services use the snapshot events to easily create materialized views for their users, without the complexity of calculating the current state themselves:

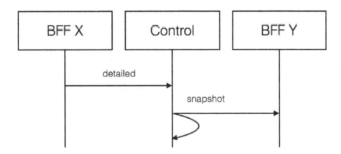

Figure 8.10 – Snapshot sequence diagram

Let's dig into snapshot events and look at how we leverage ACID 2.0 properties to calculate them.

What is ACID 2.0?

The realities of distributed systems and eventual consistency have inspired our industry to devise alternatives to distributed transactions. We have already covered the *Saga* pattern, which uses compensation transactions to return a system to a consistent state when there is a failure in a long-lived transaction. It is important to note that this is a guarantee provided by the application and not by the database itself. Instead, we, as architects, take responsibility for the eventual consistency of the system in the happy path and the failure paths.

Another transactional scenario that poses an interesting architectural challenge is when we have high contention for the same data. This includes scenarios that perform numerical calculations, such as maintaining account balances, tracking inventory, calculating bills, and accumulating metrics. The traditional approach, which locks these records and serializes the transactions, is not able to scale to high volumes or accommodate concurrent updates from distributed nodes.

To support these scenarios, we turn to an approach dubbed *ACID 2.0*. This new version of the classic acronym stands for *Associative, Commutative, Idempotent, and Distributed*. It was first documented by Pat Helland in his paper *Building on Quicksand* (`https://database.cs.wisc.edu/cidr/cidr2009/Paper_133.pdf`), and he in turn credits Shel Finkelstein for the new definition of the acronym.

Many functional requirements exhibit these mathematical properties, so let's review them before leveraging them to improve the event-sourcing pattern, as follows:

- **Associative**—When performing a calculation, the result is independent of the grouping of elements.

- **Commutative**—When performing a calculation, the result is independent of the order of elements.

- **Idempotent**—When performing a calculation, the result does not change if we receive an element more than once.

- **Distributed**—Though not a mathematical property, the other properties must hold when we distribute the calculations across many nodes, such as across multiple regions.

These properties will be more clear in the context of an example. So, let's look at how these mathematical properties help us derive the current state of domain entities from event sourcing.

Snapshot events

The performance of deriving the current state of a domain entity from event sourcing degrades as the number of events increases. To solve this problem, we record the results of a calculation as a snapshot so that we no longer have to recalculate the events that weighed into the snapshot. The next calculation starts with the latest snapshot and adds any additional events. This allows the performance of calculating the current state to remain reasonably consistent because we are limiting the number of events processed in the calculation.

A classic example of this process is tracking the balance of a bank account. We have `Deposit` events that increase the balance, `Withdraw` events that reduce the balance, and `Balance` events that provide a snapshot of the current balance. The following table includes two sets of example events side by side to demonstrate the ACID 2.0 properties:

Event Type'	Amount'	Event Type"	Amount"
Deposit	100	Deposit	100
Deposit	30	Withdraw	50
Balance	130	Balance	50
Withdraw	50	Deposit	30
Deposit	70	Deposit	20
Balance	150	Balance	100
Deposit	20	Deposit	70
Balance	170	Balance	170

Table 8.1– ACID 2.0 properties

The first thing to notice between the two sets is that the events arrived in different orders and the ending balance of both scenarios is **170**. This shows that the calculations are *commutative*. It is also the most important part because the system is eventually consistent, even if the intermediate results may vary. Next, notice that we calculated the `Balance` (that is, snapshot) events for different groupings of events, yet this did not impact the end result. This is an example of the *associative* property.

We handle the *idempotent* property by the fact that a control service collects these events in a micro events store, and the trigger function that performs the calculations will not trigger multiple times if the same event is inserted more than once. For the *distributed* property, when we deploy a control service to multiple regions, an intermediate balance event in one region may not see an event in another region, but this is no different than an event being delayed and arriving out of order.

Now, let's look at what the code for calculating a snapshot event might look like in a control service. The service collects, correlates, and collates `deposit`, `withdraw`, and `balance` events in its micro events store and emits a new snapshot event when it receives a deposit or withdraw event. You can see the code in the following snippet:

```
import { calculate } from 'aws-lambda-stream';
const RULES = [{
  id: 'c1',
  pattern: calculate,
  eventType: ['deposit', 'withdraw'],
  limit: 10,
  emit: (uow, rule, template) => {
    const { balance, triggers } = calculateBalance(uow);
    return ({
      ...template,
      type: 'balance',
      account: {
        number: uow.event.account.number,
        balance,
      },
      triggers,
    });
  },
}];
```

The `calculate` pipeline function retrieves the correlated events when a `deposit` or `withdraw` event arrives. It retrieves them in *reverse* order because we are only interested in the most recent events. We also `limit` the number of events returned, since the older events are already counted in the latest snapshot. You can see the code in the following snippet:

```
const calculateBalance = (uow) => {
  const snapIdx = uow.correlated.findIndex(e
    => e.type === 'balance');
  const snapshot = uow.correlated[snapIdx];
  const latestEvents = uow.correlated.slice(0, snapIdx);
  return {
```

```
    balance: latestEvents.reduce((balance, e) =>
      (e.type === 'deposit' ?
        balance + e.deposit.amount :
        balance - e.withdraw.amount),
      snapshot.account.balance
    ),
    triggers: [snapshot, ...latestEvents].map(({ id })
      => ({ id })),
  };
};
```

The `calculateBalance` function finds the most recent snapshot and the latest events and then reduces them to the current balance. For brevity, this example focuses on the happy path and uses an overly simple slice that ignores edge cases such as when an older detailed event arrives after a snapshot. I'll leave these kinds of edge cases for you as a thought exercise, but note that the snapshot event includes the triggers, so comparisons can be made. We could also have a pipeline that reacts to `balance` events, asserts the accuracy of the balance, and emits any adjustments. We can even do the same when the various events *expire* from the micro events store.

Next, we will look at using control services and CEP to initiate business processes as opposed to orchestrating them.

Implementing CEP logic

Up to this point, we have mostly used control services to orchestrate business processes. In the previous examples, an end user initiated a business process via publishing an event from a BFF service. Humans are excellent complex-event processors. We naturally process all kinds of inputs and quickly make decisions, but we aren't always paying attention, or there may be too many inputs to reliably and consistently process them all.

This is where we can use control services to perform CEP and emit events to alert downstream services of their findings. The processing logic is considered complex because we are not just reacting to a single event. We collect and correlate multiple events and evaluate conditions across them for actionable insights. For example, we could audit a business process and assert that it is adhering to expectations. We have already seen a basic example of CEP when joining parallel paths in a business process.

Let's look at how we can use decision tables to help reason about CEP rules, and then look at an important edge condition where we are missing events.

Decision tables

CEP is a powerful, effective, and clean approach for implementing business policies. However, reasoning about the correctness of these rules becomes more and more challenging as the number of events and conditions increases. This is because there are many more permutations to consider, especially when we account for compensation transactions and events arriving out of order.

Decision tables, such as the one shown here, are the recommended tools for modeling CEP rules. Each table presents a cohesive set of conditions:

Conditions	S1	S2	S3
Event A present	True	True	False
Event B present	True	True	False
Event C present	True	True	False
A.x <= B.y <= C.z	True	False	N/A
Actions			
Emit	audit-passed	audit-failed	N/A
Message		XYZ condition failed	
Notes			Nothing to process

Table 8.2 – An example of a decision table

The first column lists the conditions and the action to take when all the conditions are met. The remaining columns enumerate all the interesting permutations of the conditions. The cell values are true, false, and **not applicable (N/A)**. The bottom of the table declares the parameters to use when performing the actions.

The major advantage of this approach is that it is easier to see when a condition or a permutation is unaccounted for. This can be particularly helpful when reasoning about events arriving out of order. Another advantage is that they are easily translated into the rules and corresponding test cases.

In this example, we are interested in three types of events. When all the events are present, we expect the data will match the given expression. If everything is fine, then we emit an audit-passed event; otherwise, we emit an audit-failed event with the given message. Some of the scenarios, such as S3, do not need to be translated into rules, but they are included in the table for completeness. It is also helpful to include notes with supporting information.

Now, let's look at what the code for CEP might look like in a control service. The service *collects, correlates, and collates* A, B, and C events in its micro events store. As each of these event types arrive, the correlated events are retrieved and the conditions are *evaluated*. You can see the code in the following snippet:

```
const RULES = [{
  id: 's1',
  pattern: evaluate,
  eventType: ['A', 'B', 'C'],
  expression: (uow) => {
    const { A, B, C } = findAbcEvents(uow);
    return A & B & C & A.x <= B.y <= C.z;
  },
  emit: 'audit-passed',
}, {
  id: 's2',
  pattern: evaluate,
  eventType: ['A', 'B', 'C'],
  expression: (uow) => {
    const { A, B, C } = findAbcEvents(uow);
    return A & B & C & !(A.x <= B.y <= C.z);
  },
  message: 'XYZ condition failed',
  emit: auditFailed,
}];

const findAbcEvents = (uow) => ({
  A: uow.correlated.find((e) => e.type === 'A'),
  B: uow.correlated.find((e) => e.type === 'B'),
  C: uow.correlated.find((e) => e.type === 'C'),
});

const auditFailed = (uow, rule, template) => ({
    ...template,
    type: 'audit-failed',
    message: rule.message,
  })
```

The `findAbcEvents` helper function looks for all the event types in the `correlated` list. The first rule asserts that all three events are present and then checks that the additional condition evaluates to `true`. The second rule is similar but is asserting the inverse. It also demonstrates that rules can include custom metadata, such as parameterizing the error message. The `auditFailed` function uses this metadata when creating the `audit-failed` event.

Missing events

An interesting nuance of CEP is knowing when you are done. For example, if you are auditing a business process and there are a dozen rules that all instances of the process must pass, then how do you know when an instance has passed all the rules? It is easy to know when a long-lived business process instance has failed because it only has to fail one rule, but how do we know when all the rules have succeeded? We could wait until a process is complete and then evaluate all the rules, but that may cause an unwanted latency in finding issues.

A better option is to have the control service consume its own events and define a rule that counts the rules that have been evaluated. Every time an `audit-success` or `audit-failure` event is received, the rule counts the correlated events and emits an `audit-completed` event when the expected number is reacted. But what happens when the expected count is never reached? Maybe the business process instance was never completed, and thus the audits of the final steps were never performed.

An easier example to reason about is knowing when a single rule has completed, such as the rule in the previous section that is evaluating the combination of event types A, B, and C. Again, it is easy to know when the rule fails, but what if only two of the three expected events are ever received? This might be OK, or it might not be. Let's assume it is not OK and someone needs to be alerted when all three events did not occur. The obvious solution is to define another rule that asserts that all three events occurred, but the question becomes: *When do we evaluate this rule?*

The problem in both examples is that we are missing events but the rules are triggered by the presence of events. To solve this problem, we need to define a *time window* in which we expect the events to occur and set up a rule that asserts the presence of all the events when the time window expires. The following code block shows what the rules might look like:

```
const RULES = [{
  id: 'w1',
  pattern: timer,
  eventType: ['A', 'B', 'C'],
```

```
    ttl: (uow) => uow.event.timestamp + 3600, // 1 hour
}, {
    id: 'w2',
    pattern: expired,
    eventType: ['A', 'B', 'C'],
    expression: (uow) => uow.correlated.find((e) =>
        ['A', 'B', 'C'].contains(e.type)).length < 3),
    message: 'ABC condition failed with missing events',
    emit: auditFailed,
}];
```

Rule w1 creates up to three timers. When each of the event types is received, a timer is created—for example, when A is received, a window timer is created for 1 hour. When ttl expires, then rule w2 checks to see if all three events are present and emits an audit-failed event if they are not. This ensures that there is coverage, no matter which of the events are received or not. For the business process audit example, there could be a single window based on the event that initiated the business process.

It can be a challenge to reason about missing events, but it is well worth the trade-off to be able to react to these complex conditions in real time. This simply highlights the benefits of using decision tables to model these rules and find all the permutations.

Now, let's look at a variation of the Control Service pattern that uses ML to look for actionable insights. This variation can be used as an alternative or a complement to CEP.

Leveraging ML for control flow

We have only scratched the surface of what can be accomplished with control services. Using rules to implement orchestration and CEP is clean and very powerful, but it is not the end of the road. We can certainly implement control flow with raw bespoke logic as well, but a very interesting approach that is emerging is the use of ML to steer control flow. For example, a control service could raise alerts based on facial recognition or fraud and anomaly detection, or a control service could generate leads and personalized recommendations based on user activity.

To leverage ML, we need to look at both sides of the equation: models and predictions. Let's look at these in turn.

Models

When it comes to ML, it is all about the data. You need data, data, and more data. The more data you have, the more accurate your models will be. Conversely, if you do not have enough data, then you will most likely be better off using rules instead of ML.

Fortunately, we have the perfect source of data for training models—the facts in the event lake. This is one of the benefits of the event-first approach. The system is continuously emitting and collecting the facts we need for analytics in general and, more specifically, for training ML models.

The data in the event lake is used to train and experiment with your initial models. If you do not have enough historical data, then you can start with rules to bridge the gap while you collect enough data. It's not unreasonable to expect that you will need a good year's worth of data or more. Once you have your models in place, you will periodically use the event lake to retrain your models. If you have enough traffic volume, you may even continuously retrain your models by consuming from the stream.

As you gain experience you will have ideas for better models. You can use the event lake to experiment with these hypotheses by replaying the events to validate the outcomes of the model against the historical results.

Predictions

A control service leverages ML to perform the *evaluation* phase of its processing logic. The objective is to *predict* whether or not an event represents something interesting. If the event is of particular interest, an event is raised so that the system can react accordingly. The following diagram depicts the resources involved:

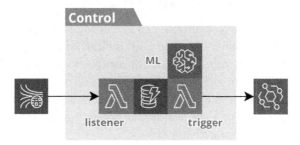

Figure 8.11 – ML control service

The **listener** function collects events in a micro events store to provide idempotence. The **trigger** function invokes an **ML** service to *evaluate* the event. If the evaluation returns an *actionable* outcome, the **trigger** function then produces an event to initiate a business process, accumulate metrics, and more.

The possibilities for *evaluation* algorithms are endless— for example, a fraud-detection algorithm would return a score regarding the likelihood that an event was fraudulent, or a facial-recognition algorithm could determine whether or not a person of interest is present in an image associated with the event. This is an exciting arena where I expect to see a lot of experimentation and discovery of new ways of evaluating events.

Now, let's look at how we can use control services to produce time-based domain events.

Implementing multi-regional cron jobs

It may seem ironic, but scheduled jobs still play a role in event-driven systems. We strive to avoid the long latency of a batch cycle, but sometimes legacy integrations necessitate scheduled jobs. In these cases, an ESG service would encapsulate those requirements, but there are still legitimate business events that happen at specific points in the day— for example, the stock market has an opening and closing bell. For these scenarios, a control service can implement the schedule and broadcast time-based domain events, as shown in the following diagram. Downstream services can then react without duplicating the scheduling logic:

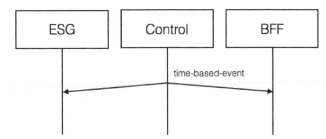

Figure 8.12 – Cron sequence diagram

As with all autonomous services, we deploy these scheduled jobs to multiple active regions to ensure that there is coverage in the case of a regional disruption. However, we do not want these scheduled jobs to execute in multiple regions and thus perform duplicate work, so one region will serve as the primary and the others as secondary. Since these events are time-based, the easternmost region is usually primary.

It is important to note that we schedule these jobs are scheduled at design time, not at runtime—in other words, they are not dynamically scheduled based on the activity of the system. We can use this to our advantage to solve the duplicate execution problem, by staggering a job across regions and leveraging replication and idempotence to ensure that it executes in only one region.

Job records and events

As is normally the case for control services, a scheduled control service is not responsible for performing the actual work. Its job is to signal when it is time to perform the work. So, we will use job records to control when we produce job events, as depicted in the following diagram:

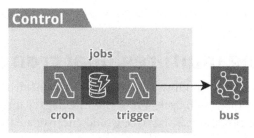

Figure 8.13 – Regional cron job

We schedule the **cron** function to execute at the desired time, such as 8 a.m. in the easternmost region. The function inserts a job record into the **jobs** table, such as AWS DynamoDB, with a deterministic identifier and body. The contents of the record must be deterministic so that the cron functions in the other regions can attempt to insert the exact same record.

The eastern region is the first to insert the deterministic job record (more on this in a moment), so the **trigger** function is invoked with an `insert` event. The function asserts that the record was inserted from the current region and publishes the appropriate time-based domain event to the **bus**. From here, downstream services take responsibility for performing the actual work.

Optionally, depending on the desired functionality, it may make sense to have the cron function call the regional health-check service, which we discussed in *Chapter 6, A Best Friend for the Frontend*. If the current region is unhealthy, then the function can decide not to insert the job record so that another region can initiate the job, which we cover next.

Replication and idempotence

The **cron** function in each region will be invoked at the scheduled time and inserts a deterministic job record, unless there is a regional disruption that prevents it. If the record already exists, then the *idempotence* of the deterministic insert will prevent the **trigger** function from being invoked, thus the time-based domain event will not be produced in that region and no duplicate work will be performed. But there is a catch—we have a `race` condition.

If we schedule all the cron functions for exactly the same time, then they will all be the first to insert the job record into their region. To eliminate this `race` condition, we leverage the regional replication feature of a serverless database, such as AWS DynamoDB, and we stagger the jobs in the secondary regions to account for the replication delay. As a result, the job will typically execute in the easternmost region until there is a disruption.

Keep in mind that this does mean that there will be a slight delay in the processing of the business functionality in a secondary region if there is a disruption in the primary region, but the objective here is to ensure that the functionality is executed. In other words, it is better late than never. If you have more than two regions, then you will need to establish an order of precedence and stagger each successive region appropriately.

There is still a small chance that multiple regions will duplicate the work—for example, if there is a replication delay that is greater then the regional offset, then another region could be the first to insert the job record in its region, but we mitigate with our ever-present requirement to make all actions idempotent. So, make certain that the work is performed based on the domain event time, not on the processing time. This also highlights that the objective is to avoid the wasted effort of doing the same work in multiple regions, but not to necessarily eliminate it. Trying to completely eliminate this duplicate work is most likely a wasted effort in and of itself.

Summary

In this chapter, we dug into the details of the Control Service pattern and you learned how to use it to implement inter-service collaboration, such that changes in business policies have minimal impact on the boundary services. We looked at variations on the pattern that handle orchestration and compensation transactions and you learned about the ACID 2.0 principles and how to use them to create event-sourcing snapshots. You also learned how we can use CEP and ML to initiate business processes, and how to implement cron jobs that can fail over across multiple regions.

In the next chapter, we will see how continuous deployment and continuous delivery work together to facilitate continuous innovation. We will cover multiple levels of planning, CI/CD pipelines, continuous testing, zero downtime deployment, and the robustness principle.

Section 3: Putting Everything in Motion

In this section, we bring everything together by describing how teams turn the crank of continuous experimentation and discovery, and we then cover some final thoughts on how to start making forward progress.

This section contains the following chapters:

- *Chapter 9, Choreographing Deployment and Delivery*
- *Chapter 10, Don't Delay, Start Experimenting*

9
Choreographing Deployment and Delivery

In *Chapter 8, Reacting to Events with More Events,* we covered the last of the three high-level autonomous service patterns. Autonomous services have fortified boundaries and own all the resources they need to continue operating when related services are down. This resilience gives teams the confidence to drive down lead times and forge ahead with changes, knowing that these boundaries will help control the blast radius when things go wrong.

We now turn our attention to the methodology of continuously building, testing, deploying, and delivering functionality to the end users. In this chapter, we focus on the best practices for keeping things from going wrong in the first place. You will learn how to choreograph the continuous deployment and delivery of services and applications with zero downtime and the confidence that all the necessary checks and balances are in place.

In this chapter, we're going to cover the following main topics:

- Optimizing testing for continuous deployment
- Focusing on risk mitigation

- Achieving zero-downtime deployments
- Planning at multiple levels
- Turning the crank

Optimizing testing for continuous deployment

In *Chapter 1, Architecting for Innovation*, we stated that the goal of software architecture is to enable change. We want to continuously deliver innovations to our end users and produce business value. To meet this goal, we strive to reduce lead times so that we can increase the rate of feedback from end users and create knowledge about what works and what does not. To this end, we have focused throughout this book on optimizing our architecture for short lead times.

Now, we need to turn our attention toward optimizing our testing processes. Traditional testing assumes that we know what is going to work, and we can gather all the requirements and acceptance criteria up front. Then, we assert that the software is correct before we deploy and release it to the end user.

However, our traditional testing practices actually work against our stated goal. They are optimized for large batch sizes, which increases deployment risk. They encourage longer lead times, which delays feedback.

So, testing is the last piece of the puzzle that we need to change to support short lead times. We need to turn our testing practices on their heads. We need to turn testing into a process of continuous discovery.

Continuous discovery

Another way of stating our goal is that we are aiming for **continuous discovery**. We need to formulate hypotheses, perform experiments, and iteratively discover the best solutions for our end users. In other words, we need a testing process that helps us build and discover the right solution, not one that asserts that we are building a solution right.

To gather feedback and discover what works, we need to put the software in the hands of the end user in the production environment. This means that we need to deploy much more frequently. Our testing processes must help us do so safely.

We need to push changes to production that are incomplete, but we need to be certain that there are no regressions. We need to assert that the system is healthy and learn which features users are actually using. To accomplish this, we certainly don't want less testing. We need more testing—a lot more testing.

As an example, let's look at the statistics for a prototypical project. We delivered 250 stories over 18 months. In the end, the code base included over 6,000 test cases, which accounted for well over 50% of the code. We completed the stories with approximately 3,000 tasks, and each task resulted in a deployment. On average, we completed eight tasks per day and wrote two test cases per task. That is a lot of testing, and *we built up the test suite incrementally*.

In other words, testing is not a separate activity—it is an integral part of each activity. Testing is the safety net that gives us the confidence to forge ahead and discover the right solution. Testing is continuous.

Continuous testing

We are changing our testing mindset to one that allows us to focus on iterating to the right solution. We are no longer waiting until the end to perform testing—we are testing all the time. After all, we are experimenting with functionality, which is a form of testing. Experiments help us eliminate the wasted effort of building the wrong solution, but we also need testing that gives us the confidence to move forward with our experiments.

Continuous testing is the overarching term for the many types of testing we perform. The following word cloud highlights the scope and breadth of the continuous testing effort. It presents the relative relationship of the testing techniques and approaches that we bring to bear to help give us the confidence to perform more frequent deployments:

Figure 9.1 – Continuous testing: word cloud

We have covered many of these topics throughout this book, and we cover more in this chapter. For example, in *Chapter 2, Defining Boundaries and Letting Go,* we introduced the new `TestOps` role and addressed the importance of test engineering in a highly automated environment, and we also saw how copious observability with work metrics and resource metrics, along with continuous auditing, enables a higher degree of governance without impeding innovation and progress.

Figure 9.1 depicts how we are shifting many of the traditional testing activities to the *left* on the timeline and automating them in the **continuous integration and deployment (CI/CD)** pipelines. These include static analysis, unit testing, integration testing, contract testing, and transitive end-to-end testing. But they are all performed in isolation, with test doubles, to minimize the friction that increases lead time. We will cover these in detail in the *Continuous integration pipeline* section.

It also shows how we are shifting other forms of testing to the *right* on the timeline—into production, where we monitor and alert on the signals that the system is emitting. These include automated smoke testing (that is, synthetics), which we execute on a continuous schedule, and anomaly detection, which alerts us to significant changes in **key performance indicators (KPIs)** so that we can focus on the **mean time to recovery (MTTR)** and fail forward quickly. We will cover these in detail in the *Continuous deployment pipeline* section.

But try as we might, testing cannot eliminate all errors—we need to focus on risk mitigation as well.

Focusing on risk mitigation

No process is perfect. We cannot eliminate honest human error. We can double down on our automated testing—even triple down, and more. But sooner or later, a mistake will happen, because to err is human.

The solution is not to slow down, but instead to go faster and *mitigate the risk.* We need to force ourselves to control the batch size, by decoupling deployments from releases, with the help of feature flags. And when things still go wrong—and they will—then we must be prepared to fail forward fast, while we rely on our autonomous services to limit the blast radius.

Small batch size

One of the most effective ways to mitigate risk is to control the batch size of the work units we produce. Agile methods help us mitigate the risk of building the wrong solution by delivering features more frequently. A smaller batch size allows us to elicit feedback from end users more quickly so that we can make course corrections and eliminate wasted development effort.

But we can do better. We need to control more than just the batch size of a delivery (that is, a **release**). A release can easily contain hundreds of changes. When a mistake happens, how do we know which change is the culprit? Even before a release, how can we reason about the stability of so many changes? There is often an interplay between changes that is not readily apparent.

We need to minimize the number of changes, but we can only reduce the batch size of a release so much before this is no longer useful for eliciting end-user feedback. We need a work unit that is smaller than a release. We need a unit of work that helps teams maintain the stability of the system. We need to decouple deployment from release.

Decoupling deployment from release

The smallest possible batch size is a single change. If we deploy a single change and the system breaks, then the cause should be fairly obvious. More importantly, it is much easier to reason about the correctness of a single change—not necessarily that the change is functionally correct, but whether or not it will break the functionality that is already working.

End users do not like it when we break features that they rely on—they always want more. But they don't like downtime. Downtime is equivalent to broken. We want to move fast, so we can innovate and give users more, but we certainly don't want to break things. And as we will see in the *Achieving zero-downtime deployments* section, sometimes the only way to accomplish this is by deploying the smallest possible backward-compatible change.

We need to treat deployments and releases as separate events. A deployment is just the act of deploying a change into an environment. We push the change all the way to production, and we do this many times a day without interrupting the end users. We will see how this works in the *Turning the crank* section, with automation pipelines, comprehensive testing, and appropriate gates.

The changes then sit dormant until we are ready to turn them on. We will enable them for ourselves so that we can perform controlled testing, but we wait until we have accumulated enough changes before we release the feature to the end users. At this point, the act of releasing is nothing more than flipping a switch to enable it for a set of users. These may be beta testers, or we may roll out a feature progressively across business units. We may A/B-test variations of a feature with a percentage of customers to determine the best fit.

Ultimately, we are continuously deploying small, controlled changes, many times a day, across many autonomous services. We will reach a point where we are continuously delivering new and improved features to various groups of users on a regular basis. We employ the help of feature flags to accomplish this.

Feature flags

Feature flags are not as fancy as they may sound. A **feature flag** is just conditional business logic that we add to the code to control when a feature is available and to whom. But conditional logic can get messy. It increases the complexity of the code. It increases the magnitude of the testing effort.

If not well designed, a feature flag can do more harm than good. But feature flags are instrumental in mitigating the risks of continuous innovation, so it is worth the effort to properly design and implement feature flags.

Natural feature flags are the best kind of feature flag. These are conditions that are intrinsic to the functionality—for example, most systems provide a role-based access feature that we use to control the rendering of menus and screens and that throws an error for unauthorized access. We can cleanly craft a hierarchy of roles to control access to new features.

Some systems require the user to purchase a feature. We could use the pricing model to offer a feature for free to beta users for a period of time. Other features are naturally optional, with the ability to opt in and opt out. Alternatively, we can combine natural feature flags to achieve the desired result. In the *Achieving zero-downtime deployments* section, we will see how we can use the presence of a change itself as a feature flag.

We should always favor natural feature flags over artificial feature flags. An **artificial feature flag** has no intrinsic value to the application. It is a Boolean logic that we temporarily wrap around a feature to limit access. It looks up the state of a flag and acts accordingly. After we release a feature, we need to remember to go back and remove an artificial feature flag.

Technical debt is the primary concern over feature flags. If we do not double back and remove these flags, the code can then become unwieldy. Even natural feature flags may need cleanup, such as removing a role that we no longer need. We should specifically allocate cleanup tasks to the task roadmap so that we remove any technical debt as we proceed. We will see examples of this in the *Achieving zero-downtime deployments* section, and we cover task roadmaps in the *Planning at multiple levels* section. But try and plan as we might, we must be ready to fail forward when things go wrong.

Fail forward fast

Again, no process is perfect. We cannot eliminate honest human error. We will make mistakes. So, we need to be prepared to jump into action, at a moment's notice, to fix the problem and move on.

Fortunately, the batch size of our deployments is now a single change. So, when something breaks, the cause is much clearer. We can easily triage the issue and define a path forward, not backward.

We are performing many deployments a day, and the process has become routine. We can rely on this *muscle memory* to roll out a fix quickly. The time needed to roll back the change is likely no different than the time to roll forward with the fix. So, we should favor the path forward.

Observability is crucial to minimizing the MTTR. We need to know that there is an issue before the end user does. We have covered this topic throughout the book, and we see exactly where it fits into the process in the *Turning the crank* section.

Yet in the eyes of the end user, when something breaks it is the equivalent of being down. If the user cannot use a feature, then the system is essentially offline, so our aim is always to have zero downtime. Let's look at what it takes to achieve zero-downtime deployments.

Achieving zero-downtime deployments

The days of taking a system offline for maintenance are long gone. Customers expect a system to be online at any time. Even employees, particularly regional employees, use systems around the clock. There is simply no viable window to take a system offline.

We need the ability to seamlessly perform deployments without interrupting the end users. This is one of the goals of **autonomous services** and **micro-apps**. Each piece is independently deployable and supports a different actor, which means that they deploy more quickly and they impact different groups of users. Plus, in the event of a mistake, they limit the blast radius.

However, there are still dependencies between these components. For example, suppose we need to change the name of a field in the domain model. This change has a ripple effect. It impacts the interactions between the frontend and the backend, between the backend and the data store, and between the event producer and the downstream consumers.

We also need to avoid a versioning nightmare. We are performing many small batch-size deployments, so running concurrent deployments is impractical. We will reserve versioning for significant changes in functionality, at the release level, which we will roll out to beta users, and so on.

Instead, we will leverage the small batch size of our deployments along with the *Robustness principle*.

The Robustness principle

The **Robustness principle** is a design guideline that helps us roll out incremental changes. It states the following:

> *Be conservative in what you send, be liberal in what you accept.*

Let's see how this can help us with an example scenario for changing a field name. The first part of the principle says: **be conservative in what you send**.

The backend needs to be conservative in what it sends to the frontend. If it sends a new field name to the frontend, how will the frontend react? Will the frontend ignore the field or throw an error? What if it removes a field? Will the frontend throw an error?

The backend needs to be conservative in what it sends to the data store. If it sends a new field name to the data store, how will the trigger function react? Will the trigger throw an error, or will it send out an invalid domain event without this data? How will downstream consumers react to the events with missing information?

We need to avoid all of these kinds of situations. They all constitute downtime. The second part of the principle says: **be liberal in what you accept**.

The frontend needs to be liberal in what it accepts from the backend. The backend can send both the old field and the new field, and the frontend can ignore the one it doesn't expect; or, the frontend can be modified to handle either field name and present a single field to the user.

The **trigger function** needs to be liberal in what it accepts from the data store. It can accept either field name from the data store and send both field names in the domain events. Consumers can accept either field and ignore the other.

We can think of the field names as natural feature flags. The presence of one or the other field dictates how the code will behave. Then, we string together a series of deployments to make the changes on both ends of an interaction and then remove the flags. Let's take the following as an example:

- The first deployment changes the backend to send both fields.
- The second deployment changes the frontend to switch fields.
- The third deployment changes the backend to stop sending the old field.

These three deployments can proceed over a period of just hours, with zero downtime for the users. Only the third deployment requires some delay while we wait for the cache to expire on the user's browser.

These are rapid one-two-three-punch combinations of deployments that we can only achieve when we have *decoupled deployment from release*. We add a conservative change on one side, upgrade the other side, and then double back and remove the flag from the first side.

Conversely, if we were to deploy every 2 weeks, then this process would take 6 weeks. In other words, slowing down is simply not practical. Instead, reducing lead time, inverting our testing process, and focusing on risk mitigation opens up the opportunity for new solutions to old problems.

Let's dig a little deeper into how this example scenario plays out between the different components.

Between the frontend and its backend

When we are planning out one of these three-deployment cycles for a specific change, we need to choose a side to start on. For the interaction between the frontend and its backend, this will depend on whether we are using **GraphQL** or **REpresentational State Transfer (REST)**.

For **GraphQL**, we need to start on the backend. The frontend dictates which field names to use, so the backend needs to understand the field names. We might proceed as follows:

1. Add the new field name to the schema and add resolvers to map the new field name to the old field in the data store.
2. Update the frontend to use the new field name.

3. Wait for the cache to expire.

4. Remove the old field name from the schema. Note that the data store is still using the old field name, so we will leave those resolvers in place a little longer.

For **REST**, we can start on either side, so we will start on the frontend side for contrast. We might proceed as follows:

1. Update the frontend to use either the old or new field name.

2. Wait for the cache to expire.

3. Update the backend to replace the old field name with the new field name.

4. Update the frontend to only use the new field name.

Now that we have taken care of the frontend and the immediate impact of the end user, we can move on to the downstream consumers.

Between producers and consumers

Again, we can choose whether to start on the consumer side or the producer side. However, we definitely cannot update the database first. Furthermore, we need to account for multiple consumers and we may need to coordinate with multiple teams, so the plan may drag out longer and it must account for the most vulnerable consumers.

First, before we add the new field to the domain event, we must ensure that downstream listener functions will not break. The `listener` functions should follow the **Robustness principle** and ignore fields they do not recognize. They should produce a `fault` event if required data is missing, but not if there is additional information. Once all listeners have *liberal* mapping logic, we can proceed as follows:

1. Update the trigger function to include both the old and new fields.

2. Downstream teams update their `listener` functions to support both fields. Preferably, they can do this ahead of the upstream change.

3. Wait for all downstream changes.

4. Update the trigger function to remove the old field name.

5. Optionally, downstream teams may remove support for the old field name from their `listener` functions. This will depend on how far back in time they need to support the replay of events from the event lake, because older events will only have the old field name. These will tend to be services that operate later in the *data life cycle*, such as analytics and archiving. To keep the logic clean, the teams can segregate this logic into different *pipelines* that filter on the event format.

External domain events and **External Service Gateway** (**ESG**) services play an important role here. Within an autonomous subsystem, the various teams will work closely together. This means that we can upgrade the downstream consumers within an autonomous subsystem relatively quickly, and we can remove the debt of the natural feature flags.

However, it will take external consumers longer to upgrade. This is where the *anti-corruption layer* of ESG services comes into play. The ESG services can hold the technical debt of the feature flags while we wait for the external services to upgrade. In the meantime, this allows the internal domain events, **Backend for Frontend** (**BFF**) services, and control services to stay clean and remove the feature flags quickly.

Between the backend and its data store

The traditional approach for upgrading a data store involves running a conversion process to update all the records. However, the data store is the one piece that connects all the others, so it cannot change until all the other changes are in place. We also have many different databases that may need to change. Some of these data stores may be so large that a one-shot conversion is impractical. Other data stores may be lean and have a **time to live** (**TTL**) that removes older records, so there is little need for a conversion.

Furthermore, most of our serverless data stores are schemaless. So, we will apply the Robustness principle to the data layer as well. The backend will use the presence or absence of a field as a natural feature flag on a *row-by-row basis*. The *command* and `listener` functions will save records in the *new* format, and `query` and `trigger` functions will understand *both* the old and new formats.

The deployments for `query` and `trigger` functions will proceed as follows:

1. Map either the old field or new field at the record level to both the old and new field at the interface level for a query response or a domain event.

2. Wait for the frontend and consumers to upgrade.

3. Continue to support the old and new fields at the record level, but only support the new field at the interface level.

4. Wait for all the records to convert and/or old records to expire.

5. Remove the record-level mappings for the old field name.

The deployments for `command` and `listener` functions will proceed as follows:

1. Map the incoming old field or new field to the new field at the record level and remove the old field from an existing record.

2. Wait for the frontend and producers to upgrade.

3. Remove the incoming old field mapping and continue to remove the old field from an existing record.

4. Wait for all the records to convert and/or old records to expire.

5. Remove the logic to remove the old field from an existing record.

For a large data store, it may make sense to have a conversion process as well. This process can execute concurrently with the changes made by the `command` and `listener` functions. For example, this process might process a month's worth of historical data each day until complete.

We can implement many of these various steps in parallel, but the order in which we deploy each step to production is the most important part for achieving zero downtime. This requires purposeful planning. Let's look at how we can plan our deployments and releases at multiple levels.

Planning at multiple levels

The process of **choreographing deployment and delivery** requires planning at multiple levels. We need to plan the deployments and the deliveries, and we need some planning in between. Exactly what we call these different levels isn't as important as having the right-sized units of work that enable teams to establish a workable cadence.

The following diagram illustrates the overall process. This diagram is purposefully similar to A traditional Agile snowman, but it is distinctly different in that we are continuously deploying changes and continuously delivering working functionality to the end users in production:

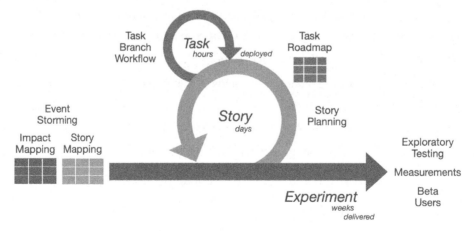

Figure 9.2 – Multiple levels of planning

The process starts out with some envisioning and event storming, as we covered in *Chapter 2, Defining Boundaries and Letting Go*, which produces an architecture of autonomous subsystems. From here, the individual subsystems can proceed, with relative autonomy and pertinent coordination, to formulate their plans. Then, the teams turn the crank, work the backlogs, evaluate feedback, and make adjustments.

For the purpose of discussion, we will call these levels of planning *experiments*, *stories*, and *tasks*. We will touch on some common alternatives to these names, but the three levels of granularity are what are most important to help control batch size and mitigate risks.

Experiments

At the top level of planning, we focus on what we will deliver to the end user, and when. It is the largest unit of work, typically measured in *weeks*. A delivery equates to released software—that is, the ability to turn a feature on for a set of users. So, we can think of this level as *release* planning, but not exactly in the traditional sense.

Early deliverables will likely be internal releases, such as the *walking skeleton* that we will cover shortly, but it is important that we deliver these to the *production* environment. Otherwise, we are accumulating a large batch size for the initial push to production that will interrupt the team's *rhythm* and increase the risk of a mistake.

We are ultimately delivering features to the end user, but we are delivering them incrementally. So, we can think of this level as *feature* planning, but it will likely take several *releases* (that is, experiments) before we are ready to turn a feature on for all users. In reality, we may have to adapt to early user feedback and change course several times before we have the right fit. So, at this level of planning, we will tend to call each unit an experiment.

We need to keep batch size down, show progress, and receive feedback. It is also good for a team to establish a cadence and have regular milestones, but we need to deliver something meaningful without going off track. Thus, limiting the scope of an experiment to a few weeks, in the early phases, is a good rule of thumb. As a product stabilizes, the experiments will likely be much smaller and more focused as we try to squeeze out more value.

Impact mapping is a common technique that teams use for planning at this level. It is *goal*-focused, such as we want to increase market share or improve efficiency by some percentage. Then, we formulate potential experiments to learn how we might achieve this impact for the specific users. The goal gives the team something measurable, so we can gauge whether or not an experiment is successful.

Epic is another common term in use at this level of planning. An epic is larger than a story and it might be smaller than a feature. It is probably larger than we want for an experiment. An epic may be a good unit of work for a modernization effort, where the team has experience with the functionality and a strong understanding of the scope of the work. However, the team should move to an experimenting mindset when they begin to introduce changes and new features.

From here, we divide experiments into stories that the individual teams divide into tasks.

Story backlog

There is plenty of discussion in the industry about the nature of **user stories**: what is a story; how do they differ from use cases; and so on.

Tactically, a **story** is just a *unit of work* that the team needs to perform to advance toward a delivery. We should measure these units of work in terms of *days*, to help control their scope so that the team can more easily reason about the impact the change will have on the production system.

We tell a story from the user's or actor's perspective. This is important because it aligns with our autonomous service patterns. Each service supports a specific actor, which makes it easy to *identify the impact* of the story.

We need to order the stories so that the team knows what to work on first, next, and so on and so forth, and we need to split large stories into right-sized stories. Story mapping is a technique that helps us do this.

Story mapping

We use **impact mapping** to help steer the *direction* of the product, and **event storming** helps us uncover the *behavior* of the system. We also divide the system into autonomous subsystems so that each can change independently. Now, we need to divide the *delivery* of a subsystem into manageable units of work we call stories. This is where **story mapping** comes in. This is a technique that helps us order and rightsize stories on the backlog.

The following diagram depicts a story-mapping board:

Figure 9.3 – Story mapping

We start by arranging user activities on the first row in the order that users perform them. Then, we add progressive details down the board for each user activity. Each card represents an ordered and right-sized story on the backlog. The team will pull the stories row by row, from left to right. Finally, we group rows into deliverables (that is, experiments).

The *first row* represents the first deliverable. It is the *walking skeleton* that forms the foundation for the subsystem. It is working software. The team identifies all the services and micro-apps, creates the repositories from templates, sets up the pipelines, and pushes everything through to production.

For example, each column aligns with a primary service. A column for a human actor will align with a micro-app and a BFF service, as we discussed in *Chapter 3, Taming the Presentation Tier*, and *Chapter 6, A Best Friend for the Frontend*. External activities will have their own columns and align with an ESG service, as we covered in *Chapter 7, Bridging Intersystem Gaps*. And the flow of activities as a whole may align with a control service, as we covered in *Chapter 8, Reacting to Events with More Events*.

At this point, the structure of the subsystem is readily visible, with menus, navigation, and placeholders for the details. It is a rough sketch that the team demonstrates to the product owner to validate that things are off to a good start.

From here, the team iterates on the details of the user activities. Each story should be right-sized. If a story will take longer than a few days, then split it into multiple stories. For example, each section of a screen can be a separate story, and rules and validations can follow in additional stories. A **user-interface-first (UI-first)** approach may also make sense, with the early stories focused on the frontend and later stories implementing the backend.

It is important not to go too deep too soon. The early deliveries should target beta users and early adopters. Their feedback may change the direction, so we don't want to waste effort on advanced details until we know we are on the right track.

Now that we have an ordered backlog of stories, the team can start pulling stories.

Story planning

Story planning is the first activity the team performs when it pulls the next story from the backlog. This is akin to sprint planning, but different. The focus is on a *single* story. The team has a conversation with the product owner to ensure they understand the intended functionality.

However, the most important output of the story-planning activity is a *task roadmap*. This roadmap enables the team to put the functionality into production with *zero downtime* so that we can perform the experiment with real users and validate the product direction.

Task roadmaps

A **task** is the smallest unit of work. We should measure tasks in terms of *hours*. Each task is an atomic unit of work that only touches a single repository. A task is a *unit of deployment* and will update production once completed and approved.

Tasks on the same repository need to be serialized. Tasks for different repositories can proceed in parallel, but it may be necessary to serialize their deployment. We define this serialization in a task roadmap.

A **task roadmap** is a well-crafted series of tasks that enables the team to put the functionality of a story into production with zero downtime, as we covered in the *Achieving zero downtime deployments* section. Each task deploys a backward-compatible portion of the functionality to production, following the *Robustness principle*.

Testing is not a task. Tasks are test-driven. A task includes writing the test cases to cover the new code. The overall test suite accumulates with each additional task.

Let's see how this works in practice.

Turning the crank

Now that we have a plan, we get to do the fun part. We get to turn the crank and do the work. We pull the next *task*, write the code, push it to *production*, and see the fruits of our labor. Right?

Actually, up to this point, the process has been very flexible. It has been a lot of talk, sticky notes, and diagrams. It has been flexible on purpose—because we are experimenting.

But now, the rubber meets the road, so to speak, and we have to get serious. After all, programming languages are notorious for doing exactly what we tell them to do, and we are about to deploy a change to production while the users are actually using the system.

So, this small part of the process needs *due diligence*. We call it *task branch workflow*. This workflow *governs* how we turn the crank and do the work. It includes both automated and manual gates. But it is a straightforward workflow that becomes *second nature* since we do it many times a day, day after day.

And it is this *muscle memory*, which we have built up day after day, that we will rely on to jump into action and fail forward when we make an honest human error.

Task branch workflow

Task branch workflow is a GitOps-style continuous deployment approach that defines the machinery for moving *focused and deliberate* changes from development into production. It joins our issue trackers, developer tools, source code repositories, and CI/CD pipelines into a cohesive system that enables us to crank out working software. It is the *automated bureaucracy* that provides needed guardrails so that we can work efficiently and safely.

The following diagram depicts the activities in a task-branch workflow:

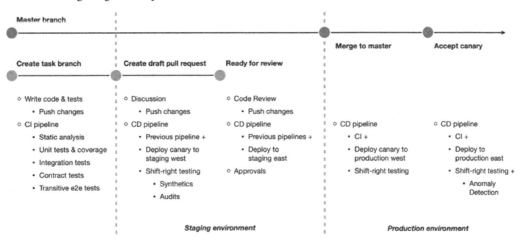

Figure 9.4 – Task-branch workflow

Let's dig into the different activities of the workflow.

Create task branch

A task-branch workflow begins when a developer pulls the next task from the backlog and creates a new branch off the master branch of the specific repository. We name the branch after the task, and all work for the task is performed on this branch. The branch will be short-lived, as a task is measured in hours.

The developer writes the new code and the all-important test cases for the new code.

We explicitly define the scope of each task when the team defines the task roadmap. Examples include seeding a new repository from a template, adding a new connector class, adding a new method to a model class, updating a mapper function for a stream processor, adding a new button to a screen, and so on. The key to success is that each change is focused and backward-compatible. In other words, the change follows the *Robustness principle*, as we covered in the *Achieving zero downtime* section.

The developer pushes the change to the remote branch, once all the tests pass. At this point, the CI pipeline will assert that all the tests pass. We will cover the details of the CI pipeline in the *Continuous integration pipeline* section.

Create draft pull request

The developer creates a draft **pull request** (**PR**) when the task is too far enough along to warrant feedback and discussion. It is important to ask for feedback early and often. A good practice is to create the draft PR after the first push.

The small size and focus of a task branch is crucial to receiving prompt feedback from fellow developers, as they are working on their own tasks. They need to be able to zero in on the essence of the change, provide constructive feedback, and then get back to their work.

Creating a draft PR also signals that it is time to deploy the change to the secondary region of the staging environment where continuous smoke tests are executing. We will cover regional canary deployments in the *Continuous deployment pipeline* section.

Ready for review

The developer moves the PR from draft mode into the ready-for-review status when the task is ready to go to production. The CI pipeline and the CD pipeline for the regional canary deployment to the staging environment must have already passed.

At this point, the developer opens the PR to a wider audience for code review and approval. How wide an audience and how many approvals will depend on the risk level of the change. If the change is to a new feature or a rarely used feature, then there is low risk. However, if it is the most critical part of the system, then it will need multiple approvals and, most likely, outside approval. The team will identify the risk level during *story planning* and notify any outside approvers in advance.

A PR for a presentation-layer change should include annotated screenshots and/or video recordings. This opens the review process to the non-technical stakeholders and provides context for the technical review.

Moving the PR to the ready-for-review status also signals that it is time to deploy the change to the primary region of the staging environment where continuous smoke tests are executing. We will cover this in the *Continuous deployment pipeline* section.

Merge to master

The team merges the PR into the master branch only after all the automated and manual gates have passed. These include all required approvals and successful execution of the following:

1. The CI pipeline
2. The CD pipelines for all the regions of the staging environment
3. All the automated smoke tests in all the regions of the staging environment

Merging the PR into the master branch will trigger the execution of the CI pipeline against the master branch. Successful execution of the CI pipeline on the master branch triggers the deployment of the change to the secondary region of the production environment. We will cover regional canary deployments in the *Continuous deployment pipeline* section.

Merging to master is a manual gate. The team may merge straight away or wait for the optimal time. Again, the team will identify the need for any delay during story planning.

Accept canary deployment

Accepting the regional canary deployment is the final manual gate for a task-level change.

At this point, the team has deployed the change to one region in the production environment. If everything has gone according to plan, then any active users in this region are none the wiser, all the continuous smoke tests have succeeded, and there were no anomalies detected.

From here, the team will wait for a predetermined amount of time and then accept the regional canary deployment. This will trigger the deployment of the change to all remaining regions in the production environment.

If the team detects a problem that they did not catch in any of the regions of the staging environment, then they stop the line and jump into action. This is where they rely on their muscle memory to fail forward fast.

The high observability of the system and the limited scope of the change facilitate **root-cause analysis (RCA)**. Meanwhile, the autonomy of the feature limits the blast radius, so upstream and downstream features continue to operate unabated.

Now, let's look closer at the pipelines.

Continuous integration pipeline

The **Continuous Integration (CI)** pipeline is the first gate in the task branch workflow. We cannot deploy the change to the staging environment, and we cannot merge the PR into the master branch until all the test cases pass.

The CI pipeline executes all the types of testing that we are automating and shifting left into the build process. These include static analysis, unit testing, integration testing, contract testing, and end-to-end testing.

Isolation from external dependencies is the key to executing all these test cases in the CI pipeline. Each pipeline must execute independently. We can achieve this more easily with autonomous services because they do not use synchronous inter-service communication, so they have a limited number of external dependencies, such as to the event hub and to their own data store.

In *Chapter 6, A Best Friend for the Frontend*, we highlighted the importance of wrapping external dependencies in *Connector* classes. These classes delineate all the locations where we need to create a *test double* to stand in for the real external service during testing, such as mock objects and VCR recordings.

It is also important for developers and the pipelines to execute the tests in the same way—for example, a developer can run all the unit tests and static analysis by executing `npm test` from the command line. Executing `npm run test:int` will run all the remaining test categories. These are the exact same commands that the pipeline executes. This allows developers to test their work before pushing a change, eliminates duplicate development effort, and decouples the test cases from the CI/CD pipeline tool.

The following example shows a fragment of a `.gitlab-ci.yml` file:

```
ci:
  stage: test
  script:
    - npm ci
    - npm test
    - npm run test:int
```

The npm scripts do the real work of the CI pipeline. The CI/CD tool only provides orchestration and the execution environment. This example invokes the CI pipeline in the test stage on any branch.

You can find examples of pipelines for popular CI/CD tools here:

```
https://github.com/jgilbert01/aws-lambda-stream/tree/master/
templates/cicd
```

Let's look into the different types of shift-left testing.

Unit testing

Unit testing is arguably the most important type of testing, because it is the first line of defense against mistakes. We are continuously deploying small changes to the production environment, and unit testing is the best way to test that a change is not doing more harm than good.

Unit tests focus on testing the business logic within the individual components. For example, in *Chapter 6, A Best Friend for the Frontend*, we introduced the concept of *Model* and *Connector* classes. The bulk of the unit-test cases will focus on the *Model* classes. These classes contain the domain logic and business rules. A fair number of test cases may be necessary to account for all the permutations in the logic. For rule-intensive logic, a portion of these tests will constitute the *acceptance tests* that assert the specified acceptance criteria.

Unit testing should constitute the overwhelming majority of test cases in a well-balanced *test automation pyramid* because they are the least difficult to write. To facilitate writing these tests, we test the business logic in isolation from their external dependencies. We accomplish this by substituting mock objects for the *Connector* classes, which we will cover in a moment.

Coverage

Unit tests are important enough that we fail the build if there is not 100% coverage. This may seem excessive at first, but with each task we only add a small amount of code, so we only need to write a small number of tests per task. Over time, these accumulate into an invaluable suite of test cases.

Without 100% coverage, it is too easy to fall into the trap of skipping these all-important tests and put the product, the process, and the mission at risk. We will make mistakes, because we are human. The reputation of the product will suffer. The continuous deployment process will receive the blame for a lack of testing, and it will likely be discarded. Ultimately, our ability to continuously innovate will be severely limited as we fall back on methods that are proven to increase lead time.

Code coverage doesn't help us write good tests, but it does keep us honest about how much testing we have and—more importantly—where it is missing. Of course, not every line of code is worth testing. So, we should make judicious use of `ignore` statements to keep coverage at 100%, without wasting effort, and keep ourselves out of the trap.

Static analysis

The first step in the unit testing process is **static analysis** (that is, **linting**). We perform this first because there is no point in unit-testing code that does not meet the guidelines.

Linting covers more than stylistic errors. It enforces best practices, automatically fixes many violations, and identifies common problems. For example, in React, we prefer functional components over class components, and linting can automatically convert class components to functional components. In essence, linting can help teach developers how to write better code.

The open source community has assembled many great rulesets, such as **eslint-config-airbnb**. Project templates should have these linting rules preconfigured so that each project gets off to the right start.

Mock objects

Testing should follow the scientific method, where we hold some variables constant, adjust the input, and measure the output. An important element of this is testing individual components in isolation from their external dependencies.

This is the primary goal of the *Connector* classes that we introduced in *Chapter 6, A Best Friend for the Frontend*. In the long term, connectors can facilitate changing an implementation decision, but in the short term, they provide immediate benefit by facilitating the testing of the business logic with mock objects.

A **mock object** is a form of *test double* that we use in unit testing to isolate external dependencies. They are pre-programmed by the developer with specific behavior to support a specific test case and substituted for the real object, following the substitution principle. The test case executes in isolation and asserts that the business logic invoked the mock object with an expected input.

However, we must handcraft the mock objects, which means they are prone to developer error, resulting in test cases that produce false positives. Furthermore, external interfaces tend to be verbose, which increases the likelihood of developer error.

Conversely, a Connector class provides a clean and simple interface to the business logic that encapsulates the details of interacting with the external resource. This greatly simplifies the work of creating mock objects for the majority of test cases and improves the reliability of the unit-test suite.

A small set of unit tests provide coverage for the connector classes themselves. For these tests, the developer spends extra effort to mock the more complex calls to the actual external interfaces. To account for developer error in these test cases, we will perform integration testing as well.

Integration testing

Integration testing picks up where the unit testing of connector classes left off. It ensures that the connectors are calling the remote services correctly.

Integration testing should constitute a small number of test cases in a well-balanced *test automation pyramid* because they are more difficult to write and maintain. This difficulty comes from the need to set up and configure the external dependencies prior to executing the tests. This includes initializing all the necessary data dependencies as well.

These calls also require the network, which is notoriously unreliable. This is the major cause of flaky tests that randomly and haphazardly fail. Flaky tests, in turn, are a major cause of poor team morale, since developers must waste valuable time tracking down the root cause of the test failures.

To solve these problems, we run the integration tests in isolation, as well, using a VCR test double.

VCR test double

We execute the integration tests in isolation by utilizing a test-double mechanism that intercepts the remote requests and replays recorded responses. We refer to this record-and-playback test double mechanism as a VCR after the video cassette recorder. Popular Node.js-based VCR tools include Replay and Polly.js. Let's look at an example of an integration test for a BFF service, as covered in *Chapter 6, A Best Friend for the Frontend.*

The following `serverless.yml` fragment configures the integration-testing environment. The `serverless-offline` plugin creates a local **HyperText Transfer Protocol (HTTP)** server that simulates the **Amazon Web Services (AWS)** API Gateway and Lambda runtimes. `baton-vcr-serverless-plugin` initializes the **Replay** VCR tool:

```
plugins:
  ...
  - baton-vcr-serverless-plugin
  - serverless-offline
```

The `npm run test:int` script starts the simulator and then executes all the integration tests. The following code block shows the integration test case for the BFF service's RESTful interface:

```
const client =
  require('supertest')('http://localhost:3001');
const THING = {...};
describe('bff command and query test', () => {
  it('should save', () =>
    client.put('/things/1')
    .send(THING)
    .expect(200);
  it('should get by id', () =>
    client.get('/things/1')
    .expect(200)
    .expect((res) => {
      expect(JSON.parse(res.text)).to.deep.equal(THING);
    }));
});
```

The test suite submits HTTP requests to the local simulator running on `localhost:3001`. The first test case saves a domain entity, and the second test case retrieves the domain entity by its identifier. The BFF service should execute the update and query operations against the DynamoDB table and return a response. The test cases assert that they received the expected responses.

When creating a test case, the developer executes the tests in recording mode to create the recordings. The VCR tool intercepts the calls to DynamoDB and saves the request-and-response pairs to the `fixtures` folder.

The integration test suite is self-initializing—in other words, it creates all the necessary test data. This simple test suite initializes the data by executing the `save` command before executing the query. A more complex suite would set up reference data and related transactions in a before-suite block. The VCR records these initialization commands as well.

With the recordings in place, the CI pipeline does not need access to the external resources. The pipeline executes the tests in playback mode. The VCR tool intercepts the calls to DynamoDB, looks for the matching recordings, and returns the recorded responses. If the code produces a different request or the VCR returns an unexpected response, then the test case will fail.

Integration testing also asserts the proper invocation of functions by cloud services. This example demonstrates how the `serveless-offline` plugin simulates the AWS API Gateway environment for `command` and `query` functions. For `listener` and `trigger` functions, we manually capture events from the log files and use them to drive the test cases. These test cases, in turn, record the calls to the data store and the event hub.

Integration tests should not cover all of the functional scenarios. That is the job of unit testing. We need just enough integration testing to be confident that we are making the remote calls correctly.

From here, we need to guard against the service side making changes that invalidate the recordings. That is the job of contract testing.

Contract testing

Contract testing and integration testing are two sides of the same coin. Integration tests ensure that a consumer is calling a service correctly, whereas contract tests ensure that a service continues to meet its obligations to a consumer and that any changes are backward-compatible.

Contract testing is unique because it is consumer-driven. This means that the consumer team writes a test case and submits a PR to the service team to add the contract test to its repository. The service team is not supposed to modify these tests.

If a contract test breaks, this indicates that the service changed in a backward-incompatible way. The service team must make the change compatible, following the Robustness principle, and then work with the consumer team to create an upgrade roadmap.

Backward-incompatible changes can manifest in subtle ways that may not violate a handcrafted contract test. For this reason, we will use the same recording from the consumer's integration test to drive the contract test in the service's test suite.

How we implement a contract test varies based on whether it is a synchronous or an asynchronous interaction. Let's look at the differences.

Synchronous

A **synchronous interaction** between a frontend and its BFF service provides a prototypical example for consumer-driven contract testing. Although a single team owns both sides of this interaction, it is still worthwhile to write contract tests. The frontend and backend have independent pipelines, so there is a chance for incompatible changes to slip through.

First, the team creates an integration test in the frontend project that records the call to the backend. Then, they copy the recording to the backend project and use it to drive a contract test. The tests on each side ensure that the code is not changing in relation to the request-and-response recordings. If these tests fail, then the team must plan out a backward-compatible roadmap for rolling out the change.

The following code block shows the contract test case for the backend:

```
const relay = require('baton-request-relay');
const client =
  require('supertest')('http://localhost:3001');
describe('contract/frontend', () => {
  it('should exec the frontend get request', () => {
    const rec = relay('./fixtures/frontend/get');
    return client[rec.request.method](rec.request.path)
      .set(rec.request.headers)
```

```
        .expect(rec.response.statusCode)
        .expect(rec.response.body);
    };
});
```

The contract test uses the same simulator environment and VCR tools that we covered in the *Integration testing* section. The test case uses the `baton-request-relay` module to parse the recording. Then, it uses the recording to execute the same request as the consumer and compares the actual response to the expected response.

Asynchronous

For an asynchronous interaction, we need to invert the process for creating and recording a consumer-driven contract test because the consumer does not initiate the interaction. The upstream service produces the domain event, and zero-to-many downstream services consume the domain event.

There is no explicit coupling between the upstream service and the downstream services, yet the definition of the domain event forms the contract that the producer must uphold. So, an asynchronous contract test ensures that the upstream service continues to produce a domain event in the expected format. It also helps to document all of the downstream dependencies.

First, a consuming team creates a contract test in the upstream project that produces and records the expected domain event. In the following example, the test case asserts that the `trigger` function continues to produce the recorded domain event for the given CDC_EVENT event. This test prevents the upstream team from making changes that will break the downstream service:

```
import CDC_EVENT from    '../../../fixtures/downstream-
consumer-x';
import { handle } from '../../../src/trigger';
describe('contract/downstream-consumer-x', () => {
  it('should publish thing-created', (done) => {
    handle(CDC_EVENT, {}, done);
  });
});
```

Then, the consuming team copy the recording of the domain event to their own project and use it to drive a `listener` test. In the following example, the test case asserts that the downstream `listener` function understands the format of the recorded `thing-created` domain event. The test case uses the `baton-event-relay` module to parse the domain event from the recording:

```
import relay from 'baton-event-relay';
import { handle } from '../../../src/listener';
describe('contract/upstream-provider-y', () => {
  it('should process the thing-created event', (done) => {
    const rec =          relay('./fixtures/upstream-provider-y/
thing-created');
    handle(rec.event, {}, done);
  });
});
```

The various teams independently create integration and contract tests as they work on their stories and tasks. When the functionality of the system begins to stabilize, the teams can coordinate and leverage these testing techniques to create a cohesive end-to-end suite. We will cover this next.

Transitive end-to-end testing

Traditional end-to-end testing is time-consuming and expensive. It favors large batch sizes and long lead times, which is the exact opposite of what we are aiming for. All too often, teams skip end-to-end testing entirely and hope for the best.

Now, we have a better option. We can leverage the integration and contract testing techniques and craft a series of test cases that form a cohesive end-to-end scenario across all the projects (that is, **services**). Each contract test case produces its own set of integration recordings, and we use these recordings to drive the next test case in the next project, and so forth.

The following diagram illustrates how these tests fit together. Borrowing from the transitive property of equality, if Test Case **1** for Service **A** produces Recording **X**, which drives Test Case **2** for Service **B** to produce Recording **Y**, which drives Test Case **3** for Service **C** to produce Recording **Z**, then we can assert that when Service **A** produces Recording **X**, then ultimately Service **C** will produce Recording **Z**:

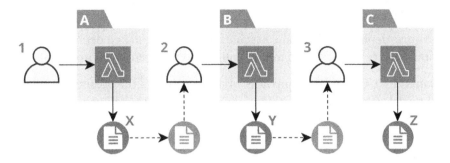

Figure 9.5 – Transitive end-to-end testing

The pipelines of the individual services remain completely independent. We only need to execute the portion of the end-to-end test suite that applies to a specific service when we modify it. There is no need to rerun all the test cases across all the projects. So long as the recordings still match, we can transitively assert the correctness of the scenario. Only a backward-incompatible change requires dependent projects to rerun their portion of the end-to-end test suite.

Transitive end-to-end testing is a powerful approach that makes end-to-end testing practical because it significantly reduces the effort of maintaining an end-to-end test suite. There is no need to maintain a dedicated testing environment because the individual pipelines constitute a virtual environment. There is no need to maintain database scripts to reset databases to a known state because the recordings embody the data.

The test engineers from across the projects must collaborate to craft the end-to-end scenarios, and the developers have to implement the test cases and generate the recordings. But this is effort well spent. We leverage it over and over with each execution of a pipeline.

It is important to point out that the effort to put an end-to-end test suite together is a unit of work in and of itself. The teams will usually collaborate on this test suite toward the end of an experiment, once the functionality starts to stabilize. With each experiment, the teams will refine the end-to-end test suite.

Once an end-to-end suite is in place, the teams must keep the suite up to date as they work on each additional story and task. Therefore, it is important to keep the scope of the end-to-end test suite in check. It should only form the tip of a well-balanced test automation pyramid. The suite should have enough coverage to give the teams the confidence to continuously deploy changes, but not be so large that maintaining it impedes experimentation and innovation.

The CI pipeline gives us enough confidence to deploy a change, but we will proceed with several additional controls in the CD pipeline.

Continuous deployment pipeline

The continuous deployment pipeline executes the fully automated deployment of an autonomous service or micro-app to the staging and production environments.

Once again, the CI/CD tool only provides orchestration and the execution environment. The pipeline delegates the heavy lifting to the npm scripts. The following example shows a fragment of a .github/workflow/cd-stg.yml file:

```
on:
  pull_request:
    branches: [ master ]
jobs:
  deploy-staging-west-canary:
    steps:

      . . .

      - run: npm run dp:stg:w
  deploy-staging-east:
    if: github.event.pull_request.draft == false
    steps:

      . . .

      - run: npm run dp:stg:e
```

This file defines the CD pipeline for the staging environment. The pipeline executes when the developer creates a PR that targets the master branch, and on any push thereafter. The canary deployment to the western region has no additional guard conditions, whereas the deployment to the eastern region asserts that the PR is not in draft mode before proceeding.

The following example shows one of the npm scripts that the pipeline executes:

```
"dp:stg:e": "sls deploy --region us-east-1 --stage stg"
```

The script calls the Serverless Framework, which in turn delegates to AWS CloudFormation to deploy all the resources of the service. You can find examples of package.json and serverless.yml files and pipeline files for popular CI/CD tools here: https://github.com/jgilbert01/aws-lambda-stream/tree/master/templates.

These fully automated and declarative deployments go a long way toward eliminating human error. But before we go all-in on the deployment, we have one more gate. We will test the water first with a regional canary deployment.

Regional canary deployments

The phrase *canary in a coal mine* refers to the former practice of taking a caged canary into a coal mine to alert miners of the presence of deadly gases. A canary is more susceptible to toxic fumes and would provide an early warning sign when it stopped singing.

In software engineering, a *canary deployment* is the practice of rolling out a change to a subset of users, before rolling it out to all the users. The subset of users acts as the canary. If there is a problem with the change then it only impacts the subset of users, and the team fails forward with a fix; otherwise, the team increments the percentage of users, such as 1%, 10%, 30%, 70%, 100%.

However, many—if not most—services will not benefit from traditional canary deployments because they do not have enough traffic; for example, a service may only receive sporadic usage. Yet, we still want the benefits of incremental deployment.

We also need to limit the risk of a deployment to an isolated environment—for example, we should not deploy a canary into the same cluster that is running the previous version of the code. The level of risk may seem low, but the consequences are significant if a mistake takes down the entire cluster.

This is where multi-regional deployments provide significant benefits because each region is an isolated environment. Whether they are running *active-active* or *active-passive*, we can leverage these isolated environments to perform regional canary deployments, and we will leverage the failover capabilities that we already have in place, which we covered in *Chapter 6, A Best Friend for the Frontend*. We need to have multiple regions anyway, so let's get the most out of them.

If a service is running in an *active-passive* configuration, then this approach is akin to a *blue-green deployment*. We treat the passive region as the green environment and the active region as the blue environment. The first deployment goes to the green region. If the smoke tests succeed in the green region, then we move ahead with the deployment and smoke tests in the blue region. Alternatively, we can flip the traffic between the different regions to achieve a more traditional blue-green approach. But it may become difficult to reason about the health of the overall system with different services actively running in different regions.

If a service is running in an *active-active* configuration, then we pick a region—usually a western region—as the canary region. The subset of users in the region acts as the canary. The first deployment goes to the canary region. We also execute the smoke tests against the canary region, since the user activity is sporadic. If the service does have a significant number of active users, then we can add weighted routing to the equations to achieve a more traditional canary deployment.

If there is a problem with the regional canary deployment, then we can leverage the failover capability and stop routing traffic to it. Once we are satisfied with the deployment in the canary region, then we move ahead with the deployment and smoke tests in the remaining regions.

We apply this approach to the staging environment as well, for an added level of protection. In the staging environment, this will tend to have a more blue-green feel, because there are far fewer testers using this environment as compared to active users in production. Regardless, we need to treat staging with the same mindset as production so that we can verify the zero-downtime task roadmap and practice the incremental deployment process.

Regional canary deployments give us the benefits of both isolation and incremental deployment, regardless of the level of user activity, on a service-by-service basis. Now, let's look at simulating user activity so that we are continuously exercising the system with smoke tests.

Synthetics

Our *shift-left testing* provides a significant level of protection because these tests must pass before we can deploy a change. However, a CI pipeline only executes the tests for the repository that is changing. Plus, we are using test doubles for all the dependencies.

The contract and transitive end-to-end tests provide strong backward-compatibility protections for the upstream and downstream services. However, there is always the potential that we might miss something—for example, a change may introduce a subtle dependency between components that we didn't intend to occur.

This is where *shift-right testing* and *synthetics* come in. These are akin to traditional end-to-end testing, but we execute them against the staging and production environments. **Synthetics** are essentially smoke tests that we automate and execute continuously.

These tests form the top of a well-balanced test automation pyramid. They cover the most critical functionality of the system. This is the 20% of the system that we use 80% of the time. They cover the functionality that must work, or else. Of course, all functionality is important, but we cannot test the entire system continuously. So, we have to make decisions.

Continuous means that we execute these tests on a schedule—for example, every 15 minutes to once an hour for the most important tests, or once a day or once a week for features that are equally important, but used far less often.

We execute these tests in the staging environment as well as the production environment so that we can find issues before approving a PR, and we execute them independently in each region to assert the stability of the canary deployments. For a regional canary deployment of a service with light usage, the synthetics will act as the canary users.

After a deployment, the team must pay extra attention to these continuous smoke tests to confirm the health and stability of the system. The bottom line is that the team needs to know about a problem before the end users so that they can fail forward fast.

Even when we are not changing the system, these tests help assert the overall health of the system. For example, if the cloud provider experiences a regional disruption, the synthetics will help trigger a regional failover.

When a synthetic test fails, then it is obvious that the team must jump into action. However, there may be an indirect problem downstream. This is where anomaly detection comes into play.

Anomaly detection

We have covered many observability topics throughout this book. Now, as we turn the crank, this is where they all come together. We are continuously collecting work metrics and resource metrics in the staging and production environments. These metrics provide teams with valuable insights on the inner workings of the system. The work metrics help us gauge the health of the features, and the resource metrics help us determine the root cause of any issues.

Having this information readily available gives teams the confidence to move forward with their experiments, because they know they have the necessary tools to fail forward fast. Without these metrics, the users will most likely find an issue first, and it will take the team longer to resolve the problem.

Anomaly detection is a form of *shift-right testing* that continuously monitors the signals that the system is emitting. Whereas synthetics continually test a fixed set of important cases, anomaly detection is continuously testing all the work metrics for unexpected spikes and dips. It applies statistical and **machine learning** (**ML**) algorithms, and alerts the team when there are deviations from the norm.

In *Chapter 4, Trusting Facts and Eventual Consistency*, we saw that the rate of a domain event is a work metric, and in *Chapter 6, A Best Friend for the Frontend*, we saw that the rate of a BFF service call is a work metric. Teams should perform anomaly detection on these two categories of work metrics.

Synthetics and anomaly detection work together to provide the team with timely information about the health of the system. Synthetics continuously exercise the system, and anomaly detection continuously tests the output signals. Together, they continuously check the system so that the team can focus on their experiments, and they notify the team when it is time to jump into action and recover quickly.

Now that we have asserted the stability of a deployment, it's time to determine if we are delivering the right functionality.

Feature flipping

Decoupling deployment from delivery gives us flexibility—it allows us to divide a delivery into a series of zero-downtime deployments. The code is available in production, but it is inactive. We can selectively activate the code for exploratory testers and early adopters, and iterate on the feedback. Then, when we have the right functionality, we deliver (that is, **activate**) the feature for general availability. In other words, we have the flexibility to flip features on and off throughout the process of discovering the right fit.

Exploratory testing

This is where the more traditional **quality assurance (QA)** activities come into play. The testers manually exercise the system to determine if a feature is fit for purpose. Once again, the focus is on discovery. The testers may have notional test scripts for what they expect to find, but this exercise is really all about finding the unexpected. What we think is right and what works in practice are not always the same, and this is an opportunity to find the gaps.

Testers usually perform exploratory testing in the staging environment, but they may test in the production environment as well. In either case, we need to turn the feature on for testers. For example, granting the necessary permissions to the `Tester` role enables a new feature for all testers.

Beta users

Feedback from beta users is invaluable. These are real users, using a feature to do real work. They are early adopters and willing participants who are vested in the outcome, and they are willing to volunteer their efforts to make the product better. They also understand that the functionality is incomplete and that their results may vary as the team experiments.

Beta users perform their work in the production environment. Again, we make the feature available to beta users with a feature flag. For example, we may create a special beta user role, and there may be a dedicated registration or invitation process.

To win the support of beta users, it may be necessary to synchronize their work with a legacy version of the functionality. A beta user's time is valuable, and they do not want to have to do their work twice. They need the ability to switch between the old and the new. For example, they can start a task in the legacy version and complete it in the new version, and vice versa. If the new version is not working correctly, then they can switch back to the legacy version and pick up where they left off, to a reasonable extent. This does increase the level of effort, but it is a valuable risk-mitigation strategy and will likely reduce the level of effort in the long run. We covered legacy integration in *Chapter 7, Bridging Intersystem Gaps*.

General availability

In due time, we make a feature available to all users. The end product may barely resemble what we thought it would look like in the beginning, but that is OK. We needed to experiment to find the right solution for the end user.

We typically refer to this as a **General Availability (GA)** release. We might call exploratory testing an alpha release, and beta users use a beta release, but this time it is official, and with it comes a new level of responsibility.

We have turned the new feature on for all users, and it is time to remove the technical debit of any feature flags that we no longer need. For example, the standard user role now has all the necessary permissions, so we need to remove the specific tester and beta user roles. We also need to remove any references to these roles from the code, along with any artificial feature-flag logic, and push a cleanup deployment.

From here, any changes to a GA feature require additional scrutiny during story planning to ensure zero downtime. Any major changes to a GA feature may make it the new legacy and require concurrently deployed versions and data synchronization. But this is the kind of change and evolution we designed our architecture to support, so bring it on.

Summary

In this chapter, you learned why it is important to control the batch size of a deployment and how to decouple deployment from release with feature flags. You learned about the Robustness principle, how to leverage it to achieve zero-downtime deployments, and the role that a well-planned task roadmap plays in the overall process.

We dug into the details of task-branch workflow and CI/CD pipelines, and you learned about regional canary deployments, synthetics, and anomaly detection. You also learned how to implement continuous testing that enables continuous deployment and continuous discovery, as the team iterates to the right product fit.

In the next and final chapter, we will round out our discussion on architecturing for innovation, with thoughts on getting started, gaining trust, and building momentum. We will address some of the myths and anti-patterns that keep teams from getting off the ground and cover various hurdles and impediments that teams must confront.

10
Don't Delay, Start Experimenting

In *Chapter 9, Choreographing Deployment and Delivery*, we laid out a lightweight development process that can help us decouple deployment from release and turn the crank with a task branch workflow. And we defined an approach for continuous testing that allows us to discover the requirements and continuously deliver business value.

Now it is time for the last chapter. It is time to take everything you have learned and put micro frontends and the autonomous service patterns into action. But where do we start? How do we build momentum? What pitfalls lie ahead? How do we cross the cultural divide between the old and the new? This chapter will answer these questions now. But there will always be open questions. We can't let them delay us. We need to start experimenting.

In this chapter, we're going to cover the following main topics:

- Gaining trust and changing culture
- Funding products, not projects
- Dissecting the Strangler pattern
- Addressing event-first concerns
- Poly everything

Gaining trust and changing culture

Any new effort that goes against the grain of the current culture will experience a bumpy start. It's normal. But it won't take long for the culture to start changing once the new approach proves its worth. I remember my first lift-and-shift project. It was a long uphill climb, but then things changed, almost overnight.

We initially transplanted our manual data center processes into the cloud. But we saw no real benefit from the cloud at that point, because each release of the software was still slow and painful. So, we set out to automate the deployment of the entire platform. We encountered resistance from the start. But we applied our agile, incremental development methodology and started to move forward. First, we did a quick proof of concept and then we addressed incremental pain points as we progressed toward the full solution. Along the way, we picked up support.

After a long 6 months, we had all the support we needed, and we were ready to go to production. The initial deployment was painful, but it was successful. Everyone celebrated. Announcement and congratulatory emails went out. Then we did another deployment on the next day, and more emails went out. And the same thing happened on the day after that. But on the fourth day, we did another deployment, and no emails went out. There was no big announcement, no congratulations, and no high-fives.

The culture changed that rapidly. It quickly became obvious that this was the new normal. We proved that we could perform deployments on any given day. A deployment was no longer a big event. It became routine. It made the whole process better for everyone. So, everyone was on board.

This is a repeatable process. I have seen it happen in many efforts. We need to establish a vision, build momentum, and put an architectural runway in place. Let's look at these things in more detail.

Establishing a vision

First and foremost, we need to establish an architectural vision for the system. It doesn't have to be perfect, but it does have to point the way forward. Without a vision, the system will easily devolve into a big ball of mud.

> **Tip**
>
> Have a look at these articles for more information: `https://en.wikipedia.org/wiki/Big_ball_of_mud` and `http://laputan.org/mud`.

In this book, I put forward the vision for the technical architecture of autonomous services and micro-apps, and *Chapter 9, Choreographing Deployment and Delivery,* provides a vision for the development methodology. But what we really need to move forward is a vision for the functional architecture of the system. We need at least an initial sketch of the system divided into **autonomous subsystems**. We covered this topic in *Chapter 2, Defining Boundaries and Letting Go.* We employed **event storming** to help us identify the core *actors* and the major *domain events*. With this information, we can begin to add structure to the system and visualize how the various pieces fit together.

From here we can begin to craft a plan of action. The architectural vision leads to organizational structure and funding models. We will use it to organize our cloud accounts. The shared vision facilitates inter-team communication. And most importantly, at this point, it helps us identify a good place to start making forward progress. Let's see how we can start to build momentum.

Building momentum

We need to start small and build momentum. Don't delay. Assemble the first team by seeding it with early adopters. These are skilled engineers who are excited about the possibilities. They will also be future leaders as we grow and add more teams.

We need to start with an experiment that immediately adds business value. For example, it could be a new feature that fills a troublesome gap in an existing business process. We cannot go a long time without delivering value to the business. Put a prototype of the frontend in the user's hands as soon as possible, while you work on the backend behind the scenes.

This feature should be relatively independent so that we do not get bogged down. But it should be significant enough to demonstrate the value of the new approach. You can seed the feature using the templates provided with this book: `https://github.com/jgilbert01/aws-lambda-stream/tree/master/templates` and `https://github.com/jgilbert01/micro-frontend-template`. It will be part of the first autonomous subsystem, so you can establish the process for stamping out the corresponding cloud accounts.

Find willing beta users. These users are eager to help improve the system because they see and feel the gaps in the existing system and want to make it better. They understand that this is a work in progress, and they want to be part of the experiment and vet the solution before you roll it out to a wider audience. They will also be a great source for more ideas.

Start building a roadmap of potential experiments. In *Chapter 9, Choreographing Deployment and Delivery*, we introduced *impact mapping* and *story mapping* as tools for identifying valuable features and for creating a roadmap. You will likely focus on one subsystem at first, but it is a good idea to put the walking skeleton for all the subsystems in place sooner rather than later.

And be prepared to get your hands dirty. We need to start putting an architectural runway in place for the teams and experiments that will come next so that they can get up and running smoothly. And the best way to know what works and what doesn't is to do it. Let's look at this runway next.

Constructing an architectural runway

In conjunction with the initial experiment of the previous section, we need to start putting an architectural runway in place. This runway consists of all the things that help the teams get up and running quickly and without duplication of effort. This consists of tools and templates, shared components, and more.

The initial experiment gives us an opportunity to put these capabilities in place. But we don't have much of a head start this first time around. So, we need to work in parallel with the first experiment and try to stay one step ahead. You can use the templates provided with this book to get a head start. Each subsystem will need an event hub and a main entry point for its micro frontend. We will need the ability to stamp out cloud accounts for new subsystems and seed autonomous services and micro-apps from templates.

We can also start to put shared subsystems in place. For example, we will need a subsystem that encapsulates any interactions with the legacy systems as we covered in *Chapter 7, Bridging Intersystem Gaps*. And we will look at this more in the *Dissecting the Strangle pattern* section to come. We will also want a master data model subsystem that sits upstream and manages the reference data that all downstream services leverage. And all the way downstream, we will want subsystems for analytics and archiving. The initial team won't own these forever, but we need the skeleton in place for the initial experiment.

In *Chapter 2, Defining Boundaries and Letting Go*, we covered the various cross-cutting concerns that all teams will need, such as CI/CD pipelines and monitoring. You will want to put these in place quickly, so SaaS solutions are the best way to go. You will also need to start looking at creating the teams that maintain your secured perimeter and your continuous auditing. Let's look at how we can build out teams next.

Seed and split

Seed and split is an approach for knowledge sharing and cultural change. The team that works on the initial experiment will develop new muscle memory, gain valuable experience, and establish a new culture of continuous flow as they work through the various challenges. To field the next team, we split the first team in half and seed new members into both teams. The new members will benefit from the experience of the current members and learn the new culture.

We can continue this process to build out the teams within each autonomous subsystem. Every new team should always start with several experienced members. To kick start a new subsystem, several members can join a team in an established subsystem for a brief period and then bring the knowledge and culture back with them to the new subsystem.

Within a subsystem, the teams will work closely with upstream and downstream teams and naturally share new experiences and continuously improve the methodology and culture. The same thing will happen between autonomous subsystems as organizations work with upstream and downstream organizations to iron out the overarching business processes. Slowly, but surely, the new culture will take hold as the teams continuously deliver business value and momentum builds.

We have established the vision for our architecture of autonomous subsystems and we have kick started our initial experiment with a team and architectural runway. Now, let's look at the funding model changes we need to ensure smooth sailing.

Funding products, not projects

In *Chapter 1, Architecting for Innovation*, we identified that traditional budgeting and planning practices increase lead times. These practices aim to control risk, but in reality, they increase the risk of delivering the wrong solution or delivering too late to be effective. The problem is that they focus on projects instead of products. They assume that we can define all the requirements upfront and provide realistic estimates. But we can't.

> **Tip**
>
> Have a look at these books for more information: `https://www.infoq.com/minibooks/noprojects-value-culture` and `https://www.amazon.com/Delicate-Art-Bureaucracy-Transformation-Wrestler-ebook/dp/B086XM4WCK`.

The bottom line is that we need to know how much money we are going to spend. Businesses need predictable cash flow. And we need to show that we are producing value and that the business is getting its money's worth. But it is hard to justify large multi-year budgets when we do not understand all the requirements upfront. We just can't.

Ultimately, business leaders need to know that everything is under control and that we can change course before we go off the rails and waste valuable time and effort. And this is exactly what our modern methods and architecture allow us to do. We are performing focused experiments so that we can learn and adapt. So, what we need is a funding model that matches our development practices. We need a funding model that supports products instead of projects.

As architects, we need to take the lead and drive this change in approach. Business leaders know that a change is necessary, but they need guidance. The approach I recommend is architecture- and team-driven. Let's look at these in turn.

Architecture-driven

In reality, a business is not going to stop spending money on software development. The business needs to deliver value to stay in business and software is the foundation of modern business processes. But a business will reallocate funding away from failing projects and toward the new best project idea.

This is actually what we are doing when we experiment. We are allocating a little bit of money to an experiment and then reallocating as we learn. So, our funding model needs to give teams the autonomy and authority to make these decisions. The business defines the objectives, and we determine the best way to meet those objectives through experimentation.

But the business needs to know what it is spending its money on, and this is where our architecture plays an all-important role. Our architecture defines what we are funding. It defines the autonomous subsystems and the high-level capabilities they provide. In other words, our architecture enumerates the business value it delivers. If it does not, then we need to go back to *Chapter 2, Defining Boundaries and Letting Go*, and revisit our architecture.

Our architecture defines the buckets of money that we are asking the business to provide so that we can experiment and continuously deliver business value. But now we need to decide how much money to ask for. So, let's look at allocating capacity for autonomous teams next.

Team capacity-driven

Autonomous teams build software. An autonomous team is self-sufficient, full-stack, and cross-functional. In other words, a team has all the resources it needs to deliver value and teams need team members. We, the members of a team, continuously deliver business value, and we can only do so much work in a given period. So, a business needs to field enough teams to perform the work at hand.

This means that funding products ultimately comes down to deciding how much team capacity we want to allocate. On average, each team should have the same capacity to produce value and require the same amount of funding. So, once we determine how many teams we need, we can calculate how much funding we need.

We determine the number of teams we need subsystem by subsystem. For example, is a subsystem big or small? Is its functionality stable or is it evolving? There are many factors that can go into the number of teams we need to field for each subsystem. But doing this at the subsystem (that is, architecture) level helps control the scope and provides focus. We tally up the number of teams across the subsystems and we have the total capacity that we need to fund.

Then, we let the teams turn the crank and perform their experiments. In *Chapter 2, Defining Boundaries and Letting Go*, we covered a continuous governance model that we can use to evaluate team performance. The teams determine how to allocate their capacity and we use team metrics to help determine how much capacity to allocate going forward.

This approach gives the business what it needs: predictable cash flow and the confidence that the money is in good hands. And it gives teams what they need: clear objectives and autonomy so that they can drive down lead times and continuously deliver business value.

Now, let's take a look at how we can migrate off of our legacy systems.

Dissecting the Strangler pattern

The overarching theme of this book is that we want to move fast, but we do not want to break things. This applies to our legacy systems as well. Our legacy architectures may impede change, but these systems provide valuable capabilities to our end users that they rely on every day. We must ensure that our legacy systems continue to work.

However, we do need to modernize our legacy systems and they are filled with a lot of functionality. This means that if we follow a traditional approach then it will take a long time to port the functionality and, in the meantime, the teams will not deliver any new business value. And when the time comes to cut over from the old system to the new system, this traditional all-or-nothing approach will put everything at risk. There is just too much risk to justify using the traditional approach.

Instead, we will build up new features and replacement features around the existing systems and integrate with them. Slowly, but surely, we will chip away at the features of the legacy systems until we simply no longer need them. This is known as the **Strangler** pattern. It is a risk mitigation strategy that takes into account the fact that we need to continuously deliver business value without breaking things.

But there is a right way and a wrong way to implement this pattern. Users prefer a seamless experience, and this creates the temptation to weave the new system into the old user experience. This usually involves writing an adapter layer that maps the old API to a new backend layer. And then we need to modify the legacy system so that it can toggle between the old and new endpoints.

This traditional approach does follow the **Substitution** principle, but it breaks the **Open-Closed** principle. We have to modify the legacy systems and sooner or later we will have to implement the new user experience and go through the risk of cutting over to that. So, we need an approach that does not require us to make changes to the legacy systems, just like we saw with the **EAI** integration approach that we covered in *Chapter 1, Architecting for Innovation*. And we need the ability to turn off the old systems without any cutover.

Moreover, the new features we write today will become tomorrow's legacy features. It is inevitable. So, we want to put in place an approach that allows the system to naturally evolve. Fortunately, this is exactly what we designed our new architecture to achieve. So, let's see how we can weave the old systems into the new system using our event-first and micro frontend approaches.

Event-first migration

Event-first migration is an integration-based approach for implementing the Strangler pattern. It is non-invasive to the legacy systems. In *Chapter 7, Bridging Intersystem Gaps*, we covered a variety of ways that we can leverage the **External Service Gateway** (**ESG**) pattern to create an anti-corruption layer around legacy systems.

We are essentially turning legacy systems into autonomous subsystems and services by wrapping them with a layer that produces and consumes events. It turns legacy data changes into external domain events for consumption by the new system. And it consumes external domain events from the new system and updates the legacy system. This creates a bi-directional synchronization between the new and old systems using the latching mechanism that we covered in *Chapter 5, Turning the Cloud into the Database*.

This allows users to work in both the new system and the old systems. One user can start a business process in the new system and another user can complete the process in a legacy system and vice versa. Beta users can experiment with the new version of a feature and if it falls short then they can complete their work in the legacy system, without losing a step.

Eventually, the legacy system will stop emitting events, because we no longer use it. At this point, we can simply turn it off without any impact on the new system. Along the way, we delivered new business value without taking away valuable capabilities. We did not put the legacy system at risk. And we did not create technical debt in the new system. We controlled all the risks.

Still, some users will have to bounce back and forth between the old and the new user interface. If the legacy user interface uses web technology, then we can weave it into the new micro frontend.

Micro frontend – headless mode

During a legacy migration, we want the user experience to be as seamless as possible. In the early stages, some users may only use the new user interface and beta users are happy to contribute and willing to bounce back and forth between the old and the new. As a migration progresses more users will start to use the new interface, but they may use it in one setting and the old user interface in another setting. So, it won't feel like they are bouncing around the old and new.

As we roll the system out to more and more users, we want to provide them with one entry point to the system. We want this to be the new entry point. The old entry point will still be available but without all the new capabilities. Our micro frontend approach, by virtue of its pluggability, is a natural fit. We just need to plug the old into the new.

We can accomplish this by writing thin micro-apps that wrap the legacy interface so that it snaps into the micro frontend. This is straightforward if the legacy frontend is also a single-page application. If the legacy interface uses server-side rendering, then it will take a little more elbow grease, such as wrapping it in an IFrame.

In either case, we need to make a slight modification to the legacy user interface to teach it how to run in *headless* mode. This is just a parameter that tells the application whether or not to render its banner and global navigations. The micro frontend will provide these instead when the legacy app executes as a micro-app. We will implement any other adaptations in the wrapper micro-app, such as transforming between different single sign-on approaches.

Again, sooner than later, the users will stop using these legacy screens, and we can simply unregister them with no impact on the new system. We did not force users to switch and we did not take away the old interface. We gave users a reason to want to switch by providing new business value along the way. And we controlled all the risks.

But our legacy systems may not go completely away. They may enjoy a long retirement.

Retirement

Our legacy systems may still have a long life ahead. We will reduce our dependency on them and significantly reduce their runtime cost. They will no longer impede innovation. But they will probably still add value for some time to come. This is good news for engineers and developers who are not ready to make the switch because their skill sets will remain valuable.

There are two areas in particular, where our legacy systems may still add value: *legacy interfaces* and *reporting*. Over the years, we likely developed many interfaces between the legacy systems and external systems. Replacing these interfaces will not happen overnight. It will take time to replace these, one by one. And external partners may not be willing to change on the same timetable. So, the legacy systems can continue to provide these interfaces and simply act as a pass-through to the new system. In the meantime, we can de-provision all the unused resources to reduce cost.

The legacy database may also evolve into a reporting database. In all likelihood, the legacy database already supports OLAP and reporting. Now it can continue to do so without competing for scarce database resources with the OLTP features. It can sit downstream and support the analytics phase of the data life cycle, as we covered in *Chapter 5, Turning the Cloud into the Database*. Once we have ported the last interface and we have completely separated the OLAP and OLTP features, then it will be easier for the OLAP and reporting features to evolve and modernize.

The Strangler pattern allows us to control the risk of modernizing our legacy systems by incrementally porting the features until we can simply turn the legacy systems off. Now, let's address some misconceptions about the event-first approach.

Addressing event-first concerns

Our event-first approach to building autonomous services is a bit of a paradigm shift. And as with any paradigm shift, there is plenty of opportunity for misunderstandings in the early adoption phases. This is completely understandable because we often have to unlearn the practices that we followed before. This can result in a resistance to change and the formulation of arguments against the change that turn out to be myths or anti-patterns.

As architects, we need to make the effort to understand the source of these concerns, so that we can set the record straight and lead the product in the right direction. To this end, I am including the most common misconceptions that I have encountered. Let's start with a common misunderstanding of event lakes.

System of record versus source of truth

The **event lake** is a key element of our architecture. It provides a complete audit trail of all the actions and changes that occur within a subsystem. So, it seems like a natural place for all services to pull their data from. But that is not its purpose. We have optimized the event lake for writes as opposed to reads. We have optimized the event lake to ensure that we do not lose any data. We can go back to the event lake at any point in time and recreate the state of the system. This is an invaluable capability, but it does not support real-time access and it should not.

Instead, we have purposefully decomposed the system into a set of autonomous services along the data life cycle that act as various systems of record and sources of truth, as we covered in *Chapter 5, Turning the Cloud into the Database*. Upstream services in the *create* phase of the data life cycle act as the **system of record** for the data they produce and publish. The event lake collects and consolidates all this information into an ultimate record of truth, but we will not read from it. Instead, downstream services in the *use* phase of the data life cycle are responsible for collecting and caching the data they need to access in real-time.

Further downstream, in the *analyze* and *archive* phases of the data life cycle, we design autonomous services that act as the **source of truth**, to support planning efforts, decision making, and records management. These services collect all the events and data from all the upstream services so that they can organize and transform all this data into valuable information.

All these autonomous services can evolve independently. The event lake provides the **systemwide transaction log**, which allows us to create an evolutionary system by turning the database inside out and turning the cloud into the database. It ensures that we can repair existing services and seed new services. But we don't execute queries against the transaction log.

This naturally leads to concerns about duplicate data. So, let's address that next.

Duplicate data is good

We are purposefully replicating data across our autonomous services. This allows us to optimize each service and most importantly it allows each to evolve independently. But this docs lead to concerns about duplication of data. This is a topic that we covered in detail in *Chapter 5, Turning the Cloud into the Database*, but it is important enough to repeat here briefly.

It turns out that there is a lot of duplicate data in our legacy systems. There is the transaction log, which retains every action, and the tables, which retain the most recent state. Then there are all the indexes, plus the materialized views. Next, we need to replicate the data across three availability zones and multiple regions. Furthermore, to support more and more concurrent users, we need to create more and more read replicas. And when performance is still insufficient, we inevitably create a read-through cache for each application.

So, we really aren't creating more duplicate data. We are just making the replication more visible and taking full control of it. And we may actually be creating less duplication, since we keep the data in each autonomous service very lean. But even if we do create more duplication in some cases, it is worthwhile, because we are enabling autonomous teams so that they can drive down lead times and increase the pace of innovation.

There is also a similar concern that we are duplicating software. So, let's address that as well.

Avoid false reuse

Software reuse is a double-edged sword. We are all taught as entry-level programmers to decompose our programs into reusable functions so that the code is easier to understand and maintain. In other words, reuse is supposed to help reduce lead times. But reuse also increases coupling. When multiple pieces of software share another piece of software, the shared software cannot change without careful consideration for the impact on all the dependants. This increases the need for inter-team coordination, which in turn increases lead times. Therefore, we have to make sure we reuse software wisely so that the liabilities of reuse do not outweigh the benefits.

As a general practice, we do not reuse software between autonomous services. Within the code base of a single service, we certainly strive for proper decomposition with `Model` and `Connector` classes as we covered in *Chapter 6, A Best Friend for the Frontend*. But we defer commitment to creating and using shared libraries between services. We will refactor as we learn more about the functionality.

This helps us avoid the false reuse that ties systems into knots and hinders their evolution. **False reuse** occurs early in the development of a system before we have discovered the bulk of the requirements. We look across a system and we see what looks like duplication. But we need to resist the urge to consolidate. If we are patient, we will find that many of these similar features will diverge as the needs of their individual actors emerge.

In hindsight, false reuse is easy to spot. We can find it in those shared libraries with all the complex conditional logic that no one is willing to change. As the requirements rolled in, we had to go back to what we thought was common code and torture the logic with all the minutiae of the individual actors. It inevitably turned into a convoluted set of if...then statements that are brittle and impossible to understand.

Instead, we will wait, and we will learn. The boundaries of our autonomous subsystems and services make it difficult to fall into the trap because the code lives in separate repositories. When we do find real reuse, then we can refactor. We can create a shared library and retrofit the individual services and micro-apps when and if they need to change. We can move logic upstream and produce events so that downstream services can react. But in all likelihood, the different actors really do have different requirements, and the code that looks similar now is just boilerplate.

Now, let's look at whether or not we should standardize our tools and technology or use what works best case by case.

Poly everything

We all have our preferences. You prefer a specific programming language, a specific database, and a specific cloud provider. You have lots of experience with them, so you can get the job done fast. Everyone should follow suit. Everyone should just get along and use the same tools and technologies. Or it should be the Wild West, and everyone should do what they prefer.

Well, of course, neither extreme is practical. There are limits. There has to be some governance. But as we covered in *Chapter 2, Defining Boundaries and Letting Go*, governance can impede innovation. So, we do want a balanced portfolio. We need diversification. We do not want to impede. And we need to be prepared for what might come. Let's see how we can strike the right balance with a poly-everything approach.

Polyglot programming

Polyglot programming is the idea that we want to use the right programming language for the job at hand. The different programming languages have their strengths and weakness, so we want to optimize the whole and use the different languages where they work best.

You may have noticed that the examples in this book are written in **JavaScript**. As it turns out, JavaScript is a great match for stream processing with its functional reactive programming style and asynchronous non-blocking I/O. Plus, **JavaScript Object Notation (JSON)** is native, so there is no need for additional transformations. And its lightweight startup characteristics are perfect for Serverless.

You are likely thinking, *"But we are a Java shop. We don't have JavaScript developers."* But that is not exactly true. Most new user interfaces are written in JavaScript and all those skills are transferrable to writing the serverless **Backend for Frontend** (**BFF**) services that we covered in *Chapter 6, A Best Friend for the Frontend*. An autonomous team of JavaScript developers can implement the full stack, from the micro-app to the BFF service and beyond. This is a very powerful incentive from a budgeting and capacity perspective.

Personally, I started using Java when it was born in the 1990s and thought I would never need another programming language. Then SPA applications and Serverless arrived on the scene and I had to switch. But JavaScript had matured significantly, and I was amazed at how powerful and easy it was. I haven't looked back since. Most Java developers are interested in expanding their skills and there are countless stories like mine. But as we just mentioned in the *Dissection the Strangler pattern* section, our legacy systems aren't going away any time soon, so having both JavaScript and Java skills is valuable.

All that said, machine learning is becoming more and more important. And the tools around this capability tend to be written in **Python**. So, when working in this area, it does not make sense to go against the grain and force-fit JavaScript or Java into the mix. And who knows what is coming next. We don't want to be in a situation where we only have a limited set of skills.

Our autonomous services provide natural boundaries for defining the use of a programming language because they each have their own repository and build process. We can choose the right programming language on a service-by-service basis. If a service needs two programming languages, then we should probably split it into two services. We can write our BFF services in JavaScript and we can let the requirements of our ESG and control services dictate the best choice. And this is all possible because our domain events in between the services are completely agnostic to these decisions.

Now, let's see how this approach applies to the database layer as well.

Polyglot persistence

Polyglot persistence is the idea that we want to use the right database technology for the work at hand. In *Chapter 5, Turning the Cloud into the Database*, we identified the fact that over the data life cycle, different actors use the same logical data in different ways with different access patterns and requirements. This means that different database technologies may be better suited for the different data life cycle phases.

Each autonomous service maintains its own data. This allows us to choose the right database technology on a service-by-service basis. Fortunately, our *serverless-first* approach facilitates polyglot persistence, because we are offloading the heavy lifting of running these databases to the cloud provider. This allows the teams to focus on continuously delivering business value.

But vendor lock-in is a common concern, even though it doesn't need to be. We are making these decisions per service, which means we can change direction per service. This is not a monolithic decision that we must make for the whole system. We are also structuring the code within each service to support making a switch.

We covered `Model` and `Connector` classes in *Chapter 6, A Best Friend for the Frontend*. The `Model` classes contain all the business logic and delegate to the connectors to make external calls. The `Connector` classes encapsulate our polyglot persistence decisions. For example, each cloud provider offers similar services. We can easily swap a connector for AWS DynamoDB with a connector for Azure Cosmos DB. This is the **Substitution** principle at work again.

This leads naturally to the decision for picking a cloud provider. Let's see how this approach scales up.

Polycloud

Polycloud is the idea that we want to use the right cloud provider for the work at hand. On a service-by-service basis, we choose a cloud provider to take advantage of a distinguishing capability only offered by that cloud provider. In practice, this means we pick a cloud provider at the autonomous subsystem level, even if it is a subsystem of only one service. We covered the approach for integrating between cloud providers in *Chapter 7, Bridging Intersystem Gaps*.

Polycloud is different from the notion of multi-cloud. Multi-cloud suggests that a service should be capable of running on multiple cloud providers simultaneously, to support a scenario where a cloud provider fails across all its regions at once. But this scenario has never happened. And few services can justify the expense. At the very least, it suggests that we should be able to lift and shift services from one cloud provider to another. But this is not practical or realistic either.

As it turns out, the code we write and run in the cloud is just the tip of a very big iceberg. Below the surface, there is a great deal of infrastructure that supports our services and applications. All the cloud providers offer these capabilities, but we should not underestimate their differences and the elbow grease that goes into provisioning this infrastructure. There are vendors that offer compatibility layers, but this is vendor lock-in to a smaller third party.

Instead, we want a balanced portfolio with diversification across cloud providers. For example, we could aim for an 80:15:5 ratio. We should have a preferred cloud provider for most of our services. Then we build up competence across two other cloud providers by using them to run a subset of services. This allows us to gain knowledge and put the architecture in place to quickly move services between cloud providers. Our *serverless-first* approach offloads the bulk of the iceberg to the cloud provider, while our connector classes encapsulate the cloud provider-specific interfaces. And as we covered in *Chapter 2, Defining Boundaries and Letting Go*, our observability tool should give us a single pane of glass across cloud providers and our CI/CD tools should run on a provider that is different from the services it deploys.

All in all, there is room for many tools and technologies. When choosing between the options, we should select the ones that help us drive down lead times and continuously deliver business value.

Summary

In this chapter, we covered some final thoughts on making forward progress on the path of architecting for innovation. We covered the importance of gaining trust and building momentum, as well as constructing an architectural runway. We also learned how to mold our funding model into our process of continuous experimentation and discovery. We dug into the Strangler pattern and we addressed common misconceptions about the event-first approach. We also learned how polyglot programming, polyglot persistence, and polycloud help us optimize the system as a whole and prepare for the future.

For the next step, give the various templates a try. Create an event hub and stand up a micro frontend. Then create a micro-app and a BFF service. Wrap an external system with an ESG service and have it react to the events from the BFF service and vice versa. Along the way, start thinking about your system and how you would divide it into autonomous subsystems. Who are the major actors and what domain events do they elicit? What are the core capabilities and how does this all fit together? Then start thinking about a plan of action. Most of all, have fun on your journey.

Packt.com

Subscribe to our online digital library for full access to over 7,000 books and videos, as well as industry leading tools to help you plan your personal development and advance your career. For more information, please visit our website.

Why subscribe?

- Spend less time learning and more time coding with practical eBooks and Videos from over 4,000 industry professionals

- Improve your learning with Skill Plans built especially for you

- Get a free eBook or video every month

- Fully searchable for easy access to vital information

- Copy and paste, print, and bookmark content

Did you know that Packt offers eBook versions of every book published, with PDF and ePub files available? You can upgrade to the eBook version at packt.com and as a print book customer, you are entitled to a discount on the eBook copy. Get in touch with us at customercare@packtpub.com for more details.

At www.packt.com, you can also read a collection of free technical articles, sign up for a range of free newsletters, and receive exclusive discounts and offers on Packt books and eBooks.

Other Books You May Enjoy

If you enjoyed this book, you may be interested in these other books by Packt:

Solutions Architect's Handbook

Saurabh Shrivastava, Neelanjali Srivastav

ISBN: 978-1-83864-564-9

- Explore the various roles of a solutions architect and their involvement in the enterprise landscape
- Approach big data processing, machine learning, and IoT from an architect's perspective and understand how they fit into modern architecture
- Discover different solution architecture patterns such as event-driven and microservice patterns
- Find ways to keep yourself updated with new technologies and enhance your skills
- Modernize legacy applications with the help of cloud integration
- Get to grips with choosing an appropriate strategy to reduce cost

JavaScript Cloud Native Development Cookbook

John Gilbert

ISBN: 978-1-78847-041-4

- Implement patterns such as Event Streaming, CQRS, and Event Sourcing
- Deploy multi-regional, multi-master solutions
- Secure your cloud-native services with OAuth and OpenID Connect
- Create a robust cloud-native continuous deployment pipeline
- Run services on AWS, Azure, and GCP
- Implement autonomous services to limit the impact of failures

Packt is searching for authors like you

If you're interested in becoming an author for Packt, please visit `authors.packtpub.com` and apply today. We have worked with thousands of developers and tech professionals, just like you, to help them share their insight with the global tech community. You can make a general application, apply for a specific hot topic that we are recruiting an author for, or submit your own idea.

Share Your Thoughts

Now you've finished *Software Architecture Patterns for Serverless Systems*, we'd love to hear your thoughts! Scan the QR code below to go straight to the Amazon review page for this book and share your feedback or leave a review on the site that you purchased it from.

`https://packt.link/r/1800207034`

Your review is important to us and the tech community and will help us make sure we're delivering excellent quality content.

Index

A

abort event 318-320
ACID 2.0 188, 322
Action BFF service 236, 237
action-event-reaction loop 303
Agile methods 7
Amazon Web Services (AWS) 22, 304, 360
anomaly detection, CD pipeline 369, 370
anti-corruption layer
  creating 260-262
API Gateway 56, 64
API Gateway, BFF service 224
Apollo framework 233
Application Programming
      Interface (API) 285
architectural runway
  constructing 376
architectural vision
  establishing 374, 375
architecture-driven funding model 378
Archive BFF service 239, 240
artificial feature flag 342
  asynchronous interaction,
        contract testing 363, 364

asynchronous inter-service
      communication 18
asynchronous non-blocking IO 111
autonomous service
  asynchronous inter-service
        communication 18
  autonomous teams, enabling with 16, 17
  bulkheads, creating 17, 18
  CI/CD pipeline 53
  dissecting 52
  fortified boundaries 19, 20
  functions 56
  GitOps 53
  micro-app 56
  persistence 55
  repository 52, 53
  shared libraries, using 57
  stack 54
  tests 53
  trilateral API 55
autonomous service patterns
  about 50
  Backend For Frontend (BFF) pattern 50
  control services 51
  External Service Gateway
      (ESG) pattern 51

autonomous subsystems 375
autonomous teams
    enabling, with autonomous
        service 16, 17
AWS Certificate Manager (ACM) 242
aws-kms-ee library
    reference link 214
Axis of Change 31

B

Backend for Frontend (BFF) 18,
    50, 164, 300, 347, 386
Backend for Frontend (BFF)
        service pattern
    API Gateway 224
    command functions 224
    connectors 228, 229
    datastore 222, 223
    dissecting 222
    listener function 225, 226
    models 227, 228
    query functions 224
    trigger functions 226
    user activities 218-221
backpressure 140, 141
batching 153, 154
batch integration 12
BFF metrics
    concurrency limits 252, 253
    observing 252
    throttling limits 252, 253
    work metrics 252
BFF services
    about 199
    Action BFF service 236, 237

Archive BFF service 239, 240
at rest 246
Dashboard BFF service 237, 238
federated identity 241
implementing 233
in transit 242
JSON Web Token (JWT), passing to 105
JWT assertion 243
JWT authorizers 242
JWT filter 244
last modified by 244, 245
latency-based routing 247-249
least privileges 245, 246
perimeter 241
regional failover 251
regional health checks 249-251
Reporting BFF service 238, 239
running, in multiple regions 247
Search BFF service 234-236
securing 240, 241
Task BFF service 234
BFF services, performance
    cache-control 255, 256
    cold start 254
    function memory allocation 253
    optimizing 253
    retries 254, 255
    timeouts 254, 255
build-time rendering
    versus runtime rendering 73, 74
bulkheads
    creating 17, 18
business processes
    orchestrating 311
    parallel execution 315-317
business process management (BPM) 312

C

callback function 270

capacity per query 179

capacity per reader 179

cart service

  nodes and edges 195, 196

CD pipeline

  about 366

  anomaly detection 369, 370

  regional canary deployment 367, 368

  synthetics 368, 369

CEP logic

  decision tables 326-328

  implementing 325

  missing events 328, 329

change data capture (CDC)

  about 55, 131, 166, 198, 226, 278, 304

  database-first event sourcing 198-201

  latching 203-205

  leveraging 197, 198

  phase, using 166, 167

  soft deletes 202, 203

channel topology 122, 123

chief technical officer (CTO) 4

CI/CD pipeline 53

CI pipeline

  about 356

  contract testing 361, 362

  end-to-end testing 364, 365

  integration testing 359

  unit testing 357

client-side rendering

  versus server-side rendering 72, 73

cloud providers

  integrating across 275, 276

Code splitting 79

cold start performance 254

command function 174

Command, Publish, Consume,
    Query (CPCQ) 18, 126, 174

compensating transactions

  used, for implementing Saga pattern 317

concurrency 114

concurrency limits 252, 253

consistency 112

consistency process

  chain reaction 113

  facts 113

  transparency 112

Content Delivery Network
    (CDN) 64, 80, 236, 255

context diagram 48

context mapping 47

continuous deployment (CD)

  testing, optimizing for 338

continuous discovery 338, 339

Continuous Integration (CI) 30

continuously delivering business value

  about 4

  high-velocity teamwork,

    achieving through 5

  turning, design into reality 4

continuous testing 339, 340

contract testing, CI pipeline

  about 361, 362

  asynchronous interaction 363, 364

  synchronous interaction 362, 363

Control Service 18

Control Service pattern

  about 300

  collate 306

  collect 304

  correlate 305

dissecting 303, 304
emit 308, 309
evaluate 306, 308
expire 309, 310
control services 51
Conway's Law 11
CQRS pattern
capacity per query 179
capacity per reader 179
dissecting 172, 173
inbound bulkheads 176, 177
live cache 178
materialized view 174-176
systemwide CQRS 173, 174
Create, Read, Update and Delete
(CRUD) 172, 234
Cross-Origin Resource Sharing
(CORS) 224
customer service
nodes and edges 194

D

Dashboard BFF service 237, 238
data
duplication 383, 384
data across regions
multi-master replication 206, 207
order tolerance 209, 210
protracted eventual consistency 209, 210
regional failover replication 209, 210
replicating 205, 206
round-robin replication 208, 209
database
derived data 171
inside out, turning 169, 170
transaction log 170

database-first event sourcing 130
Database Migration Service (DMS) 278
data field 192
data gravity
about 162
demands, competing 162, 163
insufficient capacity 163
intractable volumes 164
data life cycle
analyze phase 167, 168
archive phase 168, 169
data gravity, fighting 23, 24
embracing 164, 165
phase, creating 165, 166
Data Life Cycle Architecture (DLC) 165
data modeling, for operational
performance
about 188, 189
aggregates 189, 190
edges 189, 190
nodes 189, 190
partition keys 191
sharding 191
single table design, example 192
data volume
about 179, 180
projections 180
time to live (TTL) 181, 182
Dead Letter Queue (DLQ) 142
Delivery BFF 234
delivery service
nodes and edges 197
Dependency Inversion Principle (DIP)
about 34, 35, 312
translating, to architectural level 35
designing for failure
about 140
backpressure and rate limiting 140, 141

fault events 142-144

poison events 141, 142

resubmission 144

deterministic identifiers 183, 184

developer experience (DX) 19

discriminator field 192

Distributed Denial of Service (DDoS) 241

domain events

about 58, 118

event carried state transfer 121

event envelope 119, 120

internal domain events, versus
   external domain events 122

substitution 121

Domain Name System (DNS) 64, 248

domain-specific language (DSL) 308

downstream subsystem 274, 275

draft pull request

creating 354

DynamoDB Accelerator (DAX) 167

E

EAI integration approach 380

end-to-end testing, CI pipeline 364, 365

Enterprise Application Integration
   (EAI) 13, 14, 169, 277

enterprise service bus (ESB) 15

envelope encryption 213-215

ephemeral messages 21

epic 350

ESG scenario, challenges

cross-referencing 292

data enrichment 291

idempotence 290

latching 292

slow data, resynchronizing 292, 293

tackling 289

event bus 118

event carried state transfer 121

event-driven architecture (EDA) 20

event envelope 119, 120

event envelope, fields

<entity> field 120

eem field 120

id field 119

partitionKey field 119

raw field 120

tags field 120

timestamp field 119

type field 119

event-first approach

about 35

facts, valuing 20

idempotence 21

inversion of responsibility.
   creating 20, 21

ordered tolerance 21

treating, as first-class citizens 21

event-first concerns

addressing 382

data duplication 383, 384

false reuse, avoiding 384, 385

system of record, versus
   source of truth 383

event-first migration 380

event-first, technique

contracts, versus notifications 38

event storming 36

evolve 39

facts messages, versus ephemeral
   messages 37, 38

powered by, event hub 40, 41

react 39

verbs, versus nouns 37

event hub
    about 40, 49, 117, 118, 174
    channel topology 122, 123
    domain events 118
    powered by 40, 41
    publishing 116, 117
    routing 122, 123
event hub template
    reference link 118
event lake
    about 118, 127, 383
    indexing events 128
    perpetual storage 127, 128
    replaying events 129
event-sourcing
    about 320
    snapshots, calculating 320, 321
event-sourcing pattern
    associative 322
    commulative 322
    distributed 322
    dissecting 124
    event lake 127
    event stream 129, 130
    idempotent 322
    micro event store 132
    systemwide event sourcing 125, 126
event storming 36, 350, 375
event stream
    about 129, 130
    stream-first event sourcing 130-132
    temporal storage 130
event stream processor
    about 132
    batch size 133, 134
    connectors 139
    filtering 137

functional reactive programming
        (FRP) 135, 136
    mapping 138, 139
    multiplexing 137
    unit of work (uow) 136, 137
exploratory testing 370
external API
    providing 285
external API, egress interface
    query 288, 289
    webhook 288
external API, ingress interface
    command 287
    event 286
external domain events
    about 47, 347
    versus internal domain events 122
External Service Gateway (ESG)
        18, 197, 300, 347, 380
External Service Gateway (ESG) pattern
    about 47, 51, 260
    action, versus reaction 263, 264
    cloud accounts 267, 268
    connectivity 262, 263
    dissecting 262
    egress flow 264, 265
    ingress flow 266, 267
    packaging 267
    semantic transformation 263
external SPI
    providing 285
external SPI, egress interface
    query 288, 289
    webhook 288
external SPI, ingress interface
    command 287
    event 286

Extract, Transform, and Load
    (ETL) 24, 279

F

false reuse
  about 384
  avoiding 384, 385
fan-out 315
fault events
  about 142-144
  err field 143
  uow field 143
fault monitor template
  reference link 145
feature flag 342
feature flipping
  about 370
  beta users 370
  exploratory testing 370
  General Availability (GA) 371
First-in, First-out (FIFO) 115
first stream processor 187
forces, influencing lead time
  decision making 6
  dependencies 10, 11
  hardware provisioning 8
  inter-team communication 10, 11
  risk mitigation 6
  software deployment 8
  Software Development Life
      Cycle (SDLC) 7
  software structure 9
  testing and confidence 10
frontend monolith
  breaking up 75
  breaking up, by device type 76
  breaking up, by subsystem 75

breaking up, by user activity 76
breaking up, by version 77
Functional Reactive Programming
    (FRP) 111, 135, 146
Function-as-a-Service (FaaS)
    20, 56, 224, 254

G

Gatsby
  URL 73
General Data Protection Regulation
    (GDPR) 215, 216
GitOps 53
governance, without impediment
  about 57
  account creation, automating 66, 67
  audit continuously 62, 63
  culture of robustness, facilitating 61, 62
  observability, leveraging 57, 58
  perimeter, securing 64, 65
  TestOps, elevating 65, 66
graphical user interface (GUI) 13
GraphQL
  about 56, 231-233, 345
  versus Representational State
      Transfer (REST) 229, 230
grouping 153, 154

H

highland.js
  reference link 136
hot shard 152
HyperText Transfer Protocol (HTTP) 360

I

idempotence
  about 290
  implementing 182
immutable event triggers 187, 188
impact mapping 349, 350
inbound bulkhead 19
inbound bulkheads 176, 177
index 235
infrastructure-as-code (IAC) 8, 63
ingress relay 282
Initiator BFF service 313
integration styles
  batch integration 11
  dissecting 11
  enterprise application integration 13, 14
  microservices 15, 16
  real-time integration 13
  service-oriented architecture (SOA) 15
  shared database 14
  spaghetti integration 12
integration testing, CI pipeline
  about 359
  VCR test double 360, 361
inter-application communication 90, 91
Interface Segregation Principle
  (ISP) 30, 33, 34
internal domain events
  about 46
  versus external domain events 122
inter-service collaboration
  promoting 300-302
inter-service communication channel 129
Inverse Oplock Join 186
inverse optimistic locking 184-186
Inversion of Responsibility
  (IRP) 39, 126, 263, 304

J

Jamstack
  URL 73
JavaScript 385
JavaScript Object Notation (JSON) 385
JSON Web Key Set (JWKS) 242
JSON Web Token (JWT)
  about 64, 100, 241
  passing, to BFF services 105
JWT assertion 243
JWT authorizers 242
JWT filter 244

K

Kanban method 7
Key Management Service (KMS) 214
key performance indicators
  (KPIs) 25, 53, 340

L

latching 204, 292
latency-based routing 247-249
lead time
  controlling 5
Lean method 7
legacy interfaces 382
legacy systems
  Change Data Capture (CDC) 278, 279
  circuit breaker 280, 281
  Direct SQL 279
  egress relay 283
  ingress relay 282
  integrating with 277

legacy systems, egress relay
  files 284
  messages 284
legacy systems, ingress relay
  files 283
  messages 282, 283
linting 358
Liskov Substitution Principle
    (LSP) 32, 33, 39, 261, 314
listener function 131, 139, 174
live cache 178

M

machine learning (ML) 369
main app 80
manifest deployer 89, 90
materialized view 174-176
mean time to recovery
    (MTTR) 25, 60, 340
micro-app activation 85
micro-app registration 82, 83
micro event store 132
micro frontend
  about 49
  advantages 79
  approach 381
  dissecting 77-79
  inter-application communication 90, 91
  main app 80
  manifest deployer 89, 90
  micro-app 84
  micro-app activation 85
  mount point 88, 89
micro frontend
  tiers, equalizing 25

micro frontends, main app
  importmap file 81, 82
  index file 80, 81
  micro-app registration 82, 83
micro frontends, micro-app
  entry file 84, 85
  root component 85
micro frontends, micro-app activation
  manual activation 87
  micro-app life cycle 86
  route-based activation 86, 87
microliths 9, 15
microservices 15, 16
microservices death star 16
ML, leveraging for control flow
  about 329
  models 330
  predictions 330, 331
mobile
  versus web 74, 75
mock object 359
models, BFF service 227, 228
momentum
  building 375, 376
monolithic software 9
mount point 88, 89
multi-factor authentication (MFA) 64
multi-master replication 206, 207
multi-regional cron jobs
  events 332
  idempotence 332, 333
  implementing 331
  records 332
  replication 332, 333
multi-regional scenarios
  addressing 295
  egress failover 296

egress routing 296
ingress failover 297
ingress routing 297

N

natural feature flags 342
Next.js
  URL 73
npm 57

O

observability
  about 252, 343
  leveraging 57, 58
  optimizing 25
observability, metrics
  cost metrics 60
  resource metrics 59
  system events 59, 60
  team metrics 60
  work metrics 58, 59
offline micro applications
  designing 91, 92
  live updates 97
  local cache 93
  regional failover 99, 100
  transparency 92
offline micro applications, live updates
  long polling 98, 99
  WebSocket 97, 98
offline micro applications, local cache
  installation 93, 94
  read-through cache 94, 95
  write-through cache 96

offline micro applications, transparency
  inbox 93
  outbox 92
  status indicators 92
Online Analytical Processing
    (OLAP) 24, 165
Online Transaction Processing (OLTP)
  about 165
  database 24
Open-Closed Principle (OCP) 32, 39, 380
OpenID Connect (OIDC) 64,
    100, 102, 241
orchestration
  entry and exit events 312-315
order tolerance
  about 209, 210
  implementing 182
order tolerance and idempotence 115
organic evolution
  change, embracing 26
outbound bulkhead 19

P

parallel execution 315-317
parallelism 115, 116
partition key (pk) 191
partitions 114
pendulum 72
Personally Identifiable
    Information (PII) 213
pipeline patterns 150-152
poison events 141, 142
polycloud 275, 387
poly-everything approach
  about 385
  polycloud 387

polyglot persistence 386
polyglot programming 385, 386
polyglot persistence 387
polyglot programming 386
products, funding
   about 377, 378
   architecture-driven 378
   team capacity-driven 379
Progressive Web Applications (PWAs) 74
protracted eventual consistency
      158, 209, 210
Python 386

Q

quality assurance (QA) 25, 370
query function 174

R

rate limiting 140, 141
read-through cache 94, 95
real-time integration 13
Real User Monitoring (RUM) 106
regional canary deployment,
      CD pipeline 367, 368
regional failover 251
regional failover, accounting
   about 157
   protracted eventual consistency 158
   regional messaging channels 158, 159
regional failover replication 209, 210
regional health checks 249-251
regional messaging channels 158, 159
reporting 382
Reporting BFF service 238, 239

Representational State Transfer (REST)
   about 230, 231, 346
   versus GraphQL 229, 230
resource metrics
   about 59
   capacity 210
   observing 210
   performance 212
   throttling errors 211, 212
Restaurant BFF 234
restaurant service
   nodes and edges 193, 194
resubmission 144
retirement 382
risk mitigation
   deployment, decoupling from
      release 341, 342
   fail forward fast 343
   feature flag 342, 343
   focusing on 340
   small batch size 341
Robustness 77
Robustness principle 61, 344
root-cause analysis (RCA) 356
round-robin replication 208, 209
routing 122, 123
runtime rendering
   versus build-time rendering 73, 74

S

Saga pattern
   abort event 318-320
   employing 317
   implementing, with compensating
      transactions 317
Search BFF service 234-236

seed and split approach 377
sensitive data
    envelope encryption 213-215
    General Data Protection Regulation
        (GDPR) 215, 216
    redacting 212, 213
serverless-first approach
    about 387
    disposable architecture 22, 23
    knowledge, creating 22
    self-service 22
server-side rendering
    versus client-side rendering 72, 73
service-level agreement (SLA) 310
service-oriented architecture (SOA) 15
Service Provider Interface (SPI) 285
Service X 126, 174
Service Y 174
sharding 191
shared database 14
shared secrets
    API keys, using 295
    managing 294
    securing 294
Short Message Service (SMS) 316
single-page application (SPA) 25, 72
single-responsibility principle
        (SRP) 24, 31, 162, 219, 260
Single Sign-On (SSO) 64
single-spa
    URL 79
single table design, example
    about 192
    cart service 195, 196
    customer service 194
    delivery service 196, 197
    restaurant service 193, 194

snapshot events 323-325
Software Development Life Cycle
        (SDLC) methodology 7
SOLID principles
    building 30
    Dependency Inversion
        Principle (DIP) 34, 35
    Interface Segregation
        Principle (ISP) 33, 34
    Liskov Substitution Principle
        (LSP) 32, 33
    Open-Closed Principle (OCP) 32
    single-responsibility principle (SRP) 31
Some ESG service 313
Some Process control service 313
sort key (sk) 192
source of truth 383
spaghetti integration 12
Staged Event-Driven Architecture
        (SEDA) 111, 135, 146
staging
    about 111
    atomic 112
    cooperative programming 112
story backlog, zero-downtime
        deployments
    about 350
    story mapping 350, 351
    story planning 352
story mapping 350, 351
story planning 352
Strangler pattern
    about 380
    dissecting 379, 380
    event-first migration 380
    micro frontend approach 381
    retirement 382

stream-first event sourcing 130-132
stream processors
    reference link 133
substitution 121
Substitution principle 380, 387
subsystem bulkheads
    cloud accounts, separating 45, 46
    creating 45
    external domain events 46, 47
subsystem, decomposing into
        autonomous services
    about 47
    autonomous service patterns 50
    context diagram 47, 48
    event hubs 49
    micro frontend 49
subsystems
    downstream subsystem 274, 275
    integrating with 272
    upstream subsystem 272-274
synchronous interaction, contract
        testing 362, 363
synthetic 107
synthetics, CD pipeline 368, 369
system, dividing into autonomous
        subsystems
    about 41
    by actor 41, 42
    by business capability 43
    by business unit 42
    by data life cycle 43
    by legacy system 44
    subsystem bulkheads, creating 45
system events 59, 60
system of record 383
systemwide CQRS 173, 174
systemwide event sourcing 125, 126
systemwide transaction log 383

T

task 352
Task BFF service 234, 313
task branch
    creating 354
task branch workflow
    about 353
    canary deployment, accepting 355
    draft pull request, creating 354
    merge to master 355
    ready for review 354
task roadmap 352
team capacity-driven funding model 379
technical debit 343
temporal storage 130
TestOps
    elevating 65, 66
third-party systems
    API call 269
    asynchronous request response 270, 271
    integrating with 268
    webhook 270
throttling limits 252, 253
throughput
    about 145
    asynchronous non-blocking IO 146, 147
    batching and grouping 153
    batch size 146
    fault events 157
    iterator age 156
    observing 155
    optimizing 145
    pipelines and multiplexing 148, 150
    sharding 152
    work metrics 155

time to live (TTL)
  about 24, 181, 182, 347
  feature 309
trigger function 174, 344
trilateral API
  about 55
  API Gateway 56
  event-first approach 55

U

unit of work (uow)
  about 136, 137, 153
  batch field 137
  event field 136
  record field 136
unit testing, CI pipeline
  about 357
  coverage 358
  mock object 358, 359
  static analysis 358
universally unique identifiers
      (UUIDs) 306
upstream subsystem 272-274
USE method 59
user activity
  observing 105
  Real User Monitoring (RUM) 106
  synthetic 107
user experience (UX) 19
user experience (UX), security
  about 100
  conditional rendering 102, 103
  JWT, passing to BFF services 105
  OpenID Connect 102

OpenID Connect (OIDC) 100
  protected routes 104
user-interface-first (UI-first) 351
user stories 350

V

VCR test double 360, 361

W

Waterfall methodology 7
web
  versus mobile 74, 75
Web Application Firewall (WAF) 64, 241
webpack 81, 84
work metrics 58, 59, 252
worth-based development 61
write-through cache 96

Z

zero-downtime deployments
  achieving 343
  backend, versus data store 347, 348
  frontend, versus backend 345
  planning, at multiple levels 348, 349
  producers, versus consumers 346, 347
  Robustness principle 344
zero-downtime deployments, planning
  experiments 349
  story backlog 350
  task roadmaps 352

Made in the USA
Las Vegas, NV
22 December 2021